FAIROUZ AND THE ARAB DIASPORA

FAIROUZ AND THE ARAB DIASPORA

Music and Identity in the UK and Qatar

Dima Issa

I.B. TAURIS
LONDON • NEW YORK • OXFORD • NEW DELHI • SYDNEY

I.B. TAURIS
Bloomsbury Publishing Plc
50 Bedford Square, London, WC1B 3DP, UK
1385 Broadway, New York, NY 10018, USA
29 Earlsfort Terrace, Dublin 2, Ireland

BLOOMSBURY, I.B. TAURIS and the I.B. Tauris logo are trademarks of Bloomsbury
Publishing Plc

First published in Great Britain 2023
Paperback edition published 2025

Series design by Adriana Brioso
Cover image © François Lochon/Gamma-Rapho/Getty Images

A catalogue record for this book is available from the British Library.

A catalog record for this book is available from the Library of Congress.

ISBN: PB: 978-0-7556-4180-2
ePDF: 978-0-7556-4177-2
eBook: 978-0-7556-4178-9

Typeset by Deanta Global Publishing Services, Chennai, India

To find out more about our authors and books visit www.bloomsbury.com and
sign up for our newsletters.

For my parents: Mounir and Samia Issa
and
For my sun and moon: Hisham and Mounir Mansour

CONTENTS

PARTICIPANTS

The following is a short descriptive biography of the participants interviewed for this study. All their names have been changed to ensure anonymity. Their descriptions are relevant to the moment in which the interviews took place.

London sample

Abouna Youssef, 60, Lebanese

Abouna Youssef heads a Greek Catholic Melkite Christian parish in London and believes in the healing power of music. For Abouna Youssef, the music of Fairouz brings people closer to 'their God', since her voice contains the 'aria of prayers'. Abouna Youssef blames the Lebanese war for creating a 'lost generation' with 'anarchic' musical tastes who are in dire need of music therapy by Fairouz and the Rahbani brothers.

Ahmad, 35, Iraqi

Ahmad was born in Iraq and came to England with his family when he was four years old. He grew up in Yorkshire and has lived in London for about fourteen years. He studied Arabic at university. He is a researcher and his work focuses on Iraqi refugees in Syria. Ahmad became aware of Fairouz and her music through his mother.

Akram, 37, Syrian/Lebanese

Akram has lived in London since 2004 and has not been back to Lebanon or Syria in over six years. He is divorced and now lives with a Brazilian woman. Akram likes to keep to himself and rarely interacts with others in London. For Akram, Fairouz is his companion who has travelled with him and who keeps him company.

Ali, 64, Iraqi

Ali is a journalist and researcher from Southern Iraq. He left Iraq in 1979 and lived in Yemen for around ten years. He finished his PhD and moved to London in 1992. Ali's work revolves around Islamic heritage and Islamic philosophy. He is married to a Christian Iraqi woman who also enjoys listening to Fairouz.

Amin, 27, Palestinian

Amin was born and raised in 'Riham' city in Palestine. His dream was to get away from the life of 'occupation and slavery and surrender'. He has lived alone in

London for over nine years and works in the service industry. His parents still live in Palestine. Amin grew up with the music of Fairouz.

Asma, 36, Syrian

Asma is a mother of two boys who works in the financial sector in London. She has lived in Canada, Dubai, Lebanon and Syria. Asma enjoys her life in London and finds it easy to integrate into the 'Cosmopolitan' city. For Asma, Fairouz is a more private experience than a social one.

Ayman, 34, Syrian

Ayman is an actor and filmmaker from Northern Aleppo in Syria. He has refugee status in the UK, where he has lived for six years. He is eligible to apply for British citizenship in a year. Ayman is reflective and has a wonderful way with words. He intertwines Fairouz into the narrative of his life, combining them philosophically.

Charles, 49, Lebanese

Charles is a hair stylist with a bigger-than-life personality. He has lived in London for twenty-six years and is critical of the Lebanese government and their leaders. He is well connected to the Lebanese community in London. He has a son and a daughter who both listen to Fairouz because of him.

Dina, 42, Lebanese

Dina was born in Beirut in 1974. She came to London to continue her education, where she received an MA in media production. Dina is a professional video editor whose work focuses on Arab diaspora and refugees. She is married to a Frenchman and they have two boys. Dina's father is the one who deepened her love for Fairouz.

Elie, 50, Lebanese

A musician, Elie came to London in 1987 on a temporary contract for three months but ended up staying. He got married in London to an Iraqi woman and now manages his own sound recording studio. He is determined to teach his children about the music of Fairouz.

Ferial, 47, Palestinian

Ferial was born and raised in Al Quds, Palestine. She studied at a Catholic school although she identifies as a Muslim. She graduated from a university in Palestine with two degrees, one in English and another in translation. She left Palestine after graduating from university to work as a journalist in London. Her relationship with Fairouz developed at a later stage in her life, although her parents were big fans of the singer.

Helene, 52, Lebanese

Helene was married to an Englishman and has lived in the UK for more than twenty-four years. She went back to school after her divorce and obtained another university degree and a PhD. She believes her relationship with Fairouz and her music began when she was still in her mother's womb.

Hisham, 42, Lebanese
Hisham has lived in London since 2008. He has been married for two years. Hisham works in the service industry and makes it a point that Fairouz is always playing '24/7' in the Middle Eastern restaurant he owns.

Hussain, 60, Iraqi
Hussain is an artist. He left Iraq in 1978 and has only been back for a visit once. He lived in Kuwait and Morocco before moving to London in 1991. Hussain feels estranged from Iraq and from the rest of the Arab world. Fairouz is a means by which he feels connected and rooted.

Jana, 48, Palestinian/Syrian
Jana has been in England since she was nine and a half. She could hardly speak a word of English when she first moved to England. Jana has a background in education, adult and community learning. She also works in broadcasting where she plays Arabic music and features songs by Fairouz.

Kareem, 36, Egyptian
Kareem moved to London over ten years ago, where he lives with his wife and son. He has a master's degree from King's College and works as a journalist. He maintains connections with the Arab community in London and feels integrated into British society. Kareem enjoys listening to Fairouz with his wife who is also a fan of the singer.

Kathem, 23, Iraqi
Kathem is a refugee from Iraq, where he fled sectarian and religious violence. He was kidnapped by Al-Qaida for nineteen days when he was just sixteen years old. He moved to London with his father in 2009 and has been accepted to continue his education at Greenwich University. Although Kathem considers his family to be religious, Fairouz has always been a part of his upbringing.

Khaled, 38, Lebanese
Khaled has lived in London for over seventeen years. He manages a hairdressing salon, but he also sings and makes music. Khaled cannot start his day without listening to Fairouz. He plays her songs in the salon for his customers.

Leila, 30, Moroccan
Leila came to London ten years ago to continue her education and has remained since. She recently finished her PhD. Leila was initially planning on going to the United States to study, but after the events of 11 September 2001, her parents were worried about sending her there. She misses Morocco but could never live there. Fairouz reminds Leila of the positive side of the Arab world.

Maha, 35, Syrian/Lebanese

Maha is part Lebanese, part Syrian and was born in Beirut. She has lived in Iraq, Syria and Lebanon and moved to London over twelve years ago for her master's degree. She is married to an English-Italian man and has one stepdaughter. Although she disliked Fairouz when she was younger, she has grown fond of the singer, finding comfort in the familiarity of her voice.

Maher, 44, Syrian

Maher initially came to London to study English twenty-two years ago. He is from Latakia in Syria and is married to a Palestinian. He went back to school to take music classes and composed a few songs for singers from the Arabian Gulf. He has a studio at home. He really wants his daughter and his wife to enjoy Fairouz but has a hard time getting them into it.

Malik, 55, Iraqi

Malik has been living in London for over thirty-five years. He is a researcher and a publisher. He has worked at the London School of Anthropology as well as SOAS. He has been listening to Fairouz for forty-five to fifty years and describes her as 'organic'.

Mariam, 32, Qatari

Mariam is a Qatari woman who has been living in the UK for over ten years. She is a performance artist and has not been back to Doha for over two years. Her relationship with Fairouz developed because of her mother who was a big fan.

Michael, 36, Lebanese

Michael works in maintenance and is married to a 'foreign' woman. He cannot start his day if he does not listen to Fairouz in the morning.

Mounir, 37, Lebanese

Mounir grew up in Saudi Arabia and came to Lebanon when he was ten years old. He studied in Lebanon and then moved to the Gulf to work. He worked there for eight years and then came to London to do his MBA. He has since stayed in London and works there. He is trying to change his career into something more humanitarian and works closely with refugees. He has watched Fairouz in concert on many occasions and is a serious fan.

Nicholas, 47, Lebanese

Nicholas moved to London over twenty-five years ago. He works as an engineer during the week and as a choir leader on the weekends. He is married to Noor. He has two boys and has seen Fairouz in concert at the Ba'albeck International Festival.

Noor, 45, Lebanese

Noor was a teacher in Lebanon before she moved to London with her husband Nicholas. Even after twenty-three years in London, she still feels like she does not belong. However, she does not feel like she belongs in Lebanon either. Noor enjoys listening to Fairouz with her husband and is hopeful her sons will one day come to appreciate the singer.

Sara, 46, Lebanese

Sara is a performing artist who has lived in London for twenty-six years. She is married and has a 24-year-old daughter. When she was a child Sara would act out scenes from the Rahbani plays with her friends. She is very weary of people who do not like listening to Fairouz.

Tala, 41, Libyan

Tala has lived in Libya, the United States and Italy. She then moved to London as a thirteen-year-old. She studied law at SOAS, hoping to work with her father one day. However, after he suddenly passed away, she had to make some difficult life choices. She now works as a freelance journalist and is heavily connected to the Arab diaspora living in London. Her relationship with Fairouz began as a young girl in Libya.

Tarek, 36, Lebanese

Tarek is from South Lebanon. He moved to London alone when he was just fourteen years old. He had not been back to Lebanon in twenty-two years. However, he went back this year to attend his grandfather's funeral. He is married to a Russian woman and has two children. Fairouz offers Tarek a chance to travel to Lebanon through her songs.

Toufic, 58, Lebanese

Toufic works in the service industry and has been in London for twenty-two years. He has not seen his parents since he left Lebanon. He is politically affiliated with the Lebanese Christian Phalange party. His children visit Lebanon more often than he does. Toufic especially likes to listen to Fairouz's religious hymns on Good Friday.

Viviane, 56, Lebanese

Viviane was born and raised in Lebanon. She worked as a teacher there and then moved to London when she got married thirty years ago. She has three children. Viviane studied music in Lebanon and went on to join Fairouz's choir in 1981 when she toured the United States. Fairouz is Viviane's role model.

Wassim, 42, Lebanese

Wassim works in the service industry and has been in London for twelve years. He is married to a woman from Georgia and has a six-month-old son. Wassim visits Lebanon every year with his family. Fairouz gives Wassim hope for a better world.

Doha sample

Abou Aziz, 67, Kuwaiti/Qatari

Abou Aziz graduated from the Cinema Institute of Cairo. He is an avid music fan and collector. He is married to Umm Aziz and works at a local television station. Fairouz appeals to his sentimentality; however, he remains partial to Umm Kulthum.

Amar, 39, Lebanese

Amar moved to Doha from the United States over two years ago. She has two small children. She studied journalism and is passionate about research. She is well spoken and eloquent. Amar tragically lost her mother in the July 2006 war in Lebanon. This was a pivotal moment in her life. She is deeply involved with the Lebanese community in Doha. Fairouz is an integral part of her memories with her mother and she is keen to pass the music onto her children.

Umm Aziz, 65, Kuwaiti/Qatari

Umm Aziz is married to Abou Aziz. She is quiet and reserved. She hardly listens to music anymore since she no longer drives. But Fairouz reminds Umm Aziz of her childhood and her neighbours in Kuwait, who would bring back new releases on cassette tapes from their holidays in Lebanon.

Bianca, 37, Lebanese

Bianca moved to Doha from Nigeria eleven years ago. She is married with three children. When she first got married and had to move to Nigeria, the first items she packed were her CDs. She loves music especially songs by Fairouz. Bianca feels deeply connected to Fairouz and the singer plays a central role in Bianca's life.

Carmen, 70, Palestinian

Carmen has lived in Doha for almost thirty-six years. She is a mother of three and a grandmother of three. Prior to getting married, she worked at an airline company. She is involved with a few charities and is an avid card player. She has been listening to Fairouz since she was a child, because of her parents.

Clara, 44, Lebanese

Clara was born and raised in Doha. She has a bachelor of science in accounting, as well as an MBA from the United States. She worked in private banking as well as in real estate development projects in a managerial role. Clara has lived all over the world, from London to the United States, but Doha will always be home for her. Fairouz came into Clara's life from very early on and has remained a daily ritual ever since.

Ghassan, 45, Lebanese

Ghassan moved to Doha and set up a business as a middleman for a trading company. He is a father of three. When he moved to Qatar it was his first time living outside of Lebanon. He still lives the same way as he did in Lebanon and is very passionate about the old life there. Fairouz connects his old life to his new one. He takes pride in the fact that his wife and children also listen to Fairouz.

Gihane, 47, Lebanese
Gihane has lived in Doha for ten years. However, she regularly goes back to Lebanon since her kids attend universities there. She is a singer but has never pursued it professionally. Gihane is disappointed that her children do not have 'Arabic roots' but tries to play Fairouz for them.

Gilbert, 29, Lebanese
Gilbert is a single man who left Lebanon five years ago. He has a master's degree in computer science and an executive MBA. Gilbert works in electronics retail. He visits his parents in Lebanon every five months. Gilbert was taught Fairouz's songs at school and would sing them in the school choir.

Jihad, 51, Palestinian/Jordanian
Jihad has lived in Doha for more than twenty-five years. He initially worked in an auditing firm as a consultant and then opened his own business. He is married and has children who also live with him. For Jihad, Fairouz has been there for all the milestones in his life.

Karam, 39, Lebanese
Karam is a freelancer who moved to Qatar eleven years ago. He is married with two young daughters and his family moved to Doha to be with him. He is happy to live there for as long as he can. He is also a musician in his spare time and plays the keyboard. His relationship with Fairouz and her music began when he was seven years old.

Lara, 50, Palestinian
Lara has lived in Kuwait for most of her life and moved to Doha, Qatar, in 2000. She studied in the United States and double majored in economics and maths. She also holds an executive MBA from a US university. She previously worked as a banker. Her children are currently at university in the United States. Lara self-taught herself the piano and the first song she played was *Aam bit Dawi al Shams*, the sun is shining, by Fairouz.

Marwan, 73, Lebanese
Marwan has lived in Doha since 1972. He is married to a woman from Eastern Europe. His wife is fluent in Arabic. He has a son, who is married to a North American, and has kids of his own. They also live in Doha. Marwan runs his own company that deals with imports to Doha. His son works with him. Marwan's appreciation of Fairouz grew when he was studying engineering in Czechoslovakia.

Maya, 46, Lebanese
Maya was raised in the Emirates. She has a PhD in health policy and is pregnant with a girl. She has lived in Sri Lanka and London but sees herself moving back to Lebanon eventually. Fairouz plays a deeply personal and maternal role in Maya's life.

Mona, 45, Lebanese
Mona is married and lives with her husband and two children in Doha. They have been there for fourteen years. She is involved with the Lebanese community as well as the art scene in Doha. She has organized multiple events in Doha to ensure children from the Lebanese community are aware of their cultural traditions and heritage. Listening to Fairouz and watching her plays are part of that initiative.

Monzer, 79, Lebanese
Monzer has lived in Doha for more than sixty-one years. He is married and has four daughters. Monzer moved to Doha at eighteen years old with only twenty dollars in his pocket. Today he runs his own company there. Monzer enjoys listening to Fairouz in the mornings with his wife as well as on long car rides in the Qatari desert.

Nafie, 35, Sudanese
Nafie is a journalist, activist and artist who has been living in Doha for over twenty-five years. He is married and has two children, a boy and a girl. Nafie admires Fairouz for never taking a political side and for always being an artist for the people.

Nora, 37, Lebanese
Nora moved to Qatar with her family five years ago. She is an architect and works with a consultancy firm. She is often nostalgic and misses Lebanon yet she is enjoying the different experiences Qatar has to offer. Fairouz gives Nora the opportunity to bond with her husband and children, as they often listen and sing along to her music together.

Rodger, 38, Lebanese
Rodger has lived in Doha since 2007. He is married with children. He left Lebanon to establish a career for himself. He works in retail and visits Lebanon with his family once or twice a year. Rodger listens to Fairouz when he drops his sons off at school in the morning, but his wife does not like to listen to her, because she finds the singer depressing.

Rola, 29, Jordanian
Rola was born in Abu Dhabi and moved to Doha with her parents and siblings when she was five years old. She has also lived in Australia and studied media at university there. She works at a broadcasting network and lives with her parents. She used to sing in a church choir when she was younger. Fairouz was a means by which Rola was able to communicate with her parents, who were afraid she was digressing from Arab culture.

Shams, 40, Iranian/Palestinian/Lebanese/English
Shams moved to Doha when he was only six months old because of his father's job. He is married to an English woman and has two children. He is a diehard fan of the

Newcastle football club. He has a British passport but feels more at home in Doha. Fairouz is a reminder of Shams's dad, who passed away a few years ago.

Tania, 20, Palestinian

Tania has lived in Doha for over sixteen years. She is studying medicine. Her parents went to school in Doha and that is where they met. She is a straight-A student and music is the complement to her studies. Her grandfather used to take the time to explain the lyrics of Fairouz's songs to her. He passed away four years ago. Tania is well versed in the biography and discography of Fairouz. She has most of the songs memorized by heart.

Yassine, 70, Egyptian

Yassine has lived and worked in Doha for forty years. He is married and has two grown children, one of whom also lives in Doha with her family. He recently retired. His biggest hobby is to collect old recordings of concerts and archive them. Fairouz is one of the artists Yassine listens to and treasures.

Walid, 65, Lebanese

Walid lived in the United States for over thirty-four years, before moving to Doha. He has a PhD and works in the education sector. His contract is ending soon. He wants to move back to the United States with his family. Fairouz was the connection between the United States and Lebanon for Walid before the internet made communication easier.

Ziyad, 82, Iraqi

Ziyad has lived in Doha for over fifty-two years. He studied mechanical engineering in London on a scholarship from the Iraqi government. He has also lived in Beirut and Europe. He works in the petrochemical field. A friend in London introduced him to Fairouz and her music when they were at university.

Zuhair, 70, Lebanese

Zuhair has lived in Qatar for more than thirty years. He has his own business. Zuhair is married with two children, who also live in Doha. Zuhair's relationship with Fairouz was very strong when he was living in Lebanon, but after leaving he was driven away from the singer. Zuhair credits his wife for re-instilling Fairouz in their lives.

ACKNOWLEDGEMENTS

This book would never have been possible without the support and encouragement of a number of individuals to whom I am eternally grateful. I primarily would like to thank my wonderful parents, Mounir and Samia Issa, to whom I owe so much and without whom I would never have had the courage to embark on this journey. Making them proud has been my biggest motivator. My husband, Tarek Mansour, for his constant reassurance and crazy energy, whose heart is bigger than the entire universe. The lights of my life, my sun, Hisham Mansour, and my moon, Mounir Mansour, for filling each day with love and laughter. To my three sisters, Julie, Tania and Carla, my pillars of love and support, my greatest cheerleaders and sources of greatest comfort, thank you for all that you have done and continue to do. I would like to especially thank my sister Carla, who was on this journey with me from day one, reading and re-reading drafts, helping me with the kids and allowing me to vent when things got stressful (and believe me they did). I am extremely grateful for her unyielding love and support.

I would also like to thank my previous PhD Director of Studies and constant mentor Tarik Sabry, who went above and beyond in everything from advice to encouragement. He was a key instigator in the whole process of this book. I am so grateful for his patience, generosity of knowledge, friendship and incredible guidance. I am also grateful to Josh Kun at the University of Southern California, who opened my eyes (and ears) to the ways in which music can offer ways to understand culture and chronicle history.

I would also like to thank the following people for their valuable time and advice: Kenneth Habib, Sami Hermez, Joe Khalil, Samy Ofeish, Roza Tsagarousianou, Dina Matar, Atef Alshaer, Olga Heleno Walker, Mariam Al Muftah and John Hrabe.

Writing this book during a global pandemic in a country that was imploding at the seams came with its fair share of heartache, perforated with moments of magic, and I would like to thank Yasmin Garcha and Rory Gormley at Bloomsbury Publishing for their patience, understanding and support during this whole process.

I am also forever indebted to the study's participants, for every generous minute or hour (or hours) they selflessly gave me, welcoming me into their homes, meeting me in coffee shops or restaurants and opening up about Fairouz and their lives, thank you, meeting you all was an enormous privilege and I sincerely hope I have done justice to your stories.

Finally, I am forever grateful to Fairouz herself, whose voice was a source of comfort, my home away from home and my constant companion in the absence of belonging.

NOTES ON LANGUAGE AND TRANSLITERATION

Transliteration followed the *International Journal of Middle East Studies'* (IJMES) Arabic guidelines, but sometimes the Lebanese dialect was used as opposed to Modern Standard Arabic, for example, *Al-ghurba*, rather than *elghorba*. In addition, for certain words, /3/ was used instead of / '/. For example, the word '*Ya3ni*', however, for the ancient city of Ba'albeck the /'/ was used. Every effort was made to ensure translations of interviews were as accurate as possible. Some words, for example '*Ya3ni*' or '*Haram*', were kept in their Arabic format but written phonetically, because translating them would cause some of their meaning to be lost. '*Ya3ni*' and '*Haram*' roughly translate as 'I mean' and 'poor', but they require contextualization. If participants made references to Fairouz's songs they were kept in Arabic but written in phonetic English, as there are certain complexities in their translations. The word '*haneen*' proved the most difficult to translate, because of the way its meaning changes according to context. '*Haneen*' and '*Al-ghurba*' are discussed at length later in the book (Chapter 5). Names such as Fairouz, Rahbani, Umm Kulthum and Jamal Abdel Nasser are also written according to Lebanese phonetics. All translations are my own unless otherwise stated.

Chapter 1

THE INDIVIDUAL, THE SOCIAL, THE DIASPORIC AND THE MUSIC OF FAIROUZ

Her voice would breeze through the air conditioning vents, brushing my bedroom curtains open, revealing the morning sun. I would sleepily make my way across the cold, tiled floor, barefoot and yawning, to my parents, who would be seated in the glassroom, overlooking the bright bougainvillea vines, vinca plants and jasmine shrubs in our garden. They would sip their Lebanese coffee as they listened to the croons and whispers from one of her CDs. My mother would sing along almost in a trance, her beautiful voice matching every note, as my father clicked his fingers and swayed his head along to the music. Her voice comforting, but sometimes overwhelming, would envelope my parents in a sentimental embrace while simultaneously commanding their constant attention. Her songs, melancholy memory and patriotic love, would take us back to narrow alleyways, cobblestones and the Mediterranean sea, to a time of innocence and peace, of stability and acceptance. Fairouz's daily calls shaped our Lebanese heritage and cemented our displacement.

In 1953, at just eighteen years old, my father, the eldest of eight children, left his small town of Amioun, in the north of Lebanon, to provide for his family. Almost twelve years later he married my mother, and together they built a life for my sisters and me, filled with love, food and Fairouz. It was through Fairouz and her music that we felt a sense of belonging and un-belonging. On religious holidays, like Easter and Christmas, it was Fairouz's hymns that would complement our lavish meals. Her Easter songs, hauntingly poignant, would move women and men to tears, while her Christmas songs would add to the merriment of the occasion, prompting dancing and cheering. At dinner parties, her voice would serve as the audible ambience, occasionally halting conversations while guests joined her in song. On long drives through the Qatari desert, Fairouz kept us company, providing a sonic contrast to the barren sandy roads, with her vivid descriptions of lush greenery and village life. On CDs, cassette tapes and videos, my parents kept Fairouz close and accessible.

As a teenager, who grew up outside of Lebanon and attended international schools, Fairouz and her songs were foreign to me. She was part of something I felt no affiliation with. A world far away from my Nirvana CDs and Guns N' Roses mix-tapes.

In my eyes, she was for my Arabic-speaking parents – for a generation who were constantly looking for something they had left behind. It was a feeling I did not share, that is, until I left home in my twenties and travelled to pursue my masters' degree in London and then Los Angeles. Fairouz was there to comfort me, to recognize and single me out during my feelings of insignificance in big unfamiliar cities, whether on the bus, on the tube or in the confines of an empty house. Through my weathered earphones, Fairouz became both the means through which I could travel to the warmth of home and, simultaneously, the destination point.

However, Fairouz's voice does not remain confined to the private sphere of families or the home. Among Arabs, Fairouz is a harbourer of both public and private issues, symbiotically collapsing and redefining the two. The appeal of her voice is never denied but, for most listeners, Fairouz's pull is found in the content of her music, serving as a reminder of family and home, of one's individuality, of one's position in a community, and, possibly, in the diaspora, of one's inability to gain complete integration. With technological developments over the past few decades, and in the waves of revolutions across the Middle East and North Africa, since January 2011, Fairouz has been appropriated by different media and in various contexts. I remember sitting on my bed in my room in a rented house I shared with two roommates in Echo Park at the onset of the Arab uprisings. I felt far. Distant. Physically removed from Tahrir Square and Sidi Bouzid, but I was emotionally invested, connected, present. Pouring over news sites and messaging friends, hungry for any information I could find. During my search I found a slew of pages on social networking sites, adorned with Fairouz's visuals, quotes and melodies. Footage and images of protests from around the Arab world were juxtaposed with her music. Users uploaded videos of her plays, while some merely typed out lines from her songs. In whatever format, Fairouz became a tool of expression, a symbol for protest and a dream of a better world. Utilizing Fairouz's voice and songs as a form of storytelling is not a new concept; her songs about Palestine and Lebanon, of war and destruction, have been seen as a defiant force for years. But here it was alive and living, positioning the protests through lyrics that were written decades before.

Amidst the tumultuous waves of events across the Arab world since January 2011, and bearing in mind attitudes towards Arabs in the Western world since 11 September 2001 (and arguably before), Fairouz could not be more significant. Through her songs, Fairouz offers her listeners a space in which to engage, reflecting on the past but making room for the present and future. In the depths of a crumbling economy, a fraudulent government and a global pandemic, a bomb destroyed the Port of Beirut in Lebanon on 4 August 2020. Estimated to be the equivalent of 1,000 to 1,500 tonnes of TNT – a tenth of the power of the atomic bomb dropped on Hiroshima – the explosion killed hundreds, displaced thousands and badly damaged buildings, homes and property within its six-mile radius. The country went into mourning. Making matters worse, the Lebanese government took no responsibility, or even commented on the atrocity, sparking further anger and frustration among an already exhausted population. Weeks after the blast, French president Emmanuel Macron paid a visit to Lebanon. His first official visit was to Fairouz's home, where he awarded the singer with the French Legion of Honour, the highest of awards. The visit was seen as symbolic, a nostalgic appraisal of the Lebanon she had sung for and about all her life. A hopeful, idyllic and romanticized Lebanon, a stark contrast to the Lebanon of today, which was corrupt, broken and filled with despair. More importantly, the award showcased the strength of Fairouz, her emblematic position, what she stood for and what she meant, not just for Lebanon but also for her listeners across the world.

There is extensive research on Fairouz in both English and Arabic. However, it mostly focuses on her biography or discography, or discusses her relationship with Assi and Mansour Rahbani, her son Ziad, or studies her songs, through either a literary or ethnomusicology perspective. Consequently, there was a need for an audience reception study to examine the ways in which the singer factors in the lives of her listeners. While, Fairouz's music incorporates universal topics such as love, nostalgia and patriotism, the themes of homeland, pastoral nature, resistance against political and social injustice feature predominantly in her songs. In his dissertation *The Superstar Singer Fairouz and the Ingenious Rahbani Brothers*, Kenneth Habib attributes the success of Fairouz among her diverse listeners to her ability in navigating 'boundaries' drawn by 'nationality, religion, class, education and age'.[1] These 'boundaries' offer her listeners tangents to recognize and reflect on and so interest lies in how meaning is generated and understood among her listeners, especially among those who are straddling borders and boundaries at the international, domestic and individual levels.

This book is not aimed at elucidating any more information about Fairouz, but, rather, it is a means through which to understand the lives of members of the Arab diaspora who listen to her music and feel a sense of belonging in her songs.[2] Belonging here is seen as a form of negotiation, which is reliant on both individual and global factors that can converge and diverge on different planes of social construction and identity. Not only will this book explore how Fairouz's music assists in the understanding and construction of identity, but it will also shed light on how this identity factors within migratory environments.

Placing the Arab diaspora of Doha and London at the forefront, I investigate the role Fairouz's music plays in their lives while simultaneously shedding light on the circumstances shaping their diasporic experiences.

In the introduction to his book *Popular Culture and Nationalism in Lebanon*, Christopher Stone writes that Fairouz and the Rahbani brothers gained popularity during a time of 'increased internal and external migration' amidst the rapid development of media technology.[3] Stone describes this time as one where 'representations of the nation were particularly potent', contending that Fairouz and the Rahbani brothers 'were and continue to be key players' in the construction of the 'identity of this new nation'.[4] While Stone provides an illuminating argument on the role Fairouz and the Rahbani brothers play in creating 'subject-forming narratives' for Lebanese and Arab-speaking audiences, he cements the singer to a very concrete time and place, the 1998 Ba'albeck International Festival.[5] Although the discourse surrounding Fairouz and the Rahbanis may have been as

Stone claims, his argument is problematic in that there was no work conducted that adds to how these 'narratives' operated on the listeners' level, especially with Lebanese and non-Lebanese diasporic communities. Keeping Fairouz tied to a geo-historical context limits both her ability to remain relevant in times of change and narrows her reach among those who were not part of this 'subject-forming' narrative. The decision to broaden the criteria for participants in this study to incorporate individuals from all over the Arab world and the Middle East complements the aims of showcasing the ways Fairouz finds significance across fluctuating timeframes and nationalities and in different contexts.

In his discussion on identity and the self, Charles Taylor also raises the notion of 'narrative', arguing individuals should be seen in conjunction to a 'narrative', which is a 'basic condition of making sense of' the self.[6] However, while Stone's 'narrative' is limiting and exclusive, Taylor's is accommodating and flexible. It is a point of reflection by which the self is able to assess its present status, to change from 'what I have become' to 'where am I going'.[7] 'Narrative', for Taylor, has 'temporal depth',[8] expanding, growing and maturing. Here, it is important to understand narrative as a 'bloom space', something in constant motion, a place of contemplation and engagement, an affective 'hinge between the actual and potential'.[9] 'Narrative' gives way to the deliberation of the self but does not act alone. Including Bourdieu's notion of the *habitus* is necessary here to demonstrate how the 'narrative' and the self work with the *habitus* to construct and reconstruct meaning in a multi-tiered and shifting environment.

Dividing the habitus

For Pierre Bourdieu, the *habitus* is a 'product of history', which 'produces individual and collective practices'.[10] Past experiences and backgrounds are key to the ways individuals respond and interact with the present, since the *habitus* 'structures new experiences in accordance with the structures produced by past experiences'.[11] 'Past experiences' and 'new experiences' are thus forms of 'narratives' to which participants react as a consequence of their *habitus*. While Bourdieu counters the argument of a homogenized *habitus* with the example of class, to which he contends, 'the principle of the differences between individual *habitus* lies in the singularity of their social trajectories', there remains a need for another level of analysis to compensate for the rapidly changing global environment, as well as the geo-historical dynamism resulting from migratory experiences. *Habitus* cannot only be about time. It is also a spatial process, especially in view of the migratory nature of the diaspora. As a result, this book places the Arab diaspora against a backdrop of what I call the *meta-habitus*, global orders or circumstances in operation that influence the lives of participants, like war, for example, and the *micro-habitus*, more particular individual 'trajectories', such as domestic arrangements, allowing for a double level gauging of assessment to better understand how global and personal experience interact in the narrative of the self. The *meta-* and *micro-habitus* not only cater to the spatial considerations of participants but also attempt to adhere to a fluctuating global setting. Space and time are deeply integrated within the framework of the Arab diaspora, in terms of past, present and even future, shaping and contextualizing the ways in which respondents interrelate with the collective and, more specifically, the music of Fairouz. In addition, the *meta-* and *micro-habitus* provide a more flexible structure through which to explore the diversity that exists among Arab diasporic communities, especially along lines of citizenship, naturalization and notions of home and gender.

Fans are able to connect and identify with Fairouz and her music by way of these trajectories, thus proving her multidimensional nature. As a 'figure', Fairouz 'serve[s]' as social terrains', she occupies a 'body of discourse', transgressing and simultaneously emitting references towards time and space and the meanings embedded within them.[12] In his work on the reproduction of art, Walter Benjamin argues that the mechanical reproduction of art has led to a loss of 'aura', since the piece is removed from its 'unique existence at the place where it happens to be', a spatio-temporal detachment, a depreciation of the 'quality of its presence'.[13] However, I argue that the strength of Fairouz's 'aura' gains momentum and strength the further she is removed from the setting with which she is associated. Using Tarik Sabry's definitions of 'deterritorialization' and 'reterritorialization', unique and contemporary narratives can free Fairouz's 'aura' to take on deeper meanings. By 'dislocating' Fairouz from a precise time and space, she is able to take 'flight', offering newer 'planes' of 'self-reflexion and creativity'.[14]

Within these 'planes' of 'self-reflexion' lays the potential for affect, or what Brian Massumi would call 'intensity'.[15] Here, intensity is aided by the mnemonic imagination, since it 'provides the key to the mediation between experience and expectation'.[16] The mnemonic imagination, a strategic combination of memory and imagination, as defined by Emily Keightley and Michael Pickering, 'brings the temporal senses together and synthesizes them productively in order to achieve new meaning in the present' generating 'movement between the horizons of experience, expectation and possibility'.[17] Within these temporal pockets rest affect and its potentiality. However, affect is not only limited to time but also exists in space, in the 'midst of in-between-ness'.[18] The ways in which individuals operate within space are affective, in the alignment of 'individuals with communities' or through the interactions between 'bodily' and 'social space'.[19] For Sara Ahmed, affect is generated in the connection of 'bodies to other bodies'[20], or in the 'movement between signs'.[21] Even though Ahmed is specifically referring to emotions of hate, in the context of racism, her arguments regarding affect are especially relevant, since 'emotionality' is the 'interweaving of the personal with the social and the affective with the mediated'.[22] While Ahmed pinpoints the importance of movement in the articles mentioned earlier, it is her piece 'Home and Away: Narratives of Migration and Estrangement', which helps to position this study diasporically and affectively. In the process of migration there is 'a spatial reconfiguration of an embodied self',[23] a need for 'bodily space' to be reconfigured according to 'social space'. By this reconfiguration, notions of home and belonging arise, since there is a constant assessment of space and the consequent positioning within that space. By way of her music, Fairouz provides a lens through which members of the Arab diaspora are able to examine the 'self',[24] in an affective space, generating, furthering and dismissing narratives of identity and self in light of the *meta-* and *micro-habitus*. It is important here to reference Charles Taylor, who argues that the 'self' can only exist in 'relation to certain interlocutors' for it to attain 'self-definition'.[25] Taylor explains that, 'identity' needs to be put into dialogue with 'a defining community'.[26] Essentially, then, trying to dislocate the individual from the community, or 'bodily space' from 'social space', is a negation of the self and of identity. However, and as Taylor stresses, 'life moves', which means 'we are always also changing and *becoming*',[27] due to shifts in time and space. So not only does the community differ in the context of migratory 'social spaces', but also the individuals evolve when occupying different 'bodily space' and so do their relationships with Fairouz and her songs. This book attempts to unravel notions of self and identity, but also reveals the ways in which time and space operate affectively in creating forms of belonging in the context of Fairouz and her music.

Popular culture and the Arab diaspora

As a growing field, Arab cultural studies is paving the way for newer forms of understanding and representation, especially through its interest in popular culture. For Tarik Sabry, popular culture is a 'site for the production of political meaning', often ignored by Arab intellectuals.[28] Perhaps more urgently, as Sabry contends, 'Arab popular cultures have yet to be rationalized within a relational/ conjunctional structure' which investigates relationships and patterns 'between the social, political, economic, existential and the anthropological, as well as the dynamics that result from the interface between the "local" and the "global"'.[29]

From here, it is necessary to give voice to what Joanna Kadi has called 'the most invisible of the invisibles'.[30] Although Kadi is referring specifically to Arab-American communities, she depicts an isolated and inaccessible group of migrants, who are misunderstood, misrepresented and mistreated. The status change for this group in the United States, and arguably most of the Western world, occurred after the attacks on 11 September 2001 in New York, when Arab communities were transformed from 'invisible beings' to 'visible subjects'.[31] Not only is it important to find new ways to comprehend Arab diasporic groups, but it is also imperative to place them in a context away from the violence with which they are regularly associated. Often seen as a trivial, low end and sometimes damaging form of entertainment, popular culture is rarely taken seriously. However, in line with what Sabry has already said, Kathleen Karlyn argues, 'popular culture is a natural site of identity-formation and empowerment, providing an abundant store house of images and narratives valuable as less as a means of representing reality than as motifs available for contesting, rewriting and recoding'.[32] With this in mind, and in the context of Arab cultural studies, this book aims to showcase the ways in which Fairouz's music impacts upon the Arab diaspora, 'within a relational/ conjunctional structure',[33] and to shed light on the ways in which audiences consume media generally, and Fairouz's music specifically, to 'contest, rewrite and recode'.[34] By contributing to the existing field of Arab cultural studies, the objective is to elucidate upon the Arab diasporic experience both socially and culturally.

Stop and rewind: Music, place and migratory space

Acoustic space, vast and infinite, transgresses borders and oceans. Music and sound are found behind street corners, in homes, in elevators, in restaurants and in both public and private spaces. Omnipresent. Invisible. Music consumes, creates and curates cultures. It trumpets triumphs and shoulders strife. Often ignored in historical, geographical and societal work, music and sound are often trumped by the visual image, forcing them silently into the background. But it is within that shadowed muted space that stories and experiences are hidden. David Michael Levin has questioned whether 'Western culture has been dominated by an ocularcentric paradigm', which he defines as a 'vision-generated, vision-centred interpretation of knowledge, truth and reality'.[35] An anthology of essays by a number of prominent theorists, Levin's book shows the historical reliance of vision as a means to understanding, but also offers a lens through which to understand modernity. Levin does not explicitly favour vision as a cultural and social determinant, but, instead, presents prominent works by theorists who rely on vision for their philosophies.

Contesting the reliance on vision as the only way to historical and phenomenological knowledge, Susan Smith discusses, in her article 'Soundscape', how sound 'is inseparable from social landscape' and that 'music is integral to the geographical imagination'.[36] For Smith, 'sound itself has meaning and position', and music specifically, 'has the power to evoke a sense of space different from that evoked by sight'.[37] While Smith does not discredit visual 'privilege' in ethnographic research, she argues that sound and music are ignored in this stratum of academia, creating a lack of context that may otherwise 'influence, change or enrich the interpretation of particular scenes'.[38] Disregarding music and sound removes the political, social and cultural dimensions that might allow for greater depth and understanding. Smith contends, 'Music, in short, is no more isolated from politics than any other cultural form. It is one facet of the cultural contest that begins where institutional politics ends.'[39]

With the advent of digital media on the curated fields of social media, music acts as a political backdrop, a soundtrack of tensions and unity. The two can be defined as symbiotic, and as John Street says, 'they are not to be seen as separate entities', but, instead, they must be recognized as 'extensions of each other'.[40] For Street, music does not just describe and narrate political ideas but also mobilizes political action. DeNora echoes this sense of strength found with music, as she states that 'music has power'.[41] DeNora and, to some extent, Street, view music as having a potential for socialization, a method by which individuals and groups can be programmed to succumb to emotional responses generated by the sounds they hear, or a means through which to represent certain political ideologies. However, both authors are clear in mentioning that individuals and groups utilize music with a sense of agency.

While DeNora looks at music from an everyday perspective and the ways in which it is factored into the lives of individuals and groups, Street focuses on the political side of music. From the outset, Street defines what he means by the political, and the role of music within that political space, arguing that when 'music inspires forms of collective thought and action' is when 'it becomes part of politics', adding that music is political once it 'forms a site of public deliberation', and not when it is just 'a private reflection'.[42] While Street's differentiation of what constitutes the political, and how music is 'connected to the way we think and act politically', is important as it brings to the surface the notion of 'bodies' in space, and how mere presence within space is always political, no matter whether that space is 'public' or 'private'. Street contends 'what is public may not automatically be political, just as what is private may not be either'.[43] Perhaps ringing true with certain populations of listeners, this way of viewing the politicization of music, however, ignores categories of audiences who are diasporic and organically carry the weight of geopolitics in any space they occupy, whether deliberately or not. As Avtar Brah writes, 'diaspora space' holds the 'intersectionality of diaspora, border, and dis/location as a point of confluence of economic, political, cultural and psychic process'.[44]

In his introductory piece as guest editor of *Diaspora*, Mark Slobin discusses the impact of music on diaspora. For Slobin, 'Music is central to the diasporic experience, linking homeland and here-land with an intricate network of sound'.[45] This connection, Slobin argues, is consciously constructed and acts as 'cultural baggage' with which diasporic audiences are able to 'move from place to place, assembling and reassembling past and present identities'.[46] Through music, diaspora is able to transport and transform, recreate and rebuild, according to their surroundings. It is a means through which they carry moments and memories on their journeys. This, Slobin argues, works at both the individual and collective levels, and thus music 'lives at the margin of the person and the people', making it a 'crucial point of articulation in viewing diasporic life'.[47] This thus serves as further justification for examining music as a necessary element in the lives of the diaspora and in dissecting its role, politically or otherwise, in the quotidian. It is necessary here to shed some light on the broader music scene in the Arab world.

In his comprehensive chapter, 'Middle Eastern Music and Popular Culture', John Schaefer outlines significant research on the music scene in the Arab world and explores 'several key roles that music played in revolutions and upheavals following 2011'.[48] Beginning with an overview of regional popular music, Schaefer explores the ways music is connected among different nationalities in the Middle East, 'afforded by a familiarity' with '*maqamat*' or 'Eastern modes' and '*tarab*' which he describes as the 'emotional response that accompanies this familiarity'.[49] Outlining various genres of Arab music, Schaefer clarifies their individual relationships with politics and religion as well as illustrates how music operates and influences at national and regional levels. Schaefer's chapter continues by tracing Arab music's transformation alongside the 2011 Arab revolutions, where he focuses on

Egypt and the 'folk' music of Tahrir Square, since 'mass-popular singers are not structurally positioned to speak to the current moment'.[50] Sceptical of releasing 'frivolous' modern pop songs during the revolution in Egypt, the author tells of how studios in Cairo stopped production of new songs and instead 'smaller' forms of music were broadcast through different mediums. Therefore this fragmentation of music from the mass to the niche was as Schaefer argues an accompaniment to 'political and economic fragmentation'.[51] Schaefer's discussion of media and music is something Michael Frishkopf also brings to surface. Frishkopf's chapter in *Music and Media in the Arab World* looks at the evolution of technology from the 1980s onwards in the creation of 'inexpensive, catchy albums' what Frishkopf calls 'a shift from aesthetics to commerce' and also a 'transformation in the system's economic logic'.[52] Both Schaefer and Frishkopf take a more chronological approach towards music in the Middle East, discussing the economic, religious and political undertones found mainly on Egyptian airwaves.

Positioning 'political, identity and gender debates' in the 'realm of popular music' Abdel-Nabi, Agha, Choucair and Mikdashi's article examines music within social contexts.[53] The authors describe the Arab world and its culture as encompassing four main regions, 'the Maghrib, the Mashriq, the Gulf and Egypt', each offering a range of musical styles, modes and traditions.[54] Their research brings to surface the popularity of artists such as Elissa, Nancy Ajram and Najwa Karam from Lebanon, as well as Cheb Mami from Algeria and Amr Diab, Mohamed Mounir and Shaaban Abdel Rahim from Egypt, who according to the authors take on different forms of influence, ranging from sexuality to politics. Taking a more political and ethnographic standpoint, Daniel Gilman's work explores the 'emotional evocation in pop music' during the 2011 uprisings in Egypt. Gilman interviews youth in Cairo about their '*shababiyya*' music consumption and the 'visual aesthetics' of the accompanying video clips before and during the revolutions.[55] Gilman's objective is to move away from the '*highly formalized musiqa al-tarab*'[56] to one that appeals to younger generations from a larger class spectrum. Having conducted ethnographic studies both prior to and during the Egyptian revolution, Gilman focuses on the ways context shifts consumption of '*shababiyya*' music to claim a more 'political rhetoric' through 'emotional evocation'.[57] While Schaefer, Frishkopf and Gilman offer a rich and diverse body of literature on music in the Arab world, they focus on Egypt rather than the rest of the Middle East. Renowned musician and music scholar Ali Jihad Racy somewhat fills that gap with his research on the development of music in Lebanon. Racy's work is extensive, from his discussion of Arab musical terms,[58] to his unravelling of the 'ecstatic experience' of *tarab* music,[59] to research on Arabic folklore,[60] which places music in a sociocultural context. However, the topics Racy covers fit under what Mansour and Sabry have described as 'skewed toward historiographical and micro-sociological studies of folkloric musical traditions'.[61] As a 'very modest' field, literature on music in the Arab world tends to take on historical overviews and technological developments in genres of music.[62]

A more exploratory piece, Nasser Al-Taee's 'Voices of Peace and the Legacy of Reconciliation: Popular Music, Nationalism, and the Quest for Peace in the Middle

East' looks at the role of music in 'raising awareness of social and political tensions' as well as its 'active participat[ion] in offering tools for understanding the shifting dynamics within a disputed territory' namely that of Palestinians and Israelis.[63] Al-Taee takes a literary analysis perspective, selecting key musical contributions that shed light on the conflict and that 'capture important moments of the struggle'.[64] One of the performers Al-Taee makes note of is Fairouz, describing her as one of the 'most revered Lebanese/Arab voices' whose strong stance for the right of a Palestinian homeland is 'a testament to rising Arab Nationalism in the 1960s and 1970s'.[65] However, responses to the music of Fairouz and others are not discussed.

Perhaps, one of the most extensive Arab music reception studies done to date is Schade-Poulsen's book on Rai music. Uncovering themes like love and morality, Schade-Poulsen's ethnographic research examines the ways in which Rai music is produced and consumed alongside social, political and historical developments in Algeria, giving insight into the attitudes of Algerian men and the social roles they occupy. It is important here to recognize the work that has been done on Arab audiences and media consumption before highlighting the contribution this book hopes to make.

Arab audiences and media consumption

Schade-Poulsen's work on Rai music in Algeria brings to surface themes of love and relationships and how they are understood according to sociocultural discourse. Amidst the backdrop of increased Islamic fundamentalism and political turmoil in Algeria in the 1990s, Schade-Poulsen conducts focus groups and interviews with male participants from different social and educational backgrounds. Seen as somewhat controversial, the Algerian press often described Rai music as being 'disruptive', 'vulgar', 'low culture' and 'a musical form in which Algerian identity was seen to be at stake'.[66] With this in mind, the author shares a number of carefully selected songs that represent key genres within Rai and asks his participants about the music and lyrics. Through his fieldwork, Schade-Poulsen is able to explore points of acceptance as well as complete rejection of Rai songs and their meanings among his respondents. In this way, the author allows for a more dynamic consideration of Rai, 'related to non-musical spheres'.[67] While respondents did not always have a positive appreciation of the songs played to them, their conversations allowed Rai to leave its purely 'musical structure' and venture into the 'social world'.[68]

Schade-Poulsen begins by looking at the poetic form of the music and the aesthetic response to the songs. He then moves on to a deeper discussion where the lines of the songs are interpreted and given meaning 'depending on the individual life experiences of the listeners'.[69] In this way, Schade-Poulsen is able to immerse his participants in a live sonic experience to both showcase personal perspectives on Rai music and highlight the lyrics embedded in a 'socioeconomic cycle'.[70]

Particularly interesting is the way Schade-Poulsen describes the difference between Rai music that covers the ideal family unit or what is called 'clean Rai' and that which is called 'dirty Rai', which includes topics of sex and drinking. Positioning the themes found in both 'clean' and 'dirty' Rai, the author unravels how the songs suggest threats towards the family unit can arise through the 'development of an independent relationship with a woman from the outside' as this can create tension with his mother.[71] These convictions of distrust against women fall in line with a changing social discourse. This discourse sees shifts in the ways the different genders conducted themselves during national and regional political and economic transformations. However, it is through the conversations about Rai music that these nuances come to light.

Schade-Poulsen's book is key in understanding how social dynamics and change play an integral role in the interpretation and understanding of music, but also how music allows for a reflection of that change. In this case Rai acts as a social and historical archive, providing opportunities for a multi-layered conversation. Participants were comfortable discussing their interpretations of the lyrics as they fell under a similar discursive dialectic. This was not the case in my fieldwork, where participants did not feel comfortable discussing Fairouz and her music in front of others. This will be covered later in the chapter. But also, while Schade-Poulsen aimed to unbox an important consequence of sociopolitical transformation in Algeria, choosing to interview only Algerian men, I wanted to highlight potential gender differences in my research. For this reason, I did not limit my interviews to only one gender, sex, nationality or religion. In addition, diasporic consumption of media is something that is relevant in the context of Fairouz and so the sampling field had to be as diverse as possible.

While Arab reception studies tend to focus more on television than music, they are important to mention, especially in the context of Arab diasporic audiences. Harb and Bessaiso examine the role of 'ethnocentrism' in the consumption of media among British Arab Muslim audiences in Cardiff, Wales, after the attacks on 11 September 2001 in the United States. The researchers argue Arab channels such as Al-Jazeera provided an alternative to 'dominant Western media narratives'[72] surrounding the attacks and that participants 'identified themselves within the ethnocentric framework' of Arabic channels.[73] Harb and Bessaiso begin their article by explaining that controversial events since the early 1980s and onto the Gulf War 'pushed Islam into the national arena'[74] While there were indications of Islamophobia from the beginning, that is before 11 September 2001, and Muslim communities in Britain were prone to more 'racist violence than other minority communities', this increased after the attacks in the United States.[75] Following 11 September 2001, there were more than '300 assaults on Muslims' in Britain, this was complemented with an 'us' and 'them' Western news discourse that vilified Islam and equated it with the Taliban regime.[76] Therefore, Arab news outlets such as Al-Jazeera gave British Muslims 'confidence to express certain views', which they were unable to with Western media, as well as supplying them with different perspectives of Arab and Muslim portrayals and essentially 'fragmenting' the British news audience and creating 'a Pan-Arabic and Muslim transnational sphere'.[77] In addition, Al-Jazeera was able to showcase the Palestinian conflict, 'the heart of present day conflicts between the West and Arab/Muslims', as an act of 'resistance and not as "terrorism" – which is how the "Western media" portray it'[78] The Palestinian conflict as a 'meta-narrative' and an 'ethical-political framework' in the consumption of media is something discussed in more detail by Dina Matar.[79] Matar's research on British Palestinian's consumption of news media highlights a negotiation of identity that is complex and oscillates between 'pre-conceived ideologies and political frameworks, collective and personal memories, but also everyday experiences of living and interacting with many cultures'.[80] Unlike Harb and Bessaiso, who focused on British Muslims, Matar's participants were a mix of Christians and Muslims; however, they mostly all identified as Palestinian leading to what Matar calls an 'over-identification' with news discourses and a 'meta-narrative of Palestinian suffering' an overarching framework that encompasses news events such as the attacks on 11 September 2001.[81] This 'over-identification', Matar argues, 'comes across in often romanticized and idealized visions of the homeland'[82] making it difficult for audiences to maintain a 'perspective of cultural difference'.[83] Matar found that transnational Arabic satellite channels such as Al-Jazeera resonated ideologically with Arab diasporic viewers 'not only in terms of utility and functionality' but also that 'informed readings' of current events gave 'audiences discursive powers' that reinforced shared 'perceptions, ideas and images'.[84] Matar's research also highlights the apprehension towards Western media outlets and a general uneasiness about the positions of Arabs and their diasporas in the West, a sentiment also expressed in Noureddine Miladi's work. Miladi's article examines the consumption and interpretation of Al-Jazeera among the Arab diaspora in London in comparison to Western news outlets such as the BBC and CNN. Resonating with Matar, Miladi argues that although an increasing number of Arabs in London 'view themselves as part of the fabric of British society' they still feel 'poorly served and represented by the British media' especially in terms of news coverage.[85]

As well as their remarks of 'inaccurate and biased reporting' by Western media, respondents in Miladi's study also commented on the lack of trust they have with their national Arab state channels in their countries of origin.[86] Instead, Miladi argues, Arab satellite channels such as Al-Jazeera create what she calls 'an emerging transnational Arab public sphere'.[87] This pan-Arab collectiveness found in such channels widens 'the debate about what should be discussed in relation to the concerns of Arab people' and thus moves away from limited nation-bound issues to offer a 'wide perspective' of 'Arab culture'.[88] Connecting this to Roza Tsagarousianou's extensive research on Muslims in Europe is significant. While Miladi expresses the notion of a 'transnational Arab public sphere' in relation to pan-Arab satellite channels, Tsagarousianou calls this 'constellation of "mainstream" and "alternative" media' the 'European Muslim mediascape'.[89] Through this space, Tsagarousianou argues, Muslim viewers across Europe are able to 'engage in processes of exchange, translation and hybridization' with others.[90] Using what she calls 'injustice frames' as central to a 'production of a common stock of experience',[91] Tsagarousianou explains how this can translate across mediascapes. Among her respondents, Tsagarousianou found a common empathy towards countries 'where Islam is practiced'.[92] This can be linked to Matar's concept of 'over-identification', where a meta-narrative consumes and infiltrates pre-conceived discourses. For all researchers mentioned earlier the underlying sentiments of Arab diasporic uncertainty, discrimination and biased media representation in host countries contribute to the 'injustice frames' highlighted by Tsagarousianou, so even though respondents hail from a number of nationalities and cultures they are united through a 'translocal lens' played by the media to interpret distant suffering and injustice as part of their daily lives.[93] It is therefore this collective 'insider-ness' as a result of feeling 'outsider-ness' within their given European societies that allows for pan-Arab media, such as Al-Jazeera, to act as a 'transnational Arab public sphere' as well as to contribute towards a 'European Muslim mediascape'.

Thus this book continues this contribution of the experience of Arab media, especially in terms of the Arab diaspora and music. It is here where we dive into the beat boxes, car radios and super speakers of Doha and London, where Arab and Arab-English diasporic communities are found listening to the crooning tunes of the Lebanese singer Fairouz. Emphasis is placed on the reasoning behind patterns of listening, looking to see when and why fans are motivated to listen to Fairouz's music, and considering whether the singer features in listeners' lives at specific moments in time, or whether she forms a natural constituent of their daily activities. This bestows upon audiences a level of agency that did not surface in Stone's book, *Popular Culture and Nationalism in Lebanon*, an invaluable resource in its thorough documentation of Fairouz and the Rahbani brothers. Stone examines the sociocultural and political roles of Fairouz in Lebanon and on the folklore genre of music. While he mentions audiences to some extent, his focus is on Lebanese audiences. Although her songs depict a very specific lifestyle, Fairouz's music has an international, inter-religious, inter-sexual and inter-gendered appeal. It is therefore important to look at how audiences are able to situate the meanings of Fairouz's songs according to their own individual experiences.

Kenneth Habib offers a more social perspective on Fairouz and her music in his doctoral dissertation. As an ethnomusicologist, Habib's dissertation is rich with factual moments in the singer's life, which he relates to key historical milestones in Lebanese and Arab history. In addition to his comprehensive discography and vocal analysis of Fairouz, Habib conducts interviews with people from Lebanon and members of the Lebanese diaspora residing in the United States. However, the objectives of the interviews are to decipher and illuminate Fairouz's various meanings, rather than to examine her significance as part of the diasporic experience and the impacts thereof. In order to give voice to the 'the most invisible of the invisibles',[94] and to ensure 'anthropological interpretations of the everyday' are not 'undermined',[95] it is vital that the Arab diasporic fans of Fairouz are materialized into research that focuses on their subjective and collective trans-experiences.

Notes on fieldwork

Fieldwork was conducted in London, England and Doha, Qatar, to offer a multidimensional, spatio-temporal, cultural and socio-economic contrast in participants. Recruitment was done through snowballing and 'site-based' methods, such as attending social and community events. In Qatar, those mostly took place in the form of private social gatherings, whereas in London, some participants were recruited through unisex hair salons and restaurants in residential areas populated by members of the Arab diaspora.

Initially, it was planned that a combination of focus groups and individual interviews would be the two methods for data gathering, but after experimenting with three focus groups during the Qatar segment of the fieldwork, it was decided that one-on-one open-ended interviews would be the sole approach. The focus groups did not provide a comfortable space for interviewees to open up about personal experiences in relation to Fairouz's music. Participants in the focus groups were hesitant about their responses, concerned about what other members thought, and reluctant to provide any emotionally significant information. In one case – a focus group that contained both males and females from Lebanon – tensions rose as the male participants mocked the females and this made for an awkward exchange, to the extent that I had to ask the males to leave. Discussing this particular focus group is important, as it brought to the surface the key differences in diasporic circumstances that stemmed from gender, falling under what Mansour and Sabry would call the 'complex politics of diasporic relations'.[96] In this group, gender relations were seen as the most prominent drivers in the responses to listening behaviours and reception of Fairouz and her music. For instance, the women in the focus group all came to Qatar with their husbands for economic reasons. While compliance with this situation was not explicitly discussed, it was hinted at through their responsive reasoning about listening to Fairouz's music. On the other hand, the men in the group were essentially their own decision-makers and left Lebanon to find work. This discrepancy meant that the very experience of 'diasporaness' – being a leader/follower diasporan – is dissimilar and carries implications that may hinder acceptance and understanding of the opposite sex's media consumption habits, thus putting them into conversation with each other can cause friction and confrontation.

Listening to Fairouz's music was often a shared experience; however, the relationship with it was deeply personal. The focus groups did not allow for an interactive and enthusiastic communal discussion. On the contrary, they were awkward and uncomfortable as participants either were reluctant to share their Fairouzian experience or were defensive with other members in the group. This showcased the ways in which focus groups can gather diasporic encounters at the 'confluence of economic, political, cultural and psychic processes'.[97] A space that hosts uneven 'power geometries' that vary among 'different individuals' who 'are placed in very distinct ways' in the 'flows and interconnections' of power.[98] Linking this gendered power imbalance to Lawler's affect theory of social exchange is significant since he argues that 'individual actors make decisions about whether to exchange, with whom to exchange, and under what terms'.[99] Affective topics, such as the role of Fairouz in diasporic life, create barriers in settings where imbalances of power were found (e.g. the choice to migrate versus having to migrate with a spouse) to be shaping the 'exchanges' among participants. Interviews, on the other hand, provided a private space for deeper questioning and discovery, permitting an opportunity for respondents to be freer with their answers. The one-on-one interviews, conducted in cafés, homes and workspaces, were more conducive, as individuals were encouraged to discuss their private listening behaviours and were open about the ways Fairouz factored in their lives.

As a former resident of Qatar, the concept of immersion did not challenge me, as I knew that it would be easy for me to integrate. However, as a female researcher, certain issues arose that were unexpected. As a woman in a relatively conservative community, approaching Arab men was tricky. The men I interviewed were either introduced to me by friends or by a common acquaintance. Meetings were mostly conducted at their place of work or in their homes in the presence of their families. While there were some exceptions, many of the middle-aged men were uncomfortable with being seen in public with a female and, in some cases, it was the wives who discouraged any such meeting. Participants recruited in Qatar without an introduction from a common acquaintance were apprehensive about talking about their experiences in general, let alone engaging in deep dialogue about Fairouz.

Valuable resources found in both sampling fields were hair stylists. Whether they had their own salons, as in London, or would come to your house, as in Doha, hair stylists played an important part in this research. In London, not only did the hair stylists I met introduce me to more interviewees, they also provided a spatial forum in which conversation about Fairouz flowed between a haircut, a wash and a blow dry. In Doha, the hair stylist who comes to our home brought up the subject of my research, saying he had heard from clients that I was working on something about Fairouz. He expressed his interest in being interviewed and also assisted me by relaying messages to his other clients about my research and asking them if they were interested in speaking to me.

Although I had previously lived and studied in London, I was unfamiliar with the diasporic communities there and expected the fieldwork to be challenging. However, social media contacts were helpful in spreading information about my research, which meant I was able to meet a wide range of people from various backgrounds and nationalities. While interviews took me all over London, there were key areas, such as Uxbridge Road, Kensington, Edgware Road, East Acton and North Acton that stuck out as being highly populated by the Arab diaspora. An Uxbridge Road café that serves Lebanese food, a hairdressing salon on Old Oak Road and a restaurant with live entertainment, all allowed for public spaces that were ideal for participant observation and spontaneous interviews, something very difficult to do with the Qatar sample.

While, originally, my research was going to take me to Detroit, Michigan, I was discouraged by the logistics of this, especially in terms of relocating there for over two months with my then almost two-year-old infant. It was thus decided to conduct my research in London, England, instead. Although I did not have ready access to the London-based Arab diasporic community, I was still able to tap into different sources to gather recipients. A contact at a renowned pan-Arab newspaper, a musician, a social worker, a hair stylist and an academic, among others, assisted by referring me to individuals to interview, in turn, those then offered introductions to other participants.

At the start of his book *Becoming Arab in London: Performativity and the Undoing of Identity*, Ramy Aly discusses the approach he used to recruit members for his study. For Aly, 'site-based' methods, such as visiting *Shisha* cafés, were key to providing 'remarkably rich insights on the ways in which people expressed their ethnicity, class and gender'.[100] Initially, this seemed an ideal way for me to target samples for my research. However, as a female researcher, I quickly learned that space was very much a gendered concept. *Shisha* cafés are typically masculine places that would be tainted with trepidation and scepticism should a female enter and strike up a random conversation with males from the Arab diaspora. In turn, as a lone woman, it was a disconcerting notion to even try to enter such spaces. Instead, I focused on neutral places, to recruit and meet members of the Arab diaspora. It is significant to note that these trips were not as successful in building rapport with respondents. In a few cases, people refused to speak to me as they were perplexed by my reasons for approaching them, and so adequate time and effort had to be given in trying to build trust among respondents to ensure interactions were comfortable and secure. Spontaneously approaching people in public places rarely resulted in responses that provided much depth. It was also necessary to give a background on myself, as a researcher, to qualify the reasoning behind my questions.

Participants were composed of native Arabic speakers, who varied in nationality, gender and age, who came from a background of voluntary or involuntary displacement, and who were living away from their countries or cities of origin. Arab nationals from the Levant region, (Lebanon, Jordan, Syria, Iraq and Palestine) were more active Fairouz listeners than those from the Gulf States, North Africa and Africa, but this did not limit the regional recruitment of participants, as long as they were fans of the singer. Since Fairouz's music has been accused of perpetuating 'the lore of the Christian folk of Mt. Lebanon',[101] it was vital that demographics stemmed from backgrounds that varied religiously, socially, politically and economically. It should be understood that this sample is in no way indicative of Fairouz's listeners universally, nor is it representative of diasporic communities specifically. Instead, this book offers a theoretical lens through which to analyse and interpret possible forms of identity construction and interpretation through the music of Fairouz as it explores the ways, in which music can shape Arab diasporic experience, amidst a dynamic backdrop of revolutions, forced migrations and changing political landscapes.

Converging and diverging on multiple points, responses from over forty hours of in-depth qualitative interviews were organized thematically and analysed individually, contextually and comparatively. A series of trajectories emerged showcasing the pivotal roles in which Fairouz and her music play on the angry streets of the Arab world, in the hushed private corners of the home and in the personal memories and minds of participants. Essentially, discussing Fairouz meant discussing diasporic life, of living in '*Al-ghurba*',[102] of perceptions of belonging and identity during a tense time in which opinions of being Arab came with a host of newly packaged negative connotations. The attributes of participants and the ways they positioned themselves in space and time brought to surface various themes, which form the chapters of this book.

Contextualizing – meta- and micro-habitus

While living in two distinctive geographical locations presented an obvious difference in diasporic experiences, it is important to stress that the interviewees came from a range of political, economic and social backgrounds, varied in nationality, religion and gender. This brought to light 'intersectional' qualities that are often ignored in diasporic conversations. Referring here to Floya Anthias who, through her thorough discussion on previous academic studies of diaspora, criticizes the reductionist use of the term to 'describe the processes of settlement and adaptation relating to a large range of transnational migration movements', which 'privileges the point of "origin" in constructing identity and solidarity' and therefore 'fails to examine transethnic commonalities and relations' also frequently disregarding 'differences of race and class'.[103] For Anthias, focusing only on 'deterritorialized ethnicity' negates the 'intersectional' qualities of the diaspora. Homogenizing diasporic experience undermines internal relationships within groups, which is what Mansour and Sabry call the 'intra-diasporic subjectification dynamics'.[104] These may materialize through trajectories such as gender, social class and 'transethnic alliances',[105] and should be taken into consideration when studying diasporic communities. It is also necessary to note that intersectional qualities are discursive, in the sense that self-classifiers, such as religion or marital status, can polarize and position members within their communities differently at various points in time. In a post-9/11 world, with the aftertaste of the controversially named 'Arab Spring', Arabs and their religion are topical, so while Anthias's argument rings true in exploring diasporic dynamics, she ignores key sociopolitical undercurrents, which also need to be examined in tandem with individual environments. Turning to Bourdieu and his notion of *habitus* provides a stepping-stone from which to best show how the intersectional qualities of Fairouz's fans, coupled with both geographical location and temporal events, provide a more holistic framework to understand and interpret diasporic experience.

For Bourdieu, *habitus* 'ensures the active presence of past experiences'.[106] It is the notion that individuals do not reach certain conclusions or decisions autonomously, but, rather, are pushed 'by historically and socially situated conditions'.[107] Bourdieu does not negate the notion of free will or free agents, instead he argues, 'the *habitus* makes possible the free production of all the thoughts, perceptions and actions inherent in the particular conditions of its production – and only those'.[108] It is this 'internalisation of externality', which drives and catalyses the fusion of 'free will' and 'external forces' to adhere to the effects of the *habitus*.[109] For Bourdieu, the past is key to explaining the notion of *habitus*, and it is the past, which produces the present and shapes the individual 'in the form we have today'.[110] But what if this present is not constant? What if circumstances are rapidly changing for those citizens who come from a variety of backgrounds and 'socially situated conditions' that they cannot keep up? What if a peaceful past *habitus* has been transformed into a violent present? What if an individual who has lived in a community ripe with belonging and dignity now combats challenges of racism and ignorance?

Although there is no argument that the 'embodied history' of an individual plays a pivotal role in the course of his/her life, the *habitus*, as a sole second-level *system*, a 'system of structured, structuring dispositions',[111] is confining. In discussions with interviewees, *habitus* took on a twofold level of influence; these will be referred to as the *meta-habitus* and the *micro-habitus*. Instances of *meta-habitus* reside as the overarching consequence of the political, social, cultural and environmental systems in which the participants reside. *Micro-habitus* refers to more concentrated situations, such as domestic arrangements, familial ties and gender roles within the *meta-habitus*. While, for Bourdieu, it is the overall *structure*, which takes on the role of the *meta-habitus* described here, it can be argued that although global *structures* are an all-consuming societal phenomenon, they often fluctuate in conjunction and irrespective of each other. So, while *structure* provides indicative qualities on aspects of life and living, it requires a second-level gauge with which to visualize and understand certain actions or reactions. This can be seen through the *meta-habitus*, which works in tandem with objective daily oscillations and the subjective *micro-habitus*. So, even though those in this study may have been brought together geographically and historically in each sampling field, the *meta-* and *micro-habitus* provide deeper analysis into the differentiation of their experience. To better understand the relationship between *meta-habitus* and the *micro-habitus*, it is necessary to turn to the samples in London and Doha.

Interviews in London were conducted during key times in which (a) the UK was gearing up to vote for or against leaving the European Union (EU), and then (b) when they actually voted 52 to 48 per cent in favour of leaving the EU, otherwise known as Brexit. During fieldwork in mid-June 2016, pre-Brexit vote, and on the way to interviews by either bus or tube, Britons wore their opinions on buttons and badges, 'I'm voting in', or 'I'm voting out', 'I'm voting remain' and 'I'm voting leave'. While multiple economic, political and social factors contributed to the vote, a main argument conceded racism and xenophobia as the leading force behind the decision.[112] In their article 'Racism, Crisis, Brexit', Virdee and McGeever 'focus on the place of race and racism in the crisis that led to *Brexit*'.[113] By 'examining the discursive dimensions of the Leave Campaign', which entailed 'a deep nostalgia for empire' and the 'Powellite narrative of retreating from a globalizing world that is no longer recognizably "British"', the authors contend, 'carefully activated long-standing racialized structures of feeling about immigration and national belonging' were triggered.[114] This is significant to mention, as the atmosphere in the UK was conflicted on Europe generally and on the idea of 'foreigners' specifically. This discrepancy in opinion found its way to the coffee shops, restaurants and parks, where members of the Arab diaspora living in London talked about Fairouz and their lives.

During dessert at the Banana Tree, a Thai fusion restaurant on Westbourne Grove, on 16 June 2016, Asma,[115] 36, has just finished being interviewed. The tape recorder has been switched off and the topic of conversation has turned to Brexit. With an air of confidence, Asma, from Syria, says she is going to vote Leave on 23 June 2016, because she does not want 'foreigners' like the 'Polish' and 'Romanians' to take over jobs in England. After pointing out that she too is a 'foreigner', she replies that it was 'different'. Further explanation of what is meant by 'different' is not asked.

On a bench in Queen's Park on 21 July 2016, Jana is answering a question about self-identifying in the city of London. '*I don't feel fully English and I don't feel fully Arab either*', she explains, '*And I think even though I have a hundred percent Arab genes, I'm a hybrid, I am of the new generation, you know second-generation immigrant that has morphed*'. After expressing admiration for Sadeeq Khan, the Mayor of London, '*not because I'm a great fan of Sadeeq Khan, I'm not, but because he was of ethnic minority and because he was a Muslim*', Jana clarifies that even though she is not '*particularly religious*', this sense of multiculturalism is what makes living in London so appealing. She is then asked how she feels about Brexit:

> *Awful. I still feel absolutely appalled but I think Angela Merkel will fight Teresa May, I cannot stand Teresa May, she is the epitome of everything English that I absolutely detest because she's conservative, she's racist, closet racism and that's the one thing about English people that is really hard to accept, is this closet racism. They will never ever tell it to your face. But you will see it manifesting itself in the smallest of ways . . . I've experienced it all the time in my community; right here in Queen's Park . . . in my work. You know, people will just, it's just that look in their eyes, just like: 'OH, really? Mm . . .' and I can see it's in the balls of their eyes: 'F**k you, you f***ing foreigner, you can piss off back to your country'. And I say well yeah I would do if I could but I can't.* (Jana, 48, Palestinian/Syrian, London)

Married to a Scottish-Englishman and living in England since she was 'nine and a half', Jana has experienced 'closet racism' by colleagues and members of social circles. For Jana, Brexit was a confirmation of that racism. In comparison, Asma, who has lived in numerous cities around the world before settling in London, who is battling the reality of war in her home in Syria and who comes from a middle-upper class background sees London as '*very diverse, you don't feel like a stranger at all, and it is very easy to integrate . . . there are a lot of Arabs*'. The difference in attitudes towards Brexit showcases the ways in which intersectional qualities, coupled with the *meta-habitus* and *micro-habitus*, allow for a more holistic analysis into quotidian behaviour and experiences, which move beyond a surface-level diasporic-washing of understanding. This context allows for a deeper interpretation of the ways in which Fairouz and her music are consumed. Whether she is a source of pride, '*She's somebody that I'm proud of, she's a role model for me*' (Jana), or whether she is a reminder of loss during a stressful time, '*And Fairouz, heiki*[116], *she brings back memories, and home, patriotism, just the sense of belonging*' (Asma).

The newly formed *meta-habitus* with Brexit in London, its implications and the significances arising from it, coupled with a glocalized *structure* of racism and apprehension, both inside and outside the UK, needs to be considered in lieu of the intersectional qualities and *micro-habitus* of participants. While Brexit may not have a direct impact on responses, as a *meta-habitus* it creates a certain ambience affecting the '*sense of belonging*' participants feel on opposite sides of the Brexit spectrum. Similarly, these traits need to be contemplated with the Qatar sample hosts of different situational dynamics.

Alliance and transience

Geographically, Qatar is at a strategic point in the Middle East and, demographically, it allowed for an illustrative spectrum of diasporic audiences in the Arab world, offering a wide range of participants to interview, varying in age, nationality, gender and religion. As a nation, Qatar affords some of its foreign residents high-paying jobs and financial peace of mind, making it a desirable place to live. However, even though statistically non-Qataris are the majority, strict citizenship rules and stringent visa regulations are applied to ensure their stay in the country is purposeful and non-permanent. Purchasing property is close to impossible and comes with a series of discouraging conditions. Non-locals are therefore constantly conscious that they may have to leave at any given moment. This is the *meta-habitus* condition of the participants, who quite often vocalized a sense of unsettlement.

Jihad has been living in Doha for over twenty-five years, but his idea of home is confusing. As a '*son from a Palestinian family, who were kicked out of Palestine like many other people in 1948*', Jihad was born and raised in Jordan. With no parents to return to in Jordan and the inability to move back to Palestine, deciding where to go with his family after Qatar is perplexing. These qualities comprise the *micro-habitus*. Even though Fairouz is not the only instigator of Jihad feeling '*homesick*', she complements the sentiment that exists independently, with or without her.

While the notion of 'home' will be explored in more detail later in the book, it is used here to highlight the differences in *micro-habitus*. There was an evident divide among the Arab diasporans interviewed, both intersectional and also as a result of their *micro-habitus*, a distinction between those who lived in Qatar for most of their lives, like Jihad, who have a vague notion of where home is, while on the other hand, those who have lived in Qatar for a shorter period and have a clearer notion of home:

For me, Lebanon is my home. You know the song Watani[117] [by Fairouz]? Yeah this is it for me. Not just because I was born there, but also because it's my home. Wherever I'll go in the world, it's temporary, but Lebanon will always be the place I belong and will go back to . . . (Bianca, 37, Lebanese, Qatar)

However, the *micro-habitus* is not just limited to the time spent in Doha, nor is it just a secure sense of home. Discussions surrounding the *micro-habitus* and notions of home will be showcased in the chapters to come, but here, it is also important to discuss the global context surrounding the timeframe of this book, which had an impact on both the *meta-habitus* and *micro-habitus* of participants in this study – the Syrian conflict.

In January 2011, a Tunisian street vendor by the name of Mohamed Bouazizi set himself on fire in protest of then president Zine al-Abidine Ben Ali's government, triggering mass demonstrations across Tunisia and forcing the ruler of twenty-three years to flee. Soon after, more anti-government protests erupted across the Arab world in Bahrain, Libya, Yemen, Egypt and Syria. While discussing the details of all these uprisings is beyond the scope of this book, the Syrian conflict is perhaps the most significant in terms of foreign interference, loss of lives, destruction and the subsequent exodus of millions of Syrian refugees. Whereas London committed to settling a small number of them, the Gulf States such as Qatar and Saudi Arabia refused to accommodate them. Thoughts among participants on the conflict were divided. Since a number of Syrian respondents were targeted, answers on the topic of Fairouz differed on how much was at stake for them, but also it shaped responses by those who worked closely with refugees, highlighting the ways the *meta-habitus* and *micro-habitus* are crucial in trying to understand the consumption of Fairouz's music.

Even when the conflict resided on the same *meta-habitus* level, with its confusing set of alliances, attitudes towards fellow Arabs, perspectives on the ways in which participants positioned themselves, and growing distrust in regional leadership were also brought up in conversations about Fairouz. The excerpt shown highlights some of the differences between two participants: Maha, a Lebanese-Syrian social worker and performing artist, who moved to London for her master's degree over twelve years ago, and Ayman, an actor and a self-classified Syrian refugee, who has been living in London for over six years, who *'flew from Syria three days before all the problems started'*:

Yeah! I stopped listening to her for a while. When the conflict started in Syria, I stopped listening to Fairouz because what I was getting from the media is that she was taking quite a hard position in support of the government. And I just feel that too many lives were being lost for anyone to be taking sides and I think I was very angry with her so I stopped listening to her. (Maha, 35, Syrian/Lebanese, London)

I'm not pro regime and I'm not pro revolution because to me they are both shit. So, people started to talk about Fairouz and Sabah Fakhry, and they would say, oh, if only she didn't support Al-Assad. What do they know about her? They wanted this

division; they didn't want people to be objective . . . whatever you say you are either
labelled to be here or there. (Ayman, 34, Syrian, London)

Under the umbrella of the Syrian conflict, opinions on Fairouz and her political
stance can be seen as a reflection of both the *meta-habitus* and *micro-habitus* and
the need to examine answers through a multi-tier framework, further highlighting
the heterogeneity of the diasporic community, even when nationality is the
constant. For Maha, Fairouz's political link to the Syrian regime was enough to
stop listening to her music for a while, it was only after her brother informed
her '*that there'd been a misinterpretation of what she had said*' that she decided
'*I'll just forgive her!*' While Maha was not explicitly pro-revolution, her distaste
for the Syrian regime and the choice to position herself against Syrian president
Bashar Al-Assad was enough to ostracize Fairouz from her life. This was different
for Ayman, who found dichotomies like this typical of the '*schizophrenic and
hypocritical nature*' of Syrians and Arabs. Frustrated with the 'with us or against
us' claims of the conflict, Ayman's interview intertwined Fairouz in all aspects of
life from home, to love and to the Syrian struggle. More specifically it highlighted
the ways in which, for him, Arabs romanticized the notion of a revolution, one
they could not in reality handle:

> *They can't use words as revolution like that. They are not singing a song for Fairouz.
> It's not a song. If they want a revolution they should do it. Uh no they won't because
> they can't live that way but they don't mind others living that way. If they can't
> handle the troubles of the revolution they should shut up.* (Ayman, 34, Syrian,
> London)

The anger expressed by Ayman is targeted at both Arabs and their leaders. Blaming
internal and external stakeholders of the conflict, Ayman's lack of trust towards
them was something he reiterated multiple times. However, this was not only
restricted to Syrian respondents. Whether speaking under the pretext of the Syrian
conflict or not, this scepticism towards Arabs and their leaders was shared by other
participants from other nationalities and from various *micro-habitual* situations.

Trying to divorce the subject of the Arab diaspora from war and violence is
challenging, especially at a time when millions have been displaced and a sense
of uncertainty is prevalent. Migrating as a result of conflict goes beyond just
classifying members of the diaspora as either being a migrant or a refugee. This
form of migration brings with it a plethora of meanings, both at the *meta-* and
micro-habitus level, whether individuals and their families are impacted by conflict
directly, or not. Many members of the diaspora interviewed left their countries of
origin due to conflict, whether it was the Lebanese civil war and its aftereffects,
or the first and second Gulf wars, in both Kuwait and Iraq, or because of the
Palestinian *Nakba* in 1948. It was evident that the Syrian struggle, like those before
it, had personal repercussions on the sense of home, of belonging and of where
to return. Whether participants were migrants or refugees, or even non-Syrians
who worked with refugees, feelings of displacement and loss were clear in all their

depictions. Due to the large scale of foreign interference, the loss of many lives and the destruction of property, the Syrian conflict reaches far beyond the public sphere parameters of nation, region, and even continent, in this way, it acts as both *structure* and *meta-habitus*, paving the way for multiple lines of merging and deviation. Telling of an era in which political alliances are fleeting and confusing, the significance of the Syrian conflict is that it showed the ways in which Fairouz is positioned according to fans' *meta-* and *micro-habitus* and the ways in which those impact upon receptions of sociopolitics and identity. It also gave insight into how participants saw themselves.

Comparing London and Doha: A discussion

This book was not intended to be a comparative study of the diaspora in London and Doha but, rather, to demonstrate the role Fairouz and her music play in the lives of her listeners. Differences were found *within* the two geographical samples, since participants came from an array of backgrounds, finding points of commonality, but also digressing on certain themes. With their distinct sets of laws, cultural codes and environments, London and Doha provide two separate backdrops against which members of the Arab diaspora reside, which diversifies the colours in the meanings through which Fairouz is transferred and interpreted. For instance, feelings of 'foreignness' experienced by respondents were manifested in different ways. In Doha, no matter how long participants lived there, attitudes to 'home', nationhood and belonging were driven by the fact that, at some point, leaving would be expected. In this way, many participants felt they were transient, 'foreign bodies' that could only stay as long as they were employed. While this was not the case in London, there was also uneasiness in social positions, since interviews took place before and after Brexit. Participants in London talked about the overt racism they experienced as Arabs from individuals in the country but, in Doha, this racism was more collectively implicit, as it is embedded in the laws of the country, which favours nationals over expatriates at various points. This ability to integrate and 'feel at home' therefore drove mixed responses in regard to Fairouz and her music, marking the difference between nostalgia as 'reclaiming what seems lost'[118] and nostalgia as something that never was and in many cases never will be.

In addition, certain themes arose among the London participants that were not mentioned by members of the study in Doha, and vice versa. For example, the discussion of women and their roles in society in the context of Fairouz and her music arose in the London sample a number of times. Many female respondents identified as feminists, and they commented on Fairouz's role as either a supporter of or an adversary to feminist thought. However, this was not the case in Doha, where four respondents candidly talked about their own social positions in regard to gender, whether it was their own experience in the workplace or the expectations put on Arab Muslim women to be veiled. In two instances, Fairouz was brought in as a standard against the hypersexualization of female performers and also as an exemplar of ideal 'motherhood'. Otherwise, trying to compare inter-samples from Doha and London was futile, because of the many intra-differences among the samples themselves. The importance of the *meta-* and *micro-habitus* in discussions on Fairouz surface here, as they provide a framework within which to assess both intra-group and inter-geographical dynamics among respondents. The intersections of these structures allowed for a levelling of the plane on which to assess listening and interpreting behaviours with regard to Fairouz's music. Being able to understand notions of identity, belonging and positions in space and time required both globalized and specialized levels of analysis amidst a fluctuating field of research.

Generational, national and domestic situations also played a part in the mixed responses given by participants, and so crediting geographical placement as the main reason for those differences would be reductive and inaccurate. To better highlight this, I would like to briefly talk about respondents based on their nationality. Beginning with Syrian nationals, the crisis in Syria has seen much division since the start of the conflict in January 2011. Due to visa restrictions placed on Syrians entering Qatar, it was difficult to secure respondents for this study who lived in Doha. So, all the Syrian partakers in this research lived in London. Participants ranged from being sympathetic with the Syrian regime to being neutral with both sides, or otherwise staunchly opposed to Bashar Al-Assad and his government. Relationships with Fairouz thus fluctuated according to these positions, further emphasizing the heterogeneity of diasporic groups and the ways the *micro-* and *meta-habitus* work together to illustrate contrasts as well as parallels.

Iraqi participants in Doha and London also differed on attitudes towards Iraq. While some Iraqi interviewees had fond memories of their childhood or past in Iraq, others felt no sense of belonging there, and they were happy to have left. Although these relationships are complicated, they are significant in that they shape the ways Fairouz is heard and understood. The relationships with the 'home' country and the reasons behind leaving play a part in how participants situate themselves in space, and in how they feel about their situation in that space. It is the difference of whether they feel that they are/were refugees, or are living in exile because they opposed a certain political leadership, or whether they are nostalgic towards their countries of origin and desire to return, and it is these differences that contribute to the attitudes and deconstruction of meaning found in Fairouz's music.

Essentially, such discussions indicate it is not only about where the diaspora is currently residing but also how they got there that is of greater importance. However, this is not to say that living conditions do not matter at all. Offering another interesting perspective, Palestinian members perhaps combined the past of getting there with present living conditions and, in the case of the Doha sample, the future questions about where to go next. Palestinian participants in London are all British citizens, but those in Doha either held Jordanian, Lebanese, American or Canadian passports, which complicated their visions for their future plans to leave Doha. In effect, this stability and instability, as part of the *micro-* and *meta-*

habitus, situated them differently in space. In general, Palestinian contributors were reminded of Palestine in the songs of Fairouz, commenting on the ways the singer brought back nostalgia for their homeland and gave them hope of returning one day. However, the difference lies in their ability to travel back to Palestine. Palestinian respondents in London travelled there frequently, while those in Doha could never go, or rarely went back. So, Fairouz's songs took on different meanings here, temporally and spatially, as a complement to the past, which can be visited in the present, or as the only means by which to travel there. To collectively compare samples in the two locations would be to polarize responses on an uneven plane, discarding the complexities that arise within the communities themselves. There needed to be an individual and collective analysis of Arab diasporic communities that looked at both their private and social role amidst the environment that they inhabit. The *micro-* and *meta-habitus* thus offer such a lens through which to be able to take into account intersectional responses towards Fairouz and her music.

Navigating the book

The book is divided into seven chapters. Chapter 2 highlights key concepts and defines relevant terminologies used in the book. Looking at past studies on Fairouz, it positions the research theoretically and outlines the rationale behind its undertaking. An overview of the Lebanese singer Fairouz is given, from a short biography of her life detailing her creative impact on the Arab music scene to situating her and her music within a local, regional and global framework. It is here that the argument against Stone's statement that Fairouz was part of a 'post-colonial, nation-building project' is outlined, explaining how Fairouz cannot be tied to a specific place or time, since she is, in effect, post-national.[119] Drawing on Benjamin's discussion on the work of art and 'aura', it is contended that, unlike Benjamin's art which requires a specific spatio-temporal context to be fully appreciated, Fairouz's 'aura' gains significance the further it is removed from the location in which it first appeared, as exemplified by members of the Arab diaspora. This chapter also provides a short background on the history of Arab migration in London and Doha. Moreover, a description of what is meant by diaspora is given, one that does away with its homogenizing and limiting connotations to one that recognizes both its diversity and its ability to morph, change and to be 'continuously reconstructed and reinvented'.[120] Using the interrelations of the *meta-* and *micro-habitus,* Chapter 3 looks at the ways in which through Fairouz's music, participants situated themselves across spectra of belonging. The *meta-* and *micro-habitus* contribute towards this belonging and unfolding of affect among the Arab diaspora. Discussions on Fairouz brought up various ideas of 'Arabness' and what it means to be an Arab, and how that translated into themes of resistance and *iltizam.*[121] Nationhood, its palpability and its intangibility, and religion, as a key identifier and social positioner are also examined through their relationships with the *meta-* and *micro-habitus.*

Looking at the spaces in which these tangents of belonging occur, Chapter 4 unravels concepts of space and the ways that members of the Arab diaspora navigate through their environments by way of Fairouz's music. As a 'figure' of 'infinitely reproducible signifiers',[122] Fairouz gives her listeners the opportunity to understand and deconstruct her songs in their own ways. Interchangeable with her music, Fairouz affiliates herself with the messages she conveys, since she hardly participates or appears in any form other than that which is associated with her songs. She is an omnipresent force; deeply ingrained in memories and linked to past spaces and moments, and it is hard for participants to remove her from such settings. In this way, she creates 'aura' with her ability to be both incorporated within and simultaneously transgressing spatio-temporal realms. Through the mnemonic imagination of participants, Fairouz moves freely across space to 'achieve new meaning in the present'.[123]

Chapter 5 continues the discussion on space, switching the conversation to the concepts of 'absence' and 'presence'. Exploring the role Fairouz plays in creating the consciousness of where participants are and where they are not. 'Presence' and 'absence' are spatial markers, but they are also indicators of how affect and the mnemonic imagination collaborate with the *micro-* and *meta-habitus*, to navigate different forms of positioned awareness. In these discussions on 'presence' and 'absence', the terms '*Al-ghurba*', expatriation, and '*haneen*', nostalgia or craving, come to the surface. In spaces of prospect, where affect is able to bloom, Fairouz stands as the opposite of '*Al-ghurba*', as she embodies the comfort found in the search for '*haneen*'.

Dislocating the notion of Heimat from its geographical and historical origins and the sociopolitical history with which it is associated, Chapter 6 'reterritorializes' the German concept of homeland and puts it into conversation with *Al-Watan*, the Arabic term for homeland, to accommodate the Arab diaspora living in London and Doha. Building on existing political connotations of *Al-Watan* and drawing on Peter Blickle's[124] detailed study, I argue that the Arab homeland or *Watan* is found within the descriptive lyrics of Fairouz. So, while the German Heimat comes with both individual and social connotations specific to the German populace, *Al-Watan* accommodates different imaginaries. It is contended that Fairouz, through her songs, provides an opportunity for both 'personal' and 'popular memory' to coalesce and reconstruct so as to form a conceptual *Watan*, which participants have acquired through both 'individual and social elements of experience',[125] those which they have lived through themselves and also those which have been told to them, through the processes of storytelling. Fairouz provides the imagery of a premodern *Watan*, through comforting and desired imagery associated with 'home', and consequently the 'self', transporting her listeners to a place they acknowledge through their mnemonic imagination, but also to one in which they will always strive to live. From outlooks on homeland to exploring public and private spaces, this chapter also investigates the ways gender articulates and shapes diasporic experience. Looking at issues of mobility, naturalization and power, gender is examined as a subjective and collective experience, dependent on amalgamating factors arising from the *meta-* and *micro-habitus*.

Chapter 7 shifts the focus from the spatial to the temporal. Emphasis here is on the ways that time produces affectively modified associations with Fairouz's music. Whether respondents talked about how Fairouz provided comfort during times of war, or in comparison to how private and social developments alter understandings of Fairouz and her songs, or the ways in which memory materializes to take on various roles within the respondents' minds or, finally, how Fairouz is an inherited artist passed through generations that form part of familial lineages. Essentially, this chapter travels through the timelessness of Fairouz and her ability to be both keeper and disseminator of time.

Together, the chapters of this book reveal the ways in which Fairouz and her music filter into the lives of the Arab diaspora in Doha and London, with the aim of understanding how these narratives are *affected by*, and in turn *affect*, time and space. Through Fairouz, diasporic experience is revealed and explored, finding significance along multiple contextual, individual and social lines, transforming and adapting along the way.

Chapter 2

FAIROUZ, 'AURA' AND THE ARAB DIASPORA

It was through the kitchen window at her parents' modest flat in the Beirut suburb of Zuqaq Al-Blat that Fairouz encountered her first, albeit unwilling, public audience member. In a documentary about her life, she explains,

> I didn't have a radio, I listened to the neighbours' radio. . . . When I heard music coming from the neighbours who lived above us, I would be in the kitchen, and our kitchen was over the window of another neighbour who worked at night and slept during the day. I'd be in the kitchen in the daytime and when I heard the music I'd start singing and that would wake him up.[1]

While her neighbour may have been unappreciative of her talents at the time, Nouhad Haddad, who would later be known as 'the nightingale-voiced singer' Fairouz, was already garnering praise for her voice at school. Born on 21 November 1935, Nouhad's passion for singing was discovered early. She was encouraged to join the Lebanese Musical Conservatory by her teachers and was hired to sing in the chorus at the Lebanese Broadcasting radio station before her fifteenth birthday. Impressed by her vocal range and sharp memory, the head of the musical division at Lebanese Broadcasting, Halim Al-Roumi, took Nouhad under his wing, providing her with opportunities to showcase her voice, suggesting she call herself Fairouz – after a famous turquoise stone – and finally introducing her to Assi, who would later become her husband and musical companion, and to his brother Mansour Rahbani.

According to thespian and historian Nabil Abu Murad, Assi was taken by Fairouz's voice from the outset, but his brother Mansour did not share his admiration. Later, Mansour admitted he did not possess the same predictive sense as his brother but acknowledged that Fairouz 'came with an aura' of true talent.[2] The trio's journey began in 1951, with the first melody composed for her by Assi, *Habbaza Ya Ghuroub*.[3] However, it was not until 1953, with the song *I'tab* or *Blame*, that the group gained popularity. *I'tab* gave Fairouz and the Rahbanis further geographical exposure, when it was played on Syrian and Egyptian airwaves, garnering a large Arab fan base. This opened the door to more regional and international releases. According to ethnomusicology professor and director of the Cal Poly Arab Music Ensemble, Kenneth Habib, the cities of Damascus and

Cairo played integral parts in the success of the Rahbanis and Fairouz. *I'tab* was recorded with high-quality equipment at Damascus Radio Station. Damascus also featured prominently on the trio's tour agenda, making it a fundamental place in the enhancement and exposure of their work and music. Cairo, on the other hand, gave the group an identity and associated them with a cause. In 1957, the group released the song *Rajioun*,[4] recorded in Cairo,[5] and while *Rajioun* does not overtly refer to Palestinians and their plight, Habib contends, 'it has been widely interpreted in terms of and as supportive of the Palestinian cause'.[6] Indeed, to support his argument, the song became an anthem for Palestine Radio.[7]

The diverse spectrum of songs allowed Fairouz and the Rahbanis a greater sphere of influence. They were thus able to distribute their songs to a wider market and consequently to a more diverse audience. Their songs about young love, of defiance and resistance, of village life and of the beauty of nature, gave listeners multiple points on which to converge and find solace. For Habib, this meant that Fairouz 'became a symbol of Lebanon to those within the country and across the Arab world'.[8] Although, Fairouz often sings for and about Lebanon, I will later discuss how, as an artist, she does not just symbolize Lebanon but instead means 'different things to wide-ranging people in varying contexts'.[9] Under the direction of the Rahbani brothers, Fairouz worked with a multitude of international composers, allowing her to experiment with different styles of songs while simultaneously exposing her voice to a variety of Arab listeners. The use of an array of European and Western musical rhythms and genres gave the trio even greater universality.

In 1959, the group performed at the Damascus International Festival, their first appearance outside Lebanon, paving the way for a series of concerts around the globe, spanning over twenty-one nations. In turn, taking their music abroad created a contingent of diasporic supporters, as well as making 'the Fairouz-Rahbani team . . . local, regional and pan-Arab superstars'.[10] Reinforcing this idea is Jan Aliksan, who, in his book on Fairouz and the Rahbanis, quotes a Sydney-based journalist reviewing one of Fairouz's concerts, 'Fairouz appeared and we transformed from migrants, and displaced strangers to happy citizens, the country moved toward us in a historical moment: Fairouz recreated us, shared our feelings, gave us back our innocent childhood in the blink of an eye'.[11] It is this transformative power of Fairouz that is significant, the ability to create a sense of belonging for 'migrants, and displaced strangers' and her ability to dissolve both time and space.

Musical moments – The significance of Fairouz and the Rahbanis

Existing research on Fairouz is mostly in Arabic and biographical, Bishalani's book, *Fairouz*,[12] is an academic piece that looks at the music and discography of Fairouz until 1991. While Bishalani's work is a rich historical resource, as well as a comprehensive reference to Fairouz's songs, at times it fluctuates from the academic to the dramatic. Her attempts at trying to understand the intricate details of the split between Fairouz and Assi Rahbani digress from her important contribution to research on Fairouz, but she still provides a structured essay on

Fairouz's life, with oral histories from family members and friends of the singer. Majid Trad and Rabi' Mohammad Khalifa's *Fairouz: Her Life and Her Songs* offers a chronological composition, with some interesting interviews and an assortment of her music. Trad and Khalifa also provide an excerpt from Father Joseph Obeid, who examines the theme of prayer and spirituality in the music and performance of Fairouz.

In his doctoral dissertation, Kenneth Habib chronicles Fairouz's work, listing her theatrical, musical and audio-visual work as part of his aspiration to have written 'the first ethnomusicological dissertation in the English language'.[13] Contextualizing Fairouz and her songs against key historical, political and social moments in Lebanon and the Arab world, Habib suggests the singer's success was partly circumstantial, being 'in the right place at the right time to play an instrumental role in this larger cultural phenomenon corresponding to Lebanon's ascendance in the Arab world and on the larger world stage'.[14] For Habib, the Lebanese civil war played a part in elevating Fairouz to fame, but the author recognizes that 'perceptions of Fairouz and the experiences of Fairouz have not remained static'.[15] Habib gives a comprehensive and insightful overview of Fairouz and her music, linking the two to various parts of Lebanese life and culture. He also conducts a number of interviews with people from Lebanon and members of the diaspora in the United States to further elucidate Fairouz's various representations and meanings. Habib illustrates the nationalistic 'Lebanese-ness' of Fairouz, which is something that is also common in Christopher Stone's work.

Christopher Stone criticizes Fairouz as verging on being a 'post-colonial, nation-building project'.[16] Although there may be validity to Stone's thesis, thrusting the artist into a vessel of 'nation-building' that lacks agency, Stone's argument is problematic in that it confines Fairouz and her songs to one nation or homeland. Also, while not disputing literature on transnationalism and diaspora, which tend to focus on the media's influence in recreating and romanticizing the homeland, such as Stone's suggestion, the key argument here is that it is not a monolithic homeland, nor is it necessarily a tangible or real place. It is malleable and subjective, with the ability to be controlled. The idea of the tangible and concrete nation will thus be disputed, as focus is consigned more to audience response and the interpretation of how the homeland is perceived and the ways in which it changes.

In *Fairouz and the Rahbanis: Nation, Nostalgia and a Lebanese Cosmopolitan Modern*, Nasr explores how, through the development of radio and radio broadcasts, Fairouz and the Rahbani brothers exemplified a 'cosmopolitan modern, and modernizing, enterprise'.[17] Nasr's thesis takes on a number of concepts, looking at how the 'national imaginary' ties into the 'notion of pastoral "nostalgia"'. Drawing on Herzfeld's concept of 'social poetics', Nasr contextualizes the songs of the Rahbani and Fairouz coalition to 'situate' the '*qabaday* phenomenon and its relationship to nation and authority'.[18]

Defining '*qabaday*' as a 'champ/hero' who 'relies on his bodily strength', Nasr argues that 'the representational aesthetics of the Rahbani stage are built around Fairouz as a modern-day *qabadaya*, the site of a social poetics cast in "the voice" of Fairouz'.[19] In addition, Nasr ushers in Svetlana Boym's discussion on nostalgia in the realm of 'motifs' in the music of the Rahbanis. Nasr divides nostalgia into an individual and a social experience, the 'nostos' or 'the object of longing' or the 'home' is 'individual', while the 'algia' or the 'longing', a 'shared emotion' is 'social'.[20] It is on this foundation that Nasr examines select songs from Fairouz and the Rahbani brothers, charting the 'motifs/references' and putting them in conversation with 'social poetics', which 'extends to a total and all-encompassing Rahbani and Fairouzian conception of power and the very possibilities of nationhood'.[21] As illustrated, a number of themes emerge when discussing Fairouz – academically, historically, musically, journalistically and conceptually. Taking a more ethnographic route, this book demonstrates the ways in which Fairouz offers her diasporic listeners opportunities for exploring identities and points of belonging, positioning them temporally and spatially.

Acknowledging the complex and multifaceted success of Fairouz and the Rahbani brothers, Habib still contends that geopolitical, economic and social forces heralded their popularity in Lebanon and abroad. For Habib, Fairouz and the Rahbanis were swept up in Lebanon's 'golden age', which saw a rise in 'artistic, technological and political developments' after it gained independence from France in 1943.[22] Their accomplishments, therefore, were juxtaposed by an era-specific boom, which catapulted them to fame. Contextualizing artists within a specific geopolitical movement allows for a deeper analysis of their initial appeal. In her book on the Egyptian singer Umm Kulthum, Virginia Danielson provides a historical backdrop in which foreign interference by the British in Egypt was received with scepticism and contempt. Danielson suggests that appreciation for the music of Umm Kulthum was, in a way, a political act of rebellion by Egyptians of all classes who were disdainful of the British's actions in their country.[23] This authenticity and the focus on 'national heritage' was thus what drew Egyptian audiences towards her.[24] Danielson's book favours a biographical path from an audience-based ethnographical approach as she examines the artist in a changing sociopolitical climate. This is significantly relevant, especially in discussions on Fairouz and the diaspora. It allows for an interpolated discussion on audience and artist that is constantly contextually shifting. It is this flux of time and place, which gives weight to the argument that Fairouz is not bound by either realm, especially in terms of migratory listeners.[25]

The Fairouz–Rahbani coalition, which after Fairouz's separation from Assi in the 1970s included her son Ziad, was responsible for the production of over 1,000 songs and in excess of twenty musicals and three motion pictures, mostly revolving around the themes of village life, the prevalence of justice, love and the need for unity, against the backdrop of a rapidly deteriorating political climate. For Christopher Stone, Fairouz and the Rahbanis served as a reminder of one's 'Lebanese-ness',[26] attributing their popularity to the ways in which 'their works *represented* Lebanon'.[27] For Stone, this representation was normalized to cater to a particular stratum of Lebanese society, thus translating Lebanese folklore to mean 'the lore of the Christian folk of Mt. Lebanon'.[28] While Stone's critique requires due consideration, Lebanon and its population were not the only demographic targeted for this book, and limiting discourse to his idea of a standardized national identity is thus disadvantageous. As Nasr argues, 'treating the categories of religion, sect, state and nation as sources of pre-constructed identities is highly problematic'.[29] Nasr contends that the artists gained popularity at a time in Lebanon that saw rapid growth in 'cosmopolitan modernization and population and demographic change' inspiring the 'themes and aesthetics' prevalent in the works of the Rahbanis and Fairouz – and this is what Nasr goes on to describe as 'intermusical motifs'.[30] Both Nasr and Stone provide interesting perspectives on Fairouz and the Rahbani brothers in light of their success and constructions of nation, respectively. It is also necessary here to usher in Habib's reference to the commercial side of the group, discussing the ways in which music becomes a source of 'cultural exchange' in societies, connecting the consumers of music to the producers. In this way, Habib argues, music is commodified and traded as both an art form and a business. Thus, the meanings and messages of these art forms are also negotiated and procured among the audiences who consume them.[31]

Tracing the journey: Fairouz, the Rahbanis and the question of 'aura'

Although Fairouz's talent was evident from the outset, her marriage to Assi Rahbani and her artistic union with him and his brother, Mansour, elevated her success. The group 'forged the Lebanese artistic personality', which differed in form, length, content, lyrics and melody from other popular Arab music at the time.[32] Trad and Khalifa list the changes the Rahbani brothers made to Arabic music, explaining, 'the words of the songs were inherent of a specific social environment. . . . The length of the songs were shortened. . . . The melody was light . . . [They blended] different musical types from different sources. . . . The dialect in which the songs were sung used the ordinary Lebanese spoken dialect'.[33] They also shaped what is known today as Lebanese folklore and, as Stone contends, the three 'were and continue to be key players in the protracted struggle over the identity of [Lebanon]'.[34] However, Fairouz's appeal does not end with Lebanese audiences and to understand this better, it is necessary to understand what Fairouz[35] represents.

In *Keywords*, Raymond Williams outlines the sociopolitical progression of the word 'representation' to mean a 'symbol or image' or 'a visual embodiment of something'.[36] For Williams, representation has become a word to describe something that can be substituted for another thing, or something, which is 'not defined in its own terms'.[37] This bears resemblance to Benjamin's description of 'aura', or a simulation of the real that is taken as the real. Benjamin's 'aura' resulted from his observations on the development of technology and specifically its impact on the art world. It is vital, however, to liberate 'representation' and 'aura' from what Schroeder, Ong or Ihde would call the 'hegemony of vision', or their visually dominating implications. In other words, Fairouz's 'aura' here is not *only* dependent on her visual image, but rather its strength lies in the reception of her songs and music. It is thus Fairouz's voice that supports and amalgamates into her representation, and that subsequently feeds into her 'visual embodiment'. While the visual needs to exist, it is not the sole determinant of her 'aura'. Instead, it is this interplay between the visual and the soundscape that creates her 'aura'.

For many, Fairouz is a harbinger of peace, of a simple life, and of a just world. Through the medium of her songs, she can navigate religious, nationalistic and gendered boundaries that are consequently consumed and manipulated, stimulating multiple 'auras' that do not conform to a single representation. In her case, it is the reality of others, which affects and impacts upon her 'aura'. Her songs are decoded and appreciated according to individual experiences, and so her messages cannot be seen to have only one main 'Christian' folkloric ideal. Instead, Fairouz occupies a hybrid identity space, one in which multiple ideologies come into play and which symbiotically mould and reflect her 'aura'.

Concurrently, for Benjamin, the development in technology and 'mechanical reproduction' had resulted in a loss of 'aura', or what he called 'the here and now of the work of art'.[38] The physical environment of the work of art is what contributes to its 'aura', thus removing it from such a place causes its uniqueness to 'fade'. While this may be true of visual works of art, in the context of Fairouz it can be argued that her music takes on deeper meanings the further it moves from its physical location, especially in terms of diasporic audiences, who appropriate her songs individually and collectively in a variety of contexts. To elaborate on this point, the concept of the 'icon' is necessary. For Charles S. Peirce, 'the icon has no dynamic connection with the object it represents; it simply happens that its qualities resemble those of that object, and excite analogous sensations in the mind for which it is a likeness'.[39] Unlike other symbols and signifiers, icons are not exclusively tied to the form or object which they represent. Their 'likeness' is instead 'aided by conventional rules'.[40] These 'conventional rules' are often socially and culturally constructed. As an 'icon', Fairouz offers a 'common meeting place' for audiences who may share 'cultural rules', such as language, but that otherwise differ in aspects such as dialect, politics, religion, tradition and, perhaps even more relevantly, are spread across assorted *geographical* locations.[41] Although the visual and sonic embodiments of Fairouz thus construct her iconicity, allowing her to be recognized and identified by her audiences, albeit in various forms. It is, in fact, her 'aura' which travels through the realms of time and place and that transforms and becomes unmatched sets of feelings and meanings. It is important to keep these in mind when discussing Stone's work, which intertwines Fairouz and her songs to a very concrete place: the ancient Lebanese city of Ba'albeck.

In 1957, Fairouz debuted at the Ba'albeck International Festival, an annual event, which brought together artists and acts from all over the world. Although Fairouz performed in multiple venues in and outside Lebanon, Stone focuses on Ba'albeck as a 'symbol for modern Lebanon'.[42] For Stone, Fairouz was a strategic player in what he called 'a nation-building project' that was 'modelled on the much narrower Lebanon of the Christian mountain village envisioned by the founders of the Ba'albeck International Festival and their political sponsors'.[43] However, the problems with Stone's argument are threefold. First, associating Fairouz with a specific nation and religion counters the argument made by Habib and others that Fairouz's appeal was 'embraced by Lebanese across religious, economic and geographic boundaries'.[44] Second, according to Nasr, Stone ignores the 'dissonances, tensions and ambivalences present in the [Fairouz Rahbani] discourse' that are found in this 'idyllic' mountain village, as well as the 'conditions of lived and social experience' surrounding Fairouz's music.[45] Third, Stone's insistence on tying Fairouz down to a physical place, such as Ba'albeck, negates her 'aura's' fluidity and ability to move beyond the nation state.

Drawing on Chatterjee's concepts of the 'appropriation of the popular' and the 'classicization of tradition', Stone maintains that Ba'albeck was a crucial link in correlating Fairouz as a symbol for Lebanon, 'The presence of the popular, literally in the space of the classicized ruins, would represent a muscular claim to the past',[46] thus Fairouz is seen as another pillar in an ancient and historically significant place. However, rooting Fairouz to such a place denies her popularity among the deterritorialized. It assumes her audience are only those who see Ba'albeck as meaningful to them, that only Lebanese listeners are fans of her music, whereas it is those who are straddling, interlinking and intersecting identities that find the greatest appreciation in her lyrics.

To better grasp the significance of Fairouz among the displaced and diasporic, it is important to draw on John Fiske, who uses Baudrillard's 'simulacrum' to explain how, through the process of reproduced reality, individuals take on 'hyperreal' versions or representations of themselves, which Fiske calls 'figures'.[47] 'Figures', Fiske argues, are products composed of 'flesh, bone, and blood and a body of infinitely reproducible signifiers'[48] that materialize because of 'historical fortuitousness' and politicized attributes that are thrust on them in a specific place and time.[49] Media use and, in this case, the circulation of Fairouz's music in creating these 'figures' is vital, as it both constructs and replicates representations or associations of the 'figures', with their cause or symbolic value. In other words, certain individuals transcend their physicality to become symbolic forms or 'social terrains'.[50] This progression is inherently political and 'figures' are usually formulated with the assistance of discourse and 'historical fortuitousness'.[51] It is significant to point out here that 'figures' are not constant; they can be sculpted and manipulated by multiple subjectivities and vantage points.[52] Fairouz, as a 'figure', who can sonically shape-shift in the minds of her listeners is a vital component of this book.

To understand the interplay between Fairouz as an iconic 'figure' and the strength of her 'aura', it is important to shed light on the theory of affect, which involves her listeners' response. For Tomkins, affect is the 'primary innate motivating mechanism' in the human body.[53] It is the instigator, which triggers a consequent response in the 'midst of *in-between-ness*'.[54] The body's relationship to its surroundings and subsequent stimuli is the basis of affect.[55] While this explanation opens up opportunities through which to view individual responses to 'aura', it freezes 'aura' to a certain time and place, ignoring the multi-layered perspective of a diasporic experience of affect. 'Aura' can travel among spatio-temporal spheres. Sara Ahmed best demonstrates this by drawing on the philosopher John Locke's work. Coining the term 'Happy Objects', Ahmed takes into account Locke's example of the pleasure in eating grapes. Ahmed states, 'Happiness thus puts us into intimate contact with things. We can be happily affected in the present of an encounter',[56] meaning that the presence of certain objects or things can instigate the affect of happiness in a person. However, and as Locke contends, even with the lack of the presence of the object, the affect of happiness remains in the memory of it, 'they sustain their place as a happy object in the event of their absence'.[57] Relating this to Fairouz and her 'aura' is significant. While audiences may have experienced Fairouz in concert, on the radio or whatever medium, the 'aura' of Fairouz remains transfixed in their memory and, based on this theory, keeps her music as a 'happy object', regardless of its proximity and consequently its 'absence'. It is important to note that this 'happy object' need not be happy, it can be translated into a plethora of emotions that are catalysed through listening to her songs or even thinking about listening to her songs. Ahmed offers an accommodating notion that can be applied to feelings of sorrow or loss that transpire through direct or indirect contact with certain media. In her article, 'Affective Economies', Ahmed contends, 'affect does not reside in an object or sign, but is an affect of the circulation between objects and signs'.[58] It is this 'circulation', or movement, of 'signs' and 'objects', which is especially significant in the context of Fairouz and the diaspora. This 'circulation' of 'signs' liquefies the 'aura' and is a stepping-stone from which to place the diaspora in conversation, experiencing Fairouz in migration or, more specifically, the affective alignment of 'individuals with communities' or 'bodily space' with 'social space'.[59] However, before looking at affect in terms of diaspora, or vice versa, it is important to provide a definition of what is meant by diaspora in this book and provide an overview of Arab migration in both London and Doha.

Understanding Arab migration and diasporic audiences

Mass migration has characterized Middle Eastern populations since classical antiquity. It is thus necessary to define a specific sociopolitical environment to allow for a focused explanation and understanding of circumstances affecting the Arab world and its diaspora over the last eighty years. Although a chronological timeline is beyond this book's scope, providing an overarching backdrop assists in understanding the context of Fairouz and her fans. Moreover, drawing attention to Lebanon, as a centre for internal strife and fleeing refugees from neighbouring Palestine, is of particular interest, especially in light of the themes found in Fairouz's songs. Arguably, the Palestinian-Israeli conflict plagues both the public and private lives of Arabs across the globe. It is the pivot on which multiple Arab identities converge and diverge, but also it is a reflection of the ways in which many Arabs view themselves; misunderstood, misrepresented and mistreated by Western nations and their allies. Consequently, the Palestinian-Israeli conflict becomes a communal form of resistance for some, a way to symbolically assert personal rights through the public plight of Palestinians. In addition, the physical effects resulting from the socio-economic and political climate generated by this conflict, as well as by the 1975–90 Lebanese civil war, led to a mass exodus of Arab migrants from the Levant – an area comprised of Lebanon, Syria, Jordan and Palestinian territories – to countries across the globe.[60]

Here, attention needs to be brought to those migrants who, according to Barnard and Pendock, would be categorized as diasporic or transnational. For Barnard and Pendock, the difference between a migrant and a diasporan rests on three main criteria: 'dispersion, a homeland orientation and boundary maintenance, i.e. the maintenance of a distinctive identity vis-à-vis the host country'.[61] Avtar Brah also explains diaspora as 'an interpretive frame referencing the economic, political and cultural dimensions of these contemporary forms of migrancy'.[62] For Brah, the concepts of borders, home, what she calls 'homing desire', and similarity and difference, defined by her as '*diachronic relationality*', are embedded in understandings of diaspora. Brah argues that conversations on diaspora should focus not only on the 'journey' or the 'circumstances of leaving' but also on the conditions of 'arrival and settling down'.[63] Notions of diaspora are thus given situational grounding or 'relational positioning' to 'deconstruct the regimes of power' which 'differentiate one group from another'.[64] Diasporic experiences are thus almost never the same. This is an important point since, as Floya Anthias argues, the diaspora cannot be seen as a homogenous group, unchanged amidst spatial and temporal shifts, and neither can their position in new space be seen as applicable to all, since 'the diaspora is constituted as much in difference and division as it is in commonality and solidarity'.[65] Significant here is this heterogeneity, both among and within diasporic groups and in the ways in which these differences translate in the reception and interpretation of Fairouz's music at both the individual and collective levels.

It is also necessary to return to the 'homing desire' discussed by Brah, which is 'distinct from a desire for a "homeland"'.[66] Rather, 'home' for Brah is a 'mythic place of desire', one of 'no return', but also 'the lived experience of locality'.[67] Through her songs, does Fairouz allow for a return to this place, or does she ignite its desire? Examining the role of diasporic media in maintaining such links, Robins and Aksoy explain, 'new media technologies are making it possible to transcend the distances that have separated "diasporic communities" around the world from their "communities of origin"'.[68] These media allow for 'new means to promote transnational bonding, and thereby sustain (ethnic, national or religious) identities and cultures at-a-distance'.[69] Similarly, Hall echoes this sentiment by attributing 'cultural discovery' to the process of 'mediation'.[70] In this case, how does Fairouz's music help sustain 'cultures at-a-distance'? Does her music 'promote transnational bonding'?

Stemming from this, it is necessary to incorporate Tsagarousianou, who reminds us that 'Diasporas should be seen not as given communities, a logical, albeit deterritorialized extension of an ethnic or national group, but as imagined communities, continuously reconstructed and reinvented'.[71] Furthermore, Tsagarousianou argues, 'media technologies and diasporic media become crucial factors in the reproduction and transformation of diasporic identities' at this 'intersection of connectivity and cultural reinvention and reconstruction'.[72] It is therefore crucial to define diaspora as being constantly in flux, 'continuously reconstructed and reinvented'.[73] Simultaneously, they need to be seen as 'self-conscious' individuals 'who can reflect on her or his experience of and position in society, of "being oneself"'.[74]

There is a rich body of literature around Arab diasporic experience in countries like the United States, the United Kingdom and Australia, especially following the 11 September 2001 attacks on the United States. However, research on Qatar tends to be on its history, its demographics and its media channel Al-Jazeera, which interestingly plays a big role in existing research on the Arab diaspora. It is important here to provide an overview of migration in Doha and London to better understand the context surrounding diasporic communities residing in each location.

Migration to the Gulf is best described as a consequence of economic and political factors perforated with key timeframes, which expedited or halted movement. While international migration in the Middle East began shortly after the Second World War, it did not really take off till the early 1960s, when the economies of countries in the Gulf region began to develop. Asian workers, especially from India and Pakistan, were around since the 1940s, when many of the Gulf States were still colonized by the British. Palestinian refugees also found their way to the shores of the Arabian Peninsula after the 1947–8 war and with the creation of the state of Israel. However, by 1973, migration soared, catalysed mainly by oil revenues. There was a need for extensive infrastructural and urban projects and consequentially a demand for a skilled and unskilled labour force.

With a low local population, countries like Saudi Arabia, Libya, Kuwait, the United Arab Emirates and Qatar sought out international workers for numerous positions. Migrants from Europe and the Levant countries (Lebanon, Syria, Jordan, Iraq and Palestine) were usually highly educated and more skilled, whereas those from the Yemen Arab Republic, Sultanate of Oman, Iran and some South Asian countries were brought on as unskilled labour.[75] Egypt provided both skilled and unskilled labour, as many Egyptians travelled to work as educators in schools in the Gulf or as agricultural workers in Yemen. This determined not only the salaries of the workers but also whether they were able to bring over their families and settle for longer periods of time or whether their time was limited in the receiving countries. Either way migrants were unable to become citizens in the receiving countries of the Gulf States. Purchasing property or land was prohibited (although in some countries this is no longer the case).

As Thiollet writes, 'Strict nationality and citizenship laws based on lineage were enforced, preventing non-nationals from gaining access to socio-economic and political rights.'[76] Historians and researchers have stated this was mainly used as a method of control by the host countries, where in most cases the number of migrants overtook the number of locals. Such policies were aimed at curbing integration and ensuring foreign workers did not overstay their welcome.[77] In more recent years, job nationalization programmes were introduced to incite local populations to occupy senior positions in governmental and private institutions. Investment in local talent is something many organizations in the Gulf take pride in, at times sponsoring employees to further their education or training, building a strong and dedicated national workforce and warranting continuity. It is important to note here that the benefits of these migratory patterns extend beyond the Gulf. Through remittances and other forms of economic exchanges, regions all over Asia and the Middle East have profited from expatriate labour in building and developing their countries of origin.[78]

However, there were times of conflict that saw both an increase and a decrease in migration to the oil-rich nations. The Arab-Israeli conflicts in 1947, 1967 and 1973, the Iraq-Iran war from 1980 to 1988, the Gulf wars in 1991 and 2003 and the Arab uprisings in 2011 have all led to both an exodus and in-pouring of economic migrants, refugees and those searching for varying forms of stability. In addition, the ways in which the sending countries positioned themselves politically were also factors in whether their nationals were welcomed or not in the oil-rich countries. For example, between 1985 and 1987, Kuwait deported hundreds of Iranian and Lebanese Shi'a workers because of their affiliation with the Iranian-backed Lebanese Amal movement.[79] The First Gulf War in 1991 also saw a massive surge of voluntary and involuntary departures of foreign workers from Kuwait and Iraq. As governments of Jordan, Yemen and the Palestinian authority expressed solidarity with Iraq, Kuwait and Saudi Arabia deported around 731,000 Yemeni workers and 450,000 Palestinians[80] and expelled over 800,000 Egyptians, showcasing the ways in which politics can determine migratory patterns. With almost two million Arabs leaving the Gulf, labourers from Asia and Southeast Asia quickly replaced them.[81]

Two decades later, with the Arab uprisings and the consequential conflict that ensued, millions of Syrians fled their homes. It is estimated there are almost 6.7 million Syrians who 'live outside their homeland spread across one hundred and twenty-eight countries'.[82] Not all countries welcomed the refugees and it further indicated tensions between the countries in the Gulf and the ideologies and politics of the countries of the Levant. Attitudes towards refugees by oil-rich nations fluctuate according to political, religious and sectarian partisanship, which in turn affect whether certain nationalities can gain entry to the Arabian Peninsula.

Around 1975, it was estimated that Arab migrants made up 75 per cent of the 1.6 million foreign labourers in the Gulf.[83] By 1983, the number of foreign workers increased to five million, 55 per cent of them coming from Arab nations.[84] Just before the 1991 Gulf War, the World Bank estimated a foreign population of more than seven million in the Gulf States.[85] As of 2021 Qatar's population stands at over 2.5 million people. However, it is estimated only 15 per cent of the population is indigenously Qatari, whereas the rest are compiled of Asian, South East Asian and Arab nationals.[86] The large number of construction, development and socio-economic projects guarantee that international labour will always be needed. However, with policies and laws that limit the rights of migrants in the oil-rich countries, the feeling of uncertainty among them remains strong.

In his book *Becoming Arab in London*, Ramy Aly begins with an overview of Arab migration to London, where he highlights three key phases. The first phase of migration from the mid-nineteenth century to the mid-twentieth century follows the Syrian and Moroccan textile merchants; the Yemeni and Somali dock workers and then ends with the influx of students and diplomats in the late 1950s. The second phase, during the 1960s and 1970s, ushers in large communities of 'economic migrants and political exiles' who were able to apply for citizenship in the mid-1980s, with the passing of the British Nationality Act.[87] Finally, the highest rate of migration occurs in the last phase, from the 1990s until today, because of violence, war and conflict in some Arab states.[88] Given the diverse backgrounds of the Arab diaspora in London, Aly argues against homogenizing 'Arabness' as a 'socio-cultural, political and civilizational' form of 'identification', calling for a more performative perspective on ways these trajectories are communicated and understood as ways of 'doing Arab'.[89] As he ventures through *Shisha* cafés and Arab student university societies, Aly looks to explore the ways in which 'Arabness' is understood and performed.

Drawing on Judith Butler's concepts of gender 'passing' and gender 'performativity', Aly focuses on 'ethnographic narratives' to understand the axial connections found in performing gender. Aly defines these connections as 'identification, desire, mimesis, encryption and the project of survival – with performative race'.[90] Aly calls this form of performance 'doing Arab' rather than 'being Arab'.[91]

In addition, Aly asserts that although 'struggles of their respective homelands have brought Arabs in London together' he adds these struggles have also 'driven them apart through fear and suspicion'.[92] By analysing a series of articles and press reports, Aly chronicles pivotal political and historical moments to contextualize Arab diasporic experiences and their representations, bringing to surface various alliances and divisions within Arab diasporic communities across political, religious and social lines. However, it is through his ethnographic study and discussions with participants, as well as his analysis of British Arab imagery produced by students in London, that Aly gives insight into 'everyday Arabness' and also an indication on how Arab youth in London 'have reclaimed the Orient through the diasporic gaze'.[93]

Aly's book is a valuable resource for understanding Arabic diasporic life and the different positions individuals negotiate according to gender, race, religion and sociocultural expectations. Especially interesting is Aly's discussion on 'pervasive, inter-textual and powerful' discourse around the 'ethnic identification' of 'Arabs'.[94] Launching from 'internal' and 'London-based' discourses Aly cites respondents' attitudes towards other Arabs in London, namely those who came from the Arabian Gulf, as 'crass, uneducated backward'.[95] This 'othering'[96] is what Mansour and Sabry define as 'complex politics of diasporic relations' and 'insider-outsider positionality'.[97] While Mansour and Sabry's chapter outlines the challenges they faced in conducting an ethnographic study on children and media, the researchers give further insight into the ways Arab diasporic communities view those they consider as 'outside' the diasporic realm as well as illustrate the uneasiness and scepticism found among the Arab diaspora towards 'diasporic researchers' who were 'reporting back to the British system'.[98] With an increase in 'Arabophobia/ Islamophobia' since the 9/11 attacks in New York and 7/7 attacks in London, Mansour and Sabry's research brings to light how suspicion towards Arabs and Muslims 'affects British Muslim identities and their conceptions of Otherness' as well as the 'implications [this] has for access to ethnographic research with Muslim and Arab communities in the UK'.[99] A pivotal point, in which 'invisible citizens' became 'visible subjects',[100] the events of 9/11 and its aftermath feature prominently in works on Arab diaspora. Most research on the Arab diaspora and their media consumption foregrounds underlying sentiments of uncertainty, discrimination and biased media representation in host countries.[101] While this book examines such sentiments, it considers how they translate subjectively. Individualized notions of 'Arabness', identity and belonging are discussed amidst collective understandings of the terms. To better comprehend this individualized collectivity we turn to Appadurai's discussion of the imagination.

Situated and mnemonic – (Re) positioning the imagination

Ushering in imagination to the realm of economic and political conflict and the ensuing destabilizing social climate is best understood through Appadurai, who argues that, through the imagination, 'electronic media' are utilized to re-materialize the sense of belonging associated with the nation state by 'deterritorialized viewers'.[102] Here, the audio media stands for 'electronic media', since musical works are vital in their circulation of messages that are embedded with coexistence and nationhood. By way of 'nationally appropriated nostalgia',[103] and 'urban-for-village nostalgia',[104] fans revert to memories of their country of origin, presented by Fairouz's songs. In other words, this book shows that there is truth in what Fairouz has said, 'It's as if the songs have become their [her listeners'] country.'[105]

However, how do Fairouz's fans position themselves in relation to her music? On what aspects of her songs do listeners congregate or wander? To better comprehend these conjunctional qualities, it is crucial to turn to feminist literature and the concepts of 'subject positions' and 'intersectionality'. Based on Michel Foucault's theory of 'disciplinary power', a definition of 'subject positions' comes from cultural researcher and theorist Ien Ang, who claims them as a formation of 'individual identities' and constructed 'subjectivities' that arise as a consequence of 'meaning systems and discourses circulating in society and culture'.[106] 'Subject positions' are reliant on external and internal factors that affect their multidimensional properties, as well as their representation. Fairouz and her listeners thus occupy and transmit pivotal socio-historical elements that constitute their individualized 'subject positions'. Coupling this with the work of Crenshaw who, through her analysis of feminism and race conceives the term 'intersectionality' provides us with a deeper outlook on audience behaviour. For Crenshaw, 'intersectionality' is a means to explore 'various ways in which race and gender intersect in shaping structural, political, and representational aspects of violence against women of color'.[107] While Crenshaw specifically looks at 'intersectionality' in terms of violence, her concept is significant in the discussion of diasporic audiences. By viewing diasporic audiences as active and having a set of heterogeneous intersections, we immediately alleviate them from resignation. Elaborating on the relationships between 'subject positions', 'intersectionality' and imagination, it is important to revisit Appadurai, who argues that imagination is 'a social practice' that is 'central to all forms of agency' and a 'key component of the new global order'.[108]

Expanding on Appadurai's notion of the imagination, Athique ushers in Stoetlzer and Yuval-Davis's concept of the 'situated imagination'. For Athique, the 'situated imagination' bestows on audiences more agency and calls it 'a site where situated knowledge is produced and contested in a form which might be defined as anchored "in actual social practices" (that are linked, but not reducible to certain social positionings)'.[109] The 'situated imagination' can thus be seen as an amalgamation of Appadurai's imagination, Ang's 'subject positions' and Crenshaw's 'intersectionality', in which individual experience and background play a part in the reception and understanding of 'social practices', such as media consumption, but, together, they do not limit audiences to theories of belonging and identity, instead they offer a wider landscape of possibilities, through which to analyse diasporic audiences.

In their discussion on memory and imagination, Keightley and Pickering share this view of 'imaginative engagements' becoming 'interwoven with our own social and historical experience'.[110] Through the interplay between memory, imagination, nostalgia and experience, the authors argue for what they call the 'mnemonic imagination', a framework they define as 'an active synthesis of remembering and imagining, which is essential to our understandings of the relationship between past, present and future'.[111] For Keightley and Pickering, discussing imagination and memory as separate entities is problematic, and they argue that the two are symbiotic in that 'memory is a vital source for imagining and imagining is a vital process in making coherent sense of the past and connecting it to the present and future'.[112] Experiencing any situation, whether lived or mediated, is thus a result of the interplay between the two. Linking this to the 'situated imagination' allows for a discussion on memory and imagination, which is more personalized and 'vital for the construction of our narrative identity where the story of who we are involves the interweaving of who we have been, who we could have been and who we may become'.[113] This is also shared by Charles Taylor, who discusses identity and the 'self' as part of a 'narrative' that not only structures the present, 'what we are', but also accommodates the past and future, 'we are always also changing and *becoming*'.[114] However, and as the three authors stress, this subjective notion of identity with Taylor, memory and imagination with Keightley and Pickering, although detrimental to the study of audiences who are separate and complex entities in themselves, cannot be suspended in a time-space vacuum that is devoid of social and cultural influences.

For Taylor, the 'self' exists within 'webs of interlocutors', those 'conversation partners' who are 'essential' to 'achieving self-definition'.[115] As a 'defining community', these 'interlocutors' allow for a referential examination of the identity.[116] By achieving knowledge of the self through its position in social space, the mnemonic imagination thus 'becomes a site of dialogue between ourselves, and both immediate and distant others across time'.[117] This idea can be seen as feeding on a Benedict Anderson 'imagined community' sense, where 'members of even the smallest nation will never know most of their fellow-members, meet them, or even hear of them, yet in the minds of each lives the image of their communion',[118] but these authors allow for more agency with the mnemonic imagination that transgresses ideas of borders and nations, and allows for a deeper examination of individual experience in the collective framework. While Anderson focuses on the ways in which imagination provides an external sense of community and commonality that is somewhat centrifugal, in that it is sought outside the self for the self, Keightley and Pickering argue that this community already exists within the self and is centripetal, radiating outwards through the mnemonic imagination. For the authors, the mnemonic imagination 'allows us to see how individual experience and the pasts of others interconnect, how we all have individual memories but how at the same time all memory is indissolubly social, and we are all in the same historical mix whether we look backwards or forwards'.[119]

This conversation on the 'sociality of our experience' occurs in a fluctuating environment that does not allow for memory or imagination to remain constant or unilateral.[120] Applying this to the context of Fairouz indicates that the individual consumption and appropriation of her music, especially in conjunction with the diaspora, cannot be viewed as an isolated affair immune to 'different forms of socialization (family, primary groups, peer-groups) and the capacity for self-reflection and consciousness'.[121] As Slobin says, 'music lives at the margin of the person and the people'.[122] The act of listening, even if isolated, thus comes with a host of trajectories that move beyond the individual and beyond a specific place and time. While this theory is significant in discussing audiences, it also gives weight to the argument that Fairouz's 'aura' cannot be anchored in a specific spatio-temporal narrative. The dialogical nature of listeners' mnemonic imaginations ensures that they are involved in a 'complex, mutually shaping mixture of what is private to oneself and what is shared with others'.[123] It is important to return to affect here, specifically to Gibbs, who asserts, 'affect leaps from one body to another, evoking tenderness, inciting shame, igniting rage, exciting fear'.[124] In this way, affect and the mnemonic imagination are intrinsically linked, weaving their way through the collective, stitched together in a tapestry of Arab diasporic communities who not only find voice in Fairouz's 'aura' but also provide a bridged space for her 'aura' to live and continue through them. In this way, Fairouz's 'aura' is appropriated and democratized according to an individual intersectional 'subject position' and 'affective community'.[125]

This indicates that the point of contact with Fairouz's 'aura' does not necessarily need to be the same in order to be affective. As Ahmed explains, 'we are made happy by different things, we find different things delightful'.[126] In addition, Ahmed maintains that affect does not remain constant, 'bodily transformations might also transform what is experienced as delightful'.[127] The importance of this statement is twofold; first, it addresses the 'bodily transformation' or physical bodily migration that is geographical and pertinent to the study of diaspora, which subsequently touches upon the altered state of 'subject positions' in terms of relocation. Second, it hints at a change in the appropriation of Fairouz's 'aura' according to time and place. In this sense, delight can be heightened or tainted as a result of this 'bodily transformation' in migratory space. Through migration and change in site, Fairouz's music thus takes on a different form. Her 'aura' is appropriated from transfigured 'subject positions' which can henceforth alter the affective state. This gives rise to the statement that memory can never 'return to the present unmodified or always in exactly the same temporal sequence'.[128]

Discussions on affect, mnemonic imagination and migration are what Barrett et al. would consider a combination of 'context-level' and 'personal-level' constructs. In their work *Music-evoked Nostalgia*, the authors conceptualize what they call 'context-level' and 'personal-level' constructs as attributes that assist in determining a person's response to musical stimulus. 'Context-level' constructs consider elements such as individual relationships to certain songs, while 'personal-level' constructs are more about 'personality traits', such as how 'prone' a person is to 'nostalgia'.[129] Building on this, the researchers focus on the 'specific structure of music-evoked nostalgia and individual differences in the affective and mnemonic structure'.[130] For Barrett et al., nostalgia is 'inherently linked to autobiographical memories' and thus music has the capacity to evoke those forms of sentiments in its listeners.[131] Drawing on this, it can be argued that the physiological 'bodily transformation' of migration, both spatial and temporal, is a form of 'context-level' and 'personal-level' construct that can lead to nostalgia. Although Barrett et al.'s study is significant in its elaborations on affect, nostalgia and music, it is deeply rooted in psychology and uses more quantitative methods of data gathering, for example surveys, rather than interviews. Little information is given as to the participants' backgrounds, which does not allow analysis of what the subjects were nostalgic for. It is therefore necessary to revert to Keightley and Pickering, who draw on Ritivoi's work on nostalgia, which 'prompts certain important questions regarding the function of remembering'.[132]

For Ritivoi, nostalgia is a form of reflection that 'encourages one to differentiate and to contrast', thus allowing for an acknowledgement of one's individual and social positioning.[133] Boym's definition of nostalgia highlights the binaries of 'longing' and 'belonging', 'what we share' and 'what divides us'.[134] For Boym it is the attempt to 'repair longing with belonging' that leads to a breakdown in 'mutual understanding' and unity.[135] However, what if this 'belonging' is found within a cohesive 'longing'? Does Fairouz provide such a communal space? Through her music, does Fairouz create a collective 'belonging' by tapping into an individual 'longing'? Nostalgia, for Boym, is 'an ache of temporal distance and displacement'.[136] Her version of nostalgia emphasizes division and difference, since it 'remains an intermediary between collective and individual memory'.[137] Boym also focuses on nostalgia that is not just about the past, since it is both 'retrospective' and 'perspective'.[138] In addition, Boym discusses the ways in which technology 'offers solutions and builds bridges', essentially 'saving the time that nostalgia loves to waste'.[139] On the other hand, Jo Tacchi sees nostalgia's relationship with technology as more of an integrative 'productive engagement', a link between the private and 'wider society'.[140] Tacchi's discussion of nostalgia in the context of radio sound brings to the surface the 'connecting role' of radio 'for individuals and groups of people'.[141] It is a more agential form of nostalgia, something Keightley and Pickering also stress, in that nostalgia may 'move beyond compensation for mourning' and instead 'represent a more active effort at reclaiming what seems lost'.[142] It is at this intersection of experiencing and remembering, of 'belonging' and 'longing', of the individual and the social, of 'mourning' and 'reclaiming', that we converge to understand the role Fairouz's music plays among the Arab diaspora living in Doha, Qatar, and London, England.

Chapter 3

AFFECTIVE IDENTITIES

'ARABNESS', HYBRIDITY AND 'INTERCONTEXTUAL' ILTIZAM

Since the late 1990s, Qatar and its capital Doha have witnessed a number of structural, economic and sociopolitical changes that have transformed the once flat, sandy landscape into state-of-the-art skyscrapers and glistening buildings. Perhaps representative of the rapid transformations taking place across the small peninsula is the Lebanese School in Doha, a modern building erected on what was once a barren desert. Among the chatter, the heavy footsteps and the sleepy faces, Fairouz's voice is heard over the school's outdoor speakers, welcoming students and parents every morning. This initiative was executed by Mona,[1] 45, a concerned parent, who, after dropping off her children at school one day, saw two men in a heated argument over Lebanese politics in the parking lot, *'I got in my car and I started listening to Fairouz. I thought to myself, ouf, if they listened to her, I'm sure they wouldn't disagree'*, she says earnestly. Later that afternoon Mona wrote an email to Walid, the headmaster of the school, explaining the situation she saw earlier, and she proposed a solution – play Fairouz while parents are dropping off their children from 7.00 am to 7.30 am. Walid was quick to accept, for him it was an opportunity to *'preserve Lebanese heritage'* in a globalized environment that he thought was pushing the younger generations to diverge from *'Arab culture and the Arabic language'*. This idea of reminding parents and children of Fairouz, and what she stands for, is in itself a form of identity construction that Walid and Mona not only wanted to be a part of but also were keen to share with others within their sphere of influence. By consciously choosing to play Fairouz's songs, Mona and Walid set out to build a strategically affective space to encourage 'Arabness' and political understanding, but also to compensate for any shortcomings in achieving either objective. This interchange between the music of Fairouz and those who come into its realm is one of affect. Affect, as stated by Seigworth and Gregg, 'can serve to drive us toward movement, toward thought and extension', affect is 'persistent proof of a body's never less than ongoing immersion in and among the world's obstinacies and rhythms'.[2] This example highlights how affect travels through the environment, is absorbed and released, to show 'the way that bodies affect one another' socially and individually, intentionally or not, through the music of Fairouz.[3]

While the Lebanese school and its community form only a small portion of the 85 per cent of foreign workers that reside in Qatar, and are not the only nationality sought for this study, their discussion on identity, conflict, loss and belonging is significant, as it brings to the surface the ways in which diasporic practices differ along specific, shared and affective lines. The need to preserve '*Arab*' heritage among the youth hints at the desire for musical continuity among generations, especially among parents who themselves inherited Fairouz and her songs from their parents, but it also highlights a fear that younger generations growing up in '*Al-ghurba*',[4] and away from their countries of origin, are deviating from cultural artefacts that parents consider constructive in positioning their Arab identity. Coming to Qatar from the States, Walid was expecting younger members of the Lebanese community to be more in touch with the '*Arabic language and culture*' than Lebanese communities living in the West. However, he found that this was not the case, faulting parents for their reliance on non-Arab domestic help to raise their kids:[5]

> *So, this student, this child, is not getting the nationalistic care, or the care that comes with an Arab environment . . . and the heritage and valuable elements we grew up with.* (Walid, 65, Lebanese, Doha)

Although the Lebanese contingent of this sample were more vocal about their dissatisfaction that their children were moving away from '*heritage and valuable elements*', other participants talked about the sense of identity and 'Arabness' they feel with Fairouz, where they '*find the very us, the very family, the very society*' (Jihad, 51, Palestinian/Jordanian, Doha). In this way, through her songs, Fairouz is an embodiment of 'Arab culture', where participants experience a sense of belonging and a sense of self. Listening to Fairouz and her music is reminiscent of '*the very us*', which respondents not only crave but also want for their children. It is necessary here to revisit Fiske's 'figures' to better comprehend the role Fairouz plays in symbolizing Arab '*heritage and valuable elements*'. According to Fiske, a 'figure' is a 'human simulacrum' that takes on 'hyperreal' versions of themselves and 'serve[s] as social terrains whereby others engage in the figuring process'.[6] As a 'figure', Fairouz possesses 'infinitely reproducible signifiers',[7] which can be understood on varying levels by her listeners but also by those who know her, yet are not fans. Those 'signifiers' are based on 'historical fortuitousness' but are not necessarily produced solely through the actions of the 'figure'.[8] As Fiske argues, 'the body of the individual is comparatively powerless in determining the way he or she is to be figured'.[9] The audience are thus active agents in projecting various 'signifiers' onto Fairouz, and 'each figuring and refiguring' occurs at 'a different social history that used a different individual history to authenticate it'.[10] As members of the diaspora, experiencing Fairouz is expected to change according to *meta-* and *micro-habitual* situations, but also due to their status of being in '*Al-ghurba*'. Drawing here on Benjamin's notion of 'aura' is significant in order to understand how 'figuring and refiguring' can occur in different geopolitical circumstances. In discussing works of art, Benjamin[11] argues that the evolution of technology has resulted in a loss of 'aura', since artworks are no longer seen in their physical and temporal entirety. For Benjamin, removing art from its place in space and time devalues its 'aura'.

However, in the context of Fairouz, her 'aura' takes on different forms and is strengthened among the diasporic community across borders and generations. As a 'figure', Fairouz transforms accordingly. For example, when asked what Fairouz means to her in London, Helene, 52, a Lebanese woman who has lived there for '*around 24 years*' responded: '*that I'm far . . . Far from the Lebanon that I know. Far away from the mood and ambiance that I'm used to . . .* ' Helene's statement shows how Fairouz's 'aura' manipulates according to different 'individual histories' and social situations to take on deep-seated and discursive meanings. The link between Fairouz as a 'figure' in conjunction with the respondents' *meta-* and *micro-habitual* situations and their intersectional 'subject positions', shapes the different characteristics that her 'aura' takes on, and highlights how it plumes and dispels:

> *I can't express what she means to me in a word or a sentence. It is different things at different times. She presents happiness and wonderful memories. She also presents nationalism and unity, for when we were kids, and the war was going on her songs united us, especially when we were travelling to different countries and couldn't go to Lebanon.* (Clara, 44, Lebanese, Doha)

> *Love. For everything: The homeland, the family, the children . . . Palestine. Not because she sings for Palestine . . . because the way she speaks about Lebanon applies to any homeland in the world, not only Lebanon.* (Ziyad, 82, Iraqi, Doha)

> *Jerusalem, we were raised with the cause, a cause that means something to us on a personal level.* (Amar, 39, Lebanese, Doha)

> *Fairouz means a lot to me, Fairouz means childhood, the village, Jerusalem, the general situation of the Arab world, yeah.* (Carmen, 70, Palestinian, Doha)

> *I love that, because she equals Lebanon to me. I would like [my children] to see this image, especially because my children have no Arabic roots, it means nothing to them; I even try sometimes to explain it to my younger boy, because the older one doesn't even listen to me when I talk about it.* (Gihane, 47, Lebanese, Doha)

> *Politicians might stop meaning anything to people in Lebanon; however, Fairouz will always mean something for every Lebanese. She's the symbol of Lebanon.* (Karam, 39, Lebanese, Doha)

> *For me, she means Lebanon, the authenticity, the village, everything related to Lebanon. She's our ambassador, Lebanon's ambassador, and more.* (Zuhair, 70, Lebanese, Doha)

> *I don't think anyone can ever say anything negative about her, no matter where they're from . . . she's never expressed views that people are going to disagree with, she's never done anything to aggravate anyone.* (Tania, 20, Palestinian, Doha)

> *I mean, she's done a song for every . . . you know the main Arab struggles in the contemporary era. So she has that appeal . . . She doesn't upset anyone, so, yeah.* (Ahmad, 35, Iraqi, London)

The other time an old man asked me: what does Fairouz mean to you? I told him Fairouz . . . you know the 'tannour'[12] bread? He told me, yes. I told him, do you know what your mother washing your feet is? He said, yes, then I asked him: do you know what giving your dad a medicine bottle is? He said, yes. I told him, Fairouz is your identity. (Akram, 37, Syrian, London)

Nowadays we are accused of terrorism, and many other things. You have a person called Fairouz, she has an Arab consensus, because you identify with Fairouz as a singer, which means you identify with that type of Arab music which is a global language, personally, this is what identifies me with Fairouz, that she expresses me, she expresses the civilized aspect of myself, this is what really identifies me, not anything religious, because I'm not really fanatical about religion. (Ferial, 47, Palestinian, London)

Fairouz is the hope that something good may arise in our countries. (Hussain, 60, Iraqi, London)

I'm constantly on the news, constantly reading what's the latest book on identity and the Arab world, so when it comes to Fairouz, it's more of . . . she's my . . . yeah . . . she's my pillar. Like, I sit with her, you know? (Maha, 35, Syrian/Lebanese, London)

The earlier examples demonstrate how Fairouz, as a 'figure', can take on various 'social terrains' that are representative of certain beliefs and attributes. Individually and socially, Fairouz, as a 'figure', means '*different things at different times*'. For the Arab diaspora in Doha and London, she is armed with credibility as she personifies '*Arabness*', '*authenticity*', '*nationalism*', '*unity*', '*the Palestinian cause*', '*Arab struggles*', '*childhood*', missing '*Arab roots*' that parents want for their children, '*the civilized aspect of myself*', '*tannour bread*', mothers '*washing your feet*', the '*village*' and its innocence as well as '*hope*' for the Arab world. She is at once a form of subjective identity, but she also 'stands for, symbolizes *and* offers the immediate experience of collective identity'.[13] The 'collective identity' that Fairouz presents is rooted in 'Arabness', which participants interpret in individual ways. It is, as Simon Firth argues, 'music, like identity, is both performative and story, describes the social in the individual and the individual in the social'.[14] For Firth, it is within this 'collective identity' that participants are able to position themselves according to their personal narratives. So, 'Arabness', as an ontological concept, possesses a series of signifiers that are articulated and performed which, in turn, requires a set of recognizable 'expressions' and 'manners' that are understood personally but also socially.[15] 'Arabness' and 'Arab' identity are thus translated through their subsequent transmission, but also with the conscious consent of both the 'performer' of 'Arabness' and his/her audience. It is at the point of decoding the 'social terrains' of Fairouz, as a 'figure', where meanings of 'Arabness', and the components of recognizable Arab identity subsequently emerge.

Drawing on Erving Goffman, who discusses self-representation as everyday performance, gives the means to illustrate how it is not only Fairouz who performs 'Arabness' but also her listeners, by affectively recognizing, understanding and incorporating that 'Arabness' through learned and socialized scripts in their own lives. For Goffman, 'performance' refers 'to all the activity of an individual, which occurs during a period marked by his [*sic*] continuous presence before a particular set of observers and which has some influence on the observers'.[16] This form of theatrical performativity, described by Goffman, is divided into 'front' and 'back' regions. The 'front' is 'part of the individual's performance, which regularly functions in a general and fixed fashion to define the situation for those who observe the performance'.[17] These 'fronts tend to be selected, not created'.[18] Meaning that audience and performer work in tandem to set the scene, in which the individual will show his/her 'front'. The 'back' region is 'where the suppressed facts make an appearance' and is a place where 'illusions and impressions are openly constructed'.[19] This hidden side of the self is often in contrast to the 'front', the side which individuals do not like others to see.

There is a twofold dialectic relationship between 'front' and 'back', and performer and audience, which brings to light different sets of self-representation, that may complement or contest one another. As Goffman argues, 'a given social front tends to be institutionalised in terms of the abstract stereotyped expectations to which it gives rise, and tends to take on a meaning and stability apart from the specific tasks, which happen at the time to be performed in its name'.[20] In this way, putting on an 'Arab' 'social front' is a form of performance that moves beyond its simple linguistic meaning to become a set of 'selected' signifiers, which represent a series of 'expressions' and 'manners' akin to the individual performer, as well as a 'collective representation and a fact in its own right'.[21]

Converging on the notion of 'collective representation' is significant here, since it is an important lens through which to understand the concept of 'Arabness'. Although a 'collective representation' of 'Arabness' implies a communal set of 'expressions' and 'manners', it also hints at homogeneity. The model of 'Arabness' needs to be seen as a flexible framework, which is affective, discursive, negotiated, performative and imagined. Being 'Arab' is not a monolithic, tangible form of classification. It can be seen to be what Raymond Williams would call 'a structure of feeling', dependent on numerous factors at the individual, communal, social and global levels, 'the nuanced interaction between selected and interpreted beliefs and acted and justified experiences'.[22]

'Feeling' Arab, and belonging to 'Arab culture', is therefore both a private and a public 'experience', one which cannot rely solely on either sphere, but that is reliant on intersectional qualities and enhanced through affect, the *micro-* and *meta-habitus*.

Arab social fronts and iltizam

In the introductory chapter of his book *Becoming Arab in London*, Aly looks at 'Arabness' as a course of 'doing' and not 'being'. For Ramy Aly, 'Arabness is a process of becoming through acts, enunciations, objects, spaces, bodies and settings'.[23] Moving away from the political implications of 'Arabness', Aly argues 'Arabness is about connectedness'.[24] While Aly focuses primarily on Arabs in London, by drawing on feminist literature and specifically that of Judith Butler, he expands on the notion of 'gender performativity' to encompass 'ethnic performativity', of 'doing Arab'. 'Doing Arab' with the participants in this study meant various things at both the private and public levels, as evidenced by the ways in which they interpreted Fairouz as a symbol of 'Arabness':

> *You connect Fairouz to love, to patriotism, not just patriotism for Lebanon, for all the Arab patriotism . . . you connect her, you can't not, she has dimensions.* (Amar, 39, Lebanese, Doha)

> *Fairouz never sang to any specific political party or anyone. She just sang for the whole Arab world.* (Abou Aziz, 67, Kuwaiti/Qatari, Doha)

> *She represents really everything good. I look at her, as I said, as a God send, for the Arabic language, for the Arab world, not for Lebanon only. And I will not accept being told that she is purely Lebanese.* (Ziyad, 82, Iraqi, Doha)

> *So, as much as I'm not a fan of Arab nationalism, she represents that. But you know that union, that if we just have another way of linking the countries rather than nationalism.* (Leila, 30, Moroccan, London)

> *She is one of the things that unites us. Fairouz, as a name, song, and lyrics, combines all elements together, like Umm Kulthum, Umm Kulthum also congregates Arab people, unifies them and represents them, all Arabs loved Umm Kulthum, she used to sing to all Arabs, regardless of one's religious affiliation, and so does Fairouz, and everyone gets enlightened by listening to Fairouz, she is definitely a unifying tool for the Arabs living here.* (Ferial, 46, Palestinian, London)

> *The life when people had each other's backs, and when the neighbour had the support of the other neighbour, the authentic Arab life that has now disappeared in the Arab world, it doesn't exist anymore. So, Fairouz gives you the feeling of being an Arab and being authentic.* (Amin, 27, Palestinian, London)

> *I think she's the Christian woman who represents all the Muslims, in the struggle against the Israelis, or Arabs, I would say, not Muslims, all Arabs against Israelis . . . yeah, you play it, you feel patriotic.* (Shams, 40, Iranian/Palestinian/Lebanese/English, Doha)

Representation of 'Arabness', and the affective ways in which it transpires, is shown in these examples. For Amar, Abou Aziz, Ziyad, Leila and Ferial, Fairouz embodies 'Arabness' separately from a particular nation. Her 'Lebaneseness' is eclipsed by her 'Arabness', one that possesses an inclusive politics (Abou Aziz) and a form of patriotism that moves beyond state borders to encompass a more regional loyalty (Amar). For Ziyad, she is '*a God send, for the Arabic language and for the Arab world*', and refuses all claims to her nationality. Ferial also sees Fairouz as a *'unifying tool for the Arabs living'* in London, *'regardless of one's religious affiliation'*. Nationality and religion are thus negated here as descriptors associated with Fairouz. It is significant to note that most participants agreed that Fairouz brought people together, whether at the national, regional, global or spiritual levels, arguably unlike other singers who may have divided audiences because of their political viewpoints or affiliations.[25]

A critic of the *'political'* implications of Arab nationalism, Leila, a Moroccan respondent, who came to London to study ten years ago and has lived there ever since, sees Fairouz as a link which unites Arab countries, separate from the pan-Arab nationalism linked to Nasserism, which she describes as *'you know, like toppling regimes'*. Leila's narrative brings to light this post-Nasserite sense of Arab nationalism expressed by El-Ariss in his discussion of *iltizam*. For El-Ariss, *iltizam*, or commitment, 'has been a key posture for Arabic cultural production in the context of struggles for self-determination and economic opportunities from the 1950s onward'.[26] Providing a historical development of the concept of *iltizam* in relation to Arabic poetry, Salma Khadra Jayyusi argues that although *iltizam* peaked in the 1950s, it appeared in literary form prior to then. By tracing the development of committed poetry, or *iltizam*, Jayyusi illustrates the ways in which Arab socialist and then Marxist writers of 1920s onwards were critical of literature that did not align with the 'arena of social struggle' and did not commit to the 'oppressed masses'.[27] Placing committed writing against a backdrop of the rising nationalism of the 1950s, Jayyusi explains the 'natural' adoption of *iltizam* by Arab Nationalist writers in their quest for 'progress'.[28] This 'campaign of "*iltizam*"', Jayyusi asserts, came with advantages and disadvantages. On the positive side, it brought to light 'a deeper consciousness' among Arab writers of 'the experiences of the nation' and connected them to 'the real struggle at home', which decreased 'the dangers of cultural alienation to which poets were often exposed'.[29] However, a negative aspect of this was that using simpler language contributed to 'the weakening of some poetic elements'.[30] Building on Jayyusi's discussion of committed writing Atef Alshaer examines the interplay of poetry and politics in the Arab world, outlining the ways *iltizam* materialized according to significant political and social milestones. Alshaer places inspiration of this form of commitment in literature, the belief that 'poets or people of letters should and do mirror the concerns of their society and times'.[31] As a way towards emphasizing the role of 'social and political transformation through writing and cultural production', El-Ariss asserts that although *iltizam* began as a pledge for the 1950s pan-Arab model envisioned by Jamal Abdel Nasser, it has essentially evolved to accommodate 'new realities'.[32] These 'new realities' can be linked to *meta-habitual* and intersectional situations and opinions, which fragmented diasporic communities, affiliate or disassociate with. *Iltizam* is thus a contested and created space in which commitment is reliant on globalized politics and subjective agendas.

Amin, a Palestinian respondent who has been in London for almost nine years, and Shams, an Iranian/Palestinian/Lebanese/English respondent who has lived in Doha for most of his life, were more specific about their ideas of 'Arabness' and *iltizam*. For Amin, Fairouz is a reminder of the loss of genuineness and camaraderie present in his affective memory of the Arab world. It is a mnemonic, nostalgic past that is associated with a certain moment in history and geography. His choice of the word '*authentic*'[33] is meaningful, especially when compared to Shams's statement. Shams brings to light two features of the Arab world that are specific to his intersectional qualities and subject positions while also hinting at another form of *iltizam* pertinent to the idea of 'Arabness'. Initially, he describes Fairouz as the '*Christian woman who represents all the Muslims in the struggle against the Israelis*'. Positioning Fairouz as a '*Christian woman*' immediately situates her and Shams at a site of '*différance*', in which 'Arabness' and religion merge across narratives of symbiosis. It is a form of 'othering', which needs to be given its own weight. While discussion on religion will follow later in this chapter, it is interesting to note how religion and 'Arabness' can be intertwined to show new forms of *iltizam*, one encompassing both the *meta-* and *micro-habitus*. However, before that, it is significant to note that Shams rewords his statement to say '*all Arabs against Israelis*' instead of just '*Muslims*'. The '*struggle against the Israelis*' is a form of 'collective representation', which, in Shams's opinion, not only categorizes 'Arabness' but also unites them in its plight. For most respondents, the Palestinian cause was a key constituent of Arab *iltizam*, by first positioning them against a common Israeli occupier enemy and, second, by sharing the affective sentiment of solidarity. This was not the case in responses to the more recent Syrian conflict, which divided Arabs and the diaspora along different lines of *iltizam*. In this way, for participants in both sampling fields, *iltizam* is a lens through which to magnify the politics of 'intra-diasporic subjectification dynamics'.[34] These dynamics, in return, are manifested in affect, since 'The body "itself" – whether a social body or an individual human being – is in a constant state of de- and re-composition in relation to other bodies'.[35] In this way, affect becomes both a catalyst and driver of *iltizam*, and also *iltizam* becomes a motivator of affect. This cyclic formation between affect and *iltizam* is dependent on 'affective-evaluative coupling', which relies on the examination of the individual in the social.[36]

Religion, as a divisive classifier in the Arab world, is another popular way to 'other' members of ethnic communities. 'Otherness' is also a system of self-representation in which an individual 'forgoes all claims to be things he [*sic*] does not appear to be',[37] or as Michael Pickering states, identity is 'dependent on the difference that has been translated into Otherness'.[38] In other words, defining yourself by what you are not is an integral part of self-representation, one that can be primarily understood through affect. Sara Ahmed explains this 'othering' as a form of affective economics. Although Ahmed specifically looks at hate and fear in Western depictions of terrorism, her discussion on the way affect is formulated can be applied to the demarking of attributes on the quest for self-representation. For Ahmed, hate is able to '*circulate in an economic sense*' in the process of distinguishing '*some others from other others*'.[39]

While '*hate*' may be too strong an emotion for this conversation, Ahmed's thesis brings to the surface the ways in which affect works to police self-identity in relation to 'Others'. This '*differentiation*'[40] was evident among participants, who were keen to outline the ways in which Fairouz represented them by highlighting forms of 'Otherness', which they did not believe exemplified them as individuals or as Arabs:

> *She represents our side . . . part of the world, and she does it with such grace, and she's so undeniably, if not the best, then one of the best that the world has ever seen. Though we kind of hold her up as a beacon of . . . this is where I'm from, not this, you know.* (Rola, 29, Jordanian, Doha)

> *Imagine, the world perceives you through Fairouz, not through Al Qaida, or the Taliban, as previously, or any other offspring that are not related to us in essentials, they're all foreign, some of them from Pakistan . . .* (Ferial, 46, Palestinian, London)

> *[What] it means to me? Like I told you. It's refinement, you know. In our Arab world, the hitting and the tabbel[41] and these things, I'm not fond of it. But with her, she represented the part, which is Arabic, but not the Arabic that's loud with whistling horns, and shouting, it's more the fine part of Arabic music.* (Carmen, 70, Palestinian/Jordanian, Doha)

> *Yes, this is us. She represents, me, she represents us . . . .. Us, the Lebanese people! Yes, just us Lebanese, because I really feel jealous, she's ours and not for anyone else.* (Bianca, 37, Lebanese, Doha)

> *Because now all the new singers want to be Arab and, slash, foreign, maybe they want to appeal to the new generation or something.* (Lara, 50, Palestinian, Doha)

> *[Fairouz] reminds me of everything that's nicely Middle Eastern. You know, like the lifestyle that we couldn't, we couldn't maintain or we couldn't reach, it's just the simplicity of expressing feelings without being judged, or like, you know.* (Leila, 30, Moroccan, London)

As a *'beacon of, this is where I'm from, not this'*, Rola, a respondent from Jordan, who has been in Doha since she was five, brings to light the ideal 'front', through which she wants to be seen, what can be called affective selection. *'Not this'* refers to the violence, bloodshed and terrorism often associated with the Middle East, something Rola prefers to keep in the 'back region' of her Arab representation. Selecting Fairouz to embody the ideal form of 'Arabness' is something also echoed by Ferial, a journalist working in London, who was more explicit in her rejection of being associated with terrorist groups, like *'Al Qaida, or the Taliban previously, or any other offspring that are not related to us in essentials, they're all foreign, some of them from Pakistan'*. In her opinion, being seen as part of Fairouz's world is more representative of the qualities she wants to link with 'Arabness'. The negative and violent 'other' is someone she wants to be dissociated from completely as they are *'foreign'*, *'from Pakistan'* and thus not Arab. While Rola and Ferial focused on deviating their representation from the violence and bloodshed related to the region, Carmen wanted to move away from the stereotypical image of Arabs that is correlated with coarseness, boorishness and loudness, *'the Arabic that's loud with whistling horns, and shouting'*, to one that is classier and more sophisticated. Here,

Fairouz embodies that '*refinement*', dichotomizing different or even overlapping characteristics of Arab self-representation and 'othering' than Ferial and Rola.

Bianca, a Lebanese respondent, and Lara, from Palestine, who both live in Doha, provide an interesting difference of opinion about Fairouz and 'Arabness'. For Bianca, Fairouz is a purely Lebanese singer, who is only understood by Lebanese listeners. There is a sense of ownership towards the artist, '*she's ours and not for anyone else*'. This refers to Aly's discussion on the 'construction of insider and outsiderness', a result of 'the effects of class, politics, language, education, religion and nationality' on 'people's perceptions and identifications'.[42] For Bianca, the common nationality, and perhaps the religion she shares with Fairouz, allows her to retain 'insider' rights in owning and comprehending her music, whereas other nationalities are 'outside' that scope of understanding. In this way, 'outsiderness' can be linked to 'othering' as, in both cases, divisive lines are drawn in sketching portraits of self-identity. Refusing to share Fairouz with the rest of the Arab world lies in stark contrast to Lara, who sees the singer as the epitome of 'Arabness', and comments that she is unlike newer singers who want to be '*Arab slash foreign*'. This can be linked to Amin's interchangeable notion of 'Arabness' and '*authenticity*', which is reminiscent of what Mona Mikhail defines as 'commitment as a test for authenticity'.[43]

In her article, Mikhail discusses *iltizam* in relation to Arab poets who, post-Second World War, were torn between trying to 'coexist with the inherited love of a concise, precise poetic language intended for centuries to be recited and appreciated' and 'the transmission of the newly found experiences of nationalism and revolt'.[44] Similarly, among the participants, Amin's equation of 'Arabness' and '*authenticity*', and Lara's rejection of the '*foreign*' influence in Arabic music are symbolic of deeper systems of *iltizam* for an unaltered Arabic identity and cause, which lies in tension with their diasporic history. Having lived in New York for eighteen years before moving to Qatar, Lara admits, '*all our friends were Arab . . . Uh, I tell you, my husband doesn't really like [to socialize with] Americans, he can't socialize with Americans, at all. To sit like this with the Americans and speak English all the time, and he's very funny, so what, he's going to speak and then translate words and jokes, it won't work.*' Both Lara's *meta-* and *micro-habitus* are clear instigators of this loyalty towards 'Arabness' and the Arabic language. For her, the two are strong identifiers against the foreign 'Other', but also they are important mechanisms by which she and her husband express facets of their personality.

However, the Lebanese-Christian Bianca's firm stance on Fairouz's nationality also hints at new forms of identity construction under the umbrella of *iltizam*, which shows a very different politics to Nasser's pan-Arab idea, comprising a narrower vision of citizenship that is divorced from the region and is instead confined by state borders. Bianca's '*our*' is also significantly different from Leila's '*we*'. Leila brings us back to Arab unity, which '*we couldn't maintain or we couldn't reach*'. By '*we*', Leila includes the greater part of the Arab world, who are also eager for '*simplicity*' and harmony, whereas Bianca's '*our*' is limiting and exclusive. In this way, *iltizam* can expand and contract according to participants' intersectional 'subject positions', which are defined by their principles, beliefs and attitudes to fellow Arabs. Affectively, these forms of 'othering' and belonging not only give insight into the ways that participants saw themselves within self-explained and individualized categories of 'Arabness', but also it views 'Arabness' as a whole entity, which hints at both solidarity and deviation. Along these lines, affect makes "'the collective" appear as if it were a body, in the first place'.[45]

Hybridity, iltizam and the 'intercontextual'

Amalgamating and changing, personifying and triggering, Fairouz and her 'aura' invite listeners to receive and appropriate her music in a plethora of ways. Through participants' various 'subject positions', Fairouz is understood and experienced on the personal and social levels by means of the 'mnemonic imagination', which 'intersects personal histories and social order, cognitive processes and cultural belonging'.[46] Juxtaposing the 'mnemonic imagination' within the context of the *meta-habitus* and the *micro-habitus* provides a multifaceted analysis of the 'individualised imprint'[47] of the Arab diaspora living in England and Qatar, highlighting the complexity of diasporic experience and showcasing the need for non-essentialist discourse on migrants. The themes discussed here therefore show the ways in which respondents are able to self-represent and understand their positioning individually, socially, culturally and globally. These themes also underscore the ways in which affect is manifested, through the gradients of 'individualised imprints', but that also amplify in accordance with environment and context. It is, as Seigworth and Gregg maintain, that 'Affect marks a body's *belonging* to a world of encounters or; a world's belonging to a body of encounters but also, in *non-belonging*, through all those far sadder (de) compositions of mutual in-compossibilities'.[48] '*Belonging*' and '*non-belonging*' bring about different forms of affect, even if one or the other are experienced, lived or imagined.

In light of this, trying to bind Fairouz to one representation is ineffective and detrimental. She needs to be seen as a *hybrid* identity space, traversing all nationalistic and emotional boundaries. Rooted in post-colonial theory, *hybridity* has been challenged by a number of theorists[49] as being a deceptive form of the internalization of ideas and ideologies enforced on colonized societies by the colonizers. Hybridity has also been criticized for being too vague, 'a floating signifier, ripe for appropriation'.[50] While discussion on Fairouz as a figure of post-colonialism has been shared by Christopher Stone, in this case, hybridity is taken to mean what May Joseph describes as a 'new hybrid identity'. For Joseph, this 'new hybrid identity' refers to a 'nexus of affiliations' that 'perform contemporary acts of citizenship' forming 'modern social and political alliances'.[51] Coupling this notion of hybridity with the diaspora 'draws on local and transnational identifications',[52] allowing it to travel beyond the colonized state, while still maintaining a sense of locality. It resonates with Homi Bhabha's 'in-between spaces', which 'provide the terrain for elaborating strategies of self-hood –singular or communal'.[53] In this way, Fairouz allows for a hybrid in-between space, where intersections of identity transit by way of the '*in-between-ness*' of affect, 'in the capacities to act and be acted upon,[54] through multiple cultural, political and religious lines feeding into what Bhabha calls the 'beyond'.[55]

Exemplary of our era, this 'moment of transit where space and time cross to produce complex figures of difference and identity, past and present, inside and outside, inclusion and exclusion'[56] situates the key components of this book in a shifting and dynamic environment. Trying to anchor Fairouz to a specific space, time and identity negates her ability to move beyond their restrictive depictions, which is why it is important to look at other points of identification, through her music, which move beyond 'Arabness':

I'm not a guy who you'd ever find in a mall drinking coffee. I feel like the recent, like, ten or twenty years, killed the very 'us', killed our culture . . . made us like copies of something we've never been, which is Globalization. Ya3ni, you go to Hong Kong, you go to Boston, you go to Amman, and you come to Doha, and you go to Beirut, you go into a mall and it's the same brands, and the same trademarks, and the same haircuts for the young girls and the same clothes for the young boys. You don't feel that identity. Fairouz is that part of that identity, part of our real faces, of our real hearts, when we love and when we hate, when we get angry, or when we are upset, or when we are happy. Now, in the music that's available, in the culture that's available, you can't find us. (Jihad, 51, Palestinian/Jordanian, Doha)

Fairouz is your identity. (Akram, 37, Syrian, London)

Um, so the best thing to do is like encourage their kids to listen to Fairouz . . . it's about performing identity and stuff, 'cause where I grew up there was hardly any Arabs around where I was growing up. (Ahmad, 35, Iraqi, London)

I mean, Fairouz, for me, means a strong link to my identity, and I don't consider this as just purely Lebanese, by the way, it's more, more of a cultural identity, I identify with most Arabs I meet, I identify with most Eastern people that I meet in London, even the people who are foreigners can appreciate Eastern music. So that's all for me, part of identity. It doesn't have to be, you know, identity card and where are you from, I don't believe that much in geo-political, you know, structure, but Fairouz, for me, is a strong link to music, and I proved it by, when people are exposed to Fairouz and they'd never heard it, her before, they also identify with her. (Nicholas, 47, Lebanese, London)

When George drives through the compound, he would have Fairouz on loudly in the car. And everyone in the compound would know that it is George passing by because of the music from the car. So, yeah, Fairouz has given us an identity. (Nora, 37, Lebanese, Doha)

That home is . . . no, that home is Lebanon, that home is my family, that home is being an Arab, um, that home is uh, is kind of my identity. It is kind of, uh, she [Fairouz] brings me back to me. (Maya, 46, Lebanese, Doha)

Whether approaching global phenomena or through immediate portrayals of childhood and loved ones, Fairouz offers a kaleidoscope through which to reflect and assess diasporic notions of identity. The earlier examples bring to the surface further forms of particularity, which include, or move beyond, 'Arabness', encompassing a wider set of characteristics. In Jihad's concept of globalization, the authenticity of *iltizam* has been eradicated, which makes him feel removed and distant. It is this global homogeneity, which pushes the need for celebrating and promoting cultural '*différance*'. Jihad, who has lived in Doha for over twenty-five years, is '*not a guy who you'd ever find in a mall drinking coffee*'. With the rapid development of Doha, numerous malls burgeoned all over the capital, which not only allowed patrons the opportunity to shop international brands but also provided spaces to meet in coffee shops and restaurants. However, Jihad resists this form of social activity. He is not a conformer with the cookie-cutter malls of the world, nor with the lifestyle that comes with it, which '*killed the very "us", killed our culture . . . made us like copies of something we've never been*'. It is interesting to note the '*us*' and the '*our*' and the '*we've*', all inclusive of a very specific stratum of community, which falls under the authenticity of *iltizam*. Jihad is talking about Arab society, one which remains committed to capturing '*part of our real faces, of our real hearts*'. For Jihad, '*Fairouz is that part of that identity*', a place where he sees himself and feels a sense of belonging in an otherwise sterile and consumer-driven environment. This sentiment was not specific to Doha, as Akram in London also echoed that, '*Fairouz is your identity*'. Akram's '*you*' is very much part of Jihad's '*us*', '*our*' and '*we've*', of this Arab unity and consideration found with Fairouz, a more affective 'collective representation', which is understood but, at the same time, is challenged and subjective.

For Ahmad in London, '*it's about performing identity*' in a place where '*there was hardly any Arabs around where I was growing up*'. The '*identity*', to which Ahmad is referring, is one that is expected from him, either through his family or through other members of the Arab community. Listening to Fairouz therefore appeases that affective 'front region' of Arab identity, which is 'performative' and aesthetic, falling into Jihad and Akram's authentic '*very "us"*'. Contextualizing Fairouz through Ahmad's childhood highlights the '*in-between*' diasporic tension in remaining true to 'preconceived ways of being' and 'performing' Arab while growing up in a non-Arab district.[57] This resonates with what Susan Ruddick says in that 'becoming' something or someone is 'a social act, a co-production'.[58] For Ahmad, who moved to the UK from Iraq when he was four years old, consuming Fairouz's music at a young age helped to instil Arab identity and form a sense of self in an environment which had '*hardly any Arabs around*'. Through the 'social act' of listening to Fairouz, Ahmed thus found a way to 'become' more in touch with his Arab 'self' in a non-Arab environment.

For Nicholas, a first-generation Lebanese man in London, Fairouz is the link with multiple layers of his identity. An avid musician, who comes from a great musical lineage and who is an expert in Middle Eastern and Byzantine music, Nicholas sees Fairouz as a method through which to absorb and appreciate Middle

Eastern music by those who are unfamiliar with it. Since music is an integral part of his life, Fairouz provides a comfortable space of acceptance. She is also able to bridge the space between the Eastern and 'foreign' cultures, where Nicholas feels a sense of belonging.

This merging of cultures is similar to what Jana, a 48-year-old, Palestinian/Syrian woman in London, calls '*morphed*'. Even though Nicholas is a first-generation diasporan, he has taken on elements from his new home as part of his '*cultural identity*', which is personified in Fairouz and her music. This can be seen as a new form of *iltizam*, which moves away from geopolitical ideologies to inhabit a fragmented form of commitment built upon a '*morphed*' culture. Lying in contrast to the '*authenticity*', mentioned by Amin, '*morphed*' culture, as defined by Nicholas, is affectively selective, an '*in-between-ness*' of different worlds, offering a glimpse of new forms of identity construction, which grows from the past to encompass present and future self-representations.

Interestingly, respondents in Qatar never discussed ways they have '*morphed*', even though they would often comment on the ways in which living there was different to their own countries. This lack of 'connectedness' leads us into a deeper discussion on the ways in which the *meta-* and the *micro-habitus* play an influential role in creating a cultural identity that has incorporated elements from the society in which participants reside in. Here, it is important to relate to Marwan Kraidy, whose thorough analysis of the evolution of the notion of hybridity provides a key insight. Outlining the different definitions of the term, Kraidy draws on Appadurai to suggest an 'intercontextual' understanding of hybridity 'that explicates transnational cultural dynamics by articulating hybridity and hegemony in a global context'.[59] Through the realm of 'international and intercultural communication', the concept of 'intercontextual hybridity' thus highlights the 'mutually constitutive interplay and overlap of cultural, economic and political forces' across transnational dialogue, allowing 'us to comprehend how under certain conditions, in certain contexts, ideological elements coalesce in a certain discourse of hybridity'.[60] Linking this to the *micro-habitus*, that is 'certain conditions', and to the *meta-habitus*, that is 'certain contexts', paves the way for a negotiated form of hybridity in which participants are not only active agents but also key determiners and sculptors of their hybridity.

By absorbing elements from their environment and everyday experience, and in the practice of interpreting the role of Fairouz in their lives, participants are able to filter cross-cultural attributes in their self-representation. It can therefore be argued that 'intercontextual hybridity' paired with both the *meta-* and *micro-habitus* show the power dynamics of 'cultural identity' in producing navigated responses to self-identity and presentation. In addition, this lack of voluntary or involuntary emersion in Qatar is indicative of the difference in identity politics between Doha and London, and it sheds light on migrants who inhabit two very different geopolitical and social spaces. These centrifugal and centripetal powers of identity are important to examine here to better comprehend the ways in which notions of the cultural self can be simultaneously enforced by surroundings but are also very much projected from within.

It is necessary to draw on Stuart Hall's definition of 'cultural identity', which he explains has at least 'two different ways' of being understood. In one sense 'cultural identity' can be seen 'in terms of one, shared culture, a sort of "one true self"'.[61] Through 'shared history and ancestry', communities convene under the umbrella of 'oneness', allowing for 'stable, unchanging and continuous frames of reference and meaning, beneath the shifting divisions and vicissitudes of our actual history'.[62] This may relate to the 'collective representation' offered by Goffman, in the sense that 'cultural identity' is comprised of shared elements, which can be understood and performed. It is also reminiscent of the 'connectedness' mentioned by Aly, who maintains 'different places and contexts should be seen as constantly leading to a reiteration of Arabness in a web of interactions between the local and the global, a process which takes place as much in the diaspora as it does in the "Arab world"'.[63] In his second description, Hall maintains that while there are multiple 'points of similarity', there are also 'critical points of deep and significant *difference*'.[64] In this way, Hall argues, cultural identity is an act of 'becoming' rather than 'being', since it is not just entrenched in the confining past but instead evolves and 'belong[s] to the future as much as to the past'.[65] While Hall roots his argument in racial colonial discourse specific to the Caribbean experience, his discussion on ways in which 'cultural identities' are a spatio-temporal process where 'unstable points of identification' are formed is particularly useful in understanding fluctuating forms of 'Arabness', as well as what can best be described as 'intercontextual' *iltizam*. For Hall, 'there is always a politics of identity, a politics of position, which has no absolute guarantee in an unproblematic, transcendental "law of origin"'.[66] This 'politics' of 'positioning', in the case of the Arab diaspora, is very much related to the *micro-* and *meta-habitus* and the ways in which they work, in tandem or in opposition, to form a sense of *iltizam*.

By appropriating the term used by Kraidy and Appadurai, 'intercontextual' *iltizam*, is both a product and an identifier of an era in which Arab alliances and points of '*différance*' are experiencing tension. Shifts in political power, the lead up and aftermath of the Arab uprisings, the Syrian conflict and increasing religious fundamentalism are some of the factors in which *iltizam* has been stretched, pulled or ripped apart. It can be argued that while *iltizam* was a purpose with which to unite, 'intercontextual' *iltizam* indicates division and fragmentation. Various perspectives on 'Arabness' and self-identity can thus be attributed to the *micro-* and *meta-habitual* ways in which *iltizam* is produced, understood and followed. It is at the crossroads of the *meta-habitus* and *micro-habitus* that *iltizam* is found. In this way, Fairouz is an axis point on the scale of '*authenticity*' and '*hybridity*' on the path to 'becoming' Arab and 'doing Arab', allowing different 'positionings' within self-identity and representation.

While other respondents discuss identity in a more general sense, Nora and Maya's depiction of Fairouz takes it to the specific. Nora's version of representative identity, in this excerpt, is precisely about her husband George, who listens to Fairouz '*loudly in the car*'. When he '*drives through the compound*',[67] hearing Fairouz on high volume becomes affiliated with him. In this sense, Fairouz is a signifier of his presence among his neighbours, a performative 'George has arrived!' This illustrates the private side of identity, which is not necessarily linked to religion, cause or ideology, but, rather, to an individual, marking him/her within his/her community. From being marked in a community to feeling adrift within it, Maya's concept of identity is very much linked to absence, which she defines covertly, '*that home is my family, that home is being an Arab . . . that home . . . is kind of my identity . . . she brings me back to me*'.

While the notion of home will be explored in depth in the next section, it is interesting to note how '*home*', '*family*', '*Arab*', '*identity*' and '*brings me back to me*' become synonymous with one another; a cross-sectional form of self-identity sewn together through the music of Fairouz. It is the '*me*', which has deeply embedded paths leading to '*home*', but essentially it is that '*home*' which turns around and leads her back to herself. In either case, there is a sense of loss implied through Maya's statement. For Fairouz to '*bring*' her '*back*' to herself indicates she had drifted away from that place of familiarity only to find it again through music. The grounding Maya feels through Fairouz and her songs can be traced to the link between mnemonically imaginative notions of '*home*', nostalgia and affect. While themes falling under the mnemonic imagination will form a key chapter in itself, it is important to shed light here on the ways in which it contributes to identity construction and structures of belonging. Keightley and Pickering argue the mnemonic imagination, a marriage between imagination and memory, weaving across different lived and projected timescales is an important tool in trying to 'sustain a sense of self-identity'[68] through temporal and environmental progressions. In this vein, 'experience becomes the interspace within which we negotiate our self-identity and our social identity, and the ways in which these do, or do not, match up to each other'.[69] With Maya, the experience of being a member of the diaspora becomes the experiential 'interspace', in which she 'negotiates' the absence of her 'self-identity' retrospectively of her positional 'social identity'. It is through the music of Fairouz, and within that 'interspace', that she is thus able to assess and formulate the identity she understands. Maya feels '*frequently sad*' when she listens to Fairouz's songs, especially those about Palestine, even though '*I'm not Palestinian, but it's . . . somehow, it's about a lost homeland, which I feel I have lost in Lebanon . . . so they make me sad*'. This nostalgia Maya feels for what she calls '*paradise lost*' is what Barrett et al. consider 'an affective process that can accompany autobiographical memories'.[70]

In their study on music-evoked nostalgia, the authors 'research the specific structures of music-evoked nostalgia and individual differences in the affective and mnemonic structures'.[71] Defining nostalgia as 'a complex emotion that gives rise primarily (albeit not exclusively) to positive affect, and serves to counteract sadness and loneliness', the authors argue that nostalgia is 'an emotion often triggered by music'.[72] To 'counteract sadness and loneliness', Maya thus resorts to nostalgia through Fairouz's music. Heightening the awareness of her loss of 'homeland' and, interchangeably, her sense of 'self', Maya is able to travel through the mnemonic imagination, via Fairouz, to reconfigure and reboot this yearned for identity, which is essentially '*Arab*', linked to her '*family*', her '*identity*' and her '*self*'.

It is also important to mention what Barrett et al. call 'autobiographical salience' and its correlation in evoking feelings of nostalgia. For these authors, 'autobiographical salience' or 'the particular associations the individual has formed between a piece of music and both past events . . . as well as basic emotions that these evoke' increase the possibility for nostalgia because of memories' 'emotional components'.[73] The '*loss of homeland*' and '*loss of self*' therefore intertwine to mean both one and the other, and the detachment associated with their subsequent components, such as '*Arab*' and '*family*', essentially leads to a detachment of '*self*'. Barrett et al. examine two paradigms, which they say 'may contribute to nostalgic experience'.[74] They call these 'context-level' and 'personal-level constructs'.

'*Context-level constructs*' look at a 'person's relationship to a given song' and the 'degree to which it is associated with a personal memory', while '*personal-level constructs*' refer to 'individual differences between listeners' and how probable they are to 'experience nostalgia'.[75] The relationship between *context-level* and *personal-level constructs* is what determines the likelihood of experiencing nostalgia. Putting this into a conversation, in which nostalgia is attributed to 'members of a specific generation or social group who feel temporally displaced, strangers in a new world that seems radically disconnected from an earlier one',[76] demonstrates how all these different components, as well as the *micro-* and *meta-habitual* situations of participants, come together to reveal very personal, but also very collective, frameworks for examining nostalgia. As someone who lives in the diaspora and is 'temporally displaced', as well as away from her family, Maya is a prime candidate for nostalgia, both through the *context-level constructs* of Fairouz's songs, which factor strongly in 'autobiographical salience' for her, and because of her feeling 'temporally displaced' at the *personal level*. Adding to this, it is important to note that 'autobiographical salience' is a mnemonic construct and is thus just as *imagined* as it is remembered. In this way Maya's sense of '*self*', which she attributes to a '*lost homeland*' and which she finds in Fairouz's songs, is essentially unattainable and intangible, thus putting her in constant tension with different aspects of herself. As Firth contends, 'identity is not a thing but a process'.[77] Feelings of loss will always be inherent due to the fluctuating and inconsistent 'process' of identity and the mnemonic imaginings of that identity in relation to '*home*'.

The feelings of loss and memory with regard to '*home*' are best explained by Sara Ahmed, who interlaces the notions of 'home' with the 'self'. In doing so, Ahmed highlights the consequential 'discomfort of inhabiting a migrant's body'. For Ahmed, 'home' and 'self' cannot be dislocated from one another, since 'the home is not exterior to a self, but implicated in it'.[78] Maya interchangeably uses the 'self' as part of her Lebanese, familial identity, providing evidence that this dis-positioning of the 'body' caused by 'leaving home' is an affective state, which is 'uncomfortable' and 'out of place'. The loss she feels is thus not only because she is a member of the diaspora but essentially because of the 'failure' she feels in accommodating her new migrant 'self'. Here, affect, through the mnemonic imagination and driven by the *meta-* and *micro-habitus*, plays an integral role – not only in the recognition of a 'home' or a 'home' lost but also in the ability to make one feel like one 'self'. Stemming from this, it is important to discuss 'home' as part of the 'process' of identity. The concept of home among the diaspora in both Doha and London was divided, some interviewees had a clear description of 'home', while others were quite confused by the notion.

Mnemonic imaginings of home

As outlined previously, Qatar's strict citizenship laws confine non-local residents to their positions in the country as workforce or labour. Purchasing property, or naturalization, is difficult and almost impossible. Residents thus often feel they are in transience, transiting to ensure a viable and secure future, even though locating where that future may be is a point of contention:

> *I've been here for 25 years . . . Obama is the son of an immigrant and he became a president. Us, every time we want to travel, we need to go and get [permission]. Is this close to any home that you can imagine?* (Jihad, 51, Palestinian/Jordanian, Doha)

Even after twenty-five years Qatar is not home for Jihad. Its confining treatment of non-locals – for example needing an exit permit to leave the country[79] – makes it a regulated environment, which gives little control and equality to non-Qataris. Jihad is also unsure of where his home is, since moving to Jordan is not an option for him or his family. However, confusion on the notion of home was not always shared; for some, home was a clear and concrete place to which participants were eager to return, as soon as they were financially ready:

> *I'm fine, I'm not stressed, I'm fine. But I'm living . . . it could be tomorrow, it could be in a year, it could be in 10 years, I don't mind, but I'm living for the day that I return to Lebanon.* (Bianca, 45, Lebanese, Doha)

Even though Jihad and Bianca are part of the same *meta-habitus*, in that they are both living in Qatar and are thus expected to leave at some point, it is their various 'subject positions' and their *micro-habitus* that differentiate their attitudes towards where they are and where they aspire to be. Although both respondents claim to be comfortable and content with their respective living conditions, their affective discrepancy shapes their opinion of homeland and nation, which emerges in their discussion of Fairouz and her music. For Bianca, Fairouz's music is reflective and serves as a reminder that she will eventually move to Lebanon and '*be a part of* the lifestyle Fairouz sings about. For Jihad, it is, however, a reminder of '*homesickness*' and loss, since '*there are songs of hers my dad used to love, and when I listen to them, this is where you feel homesickness . . . I wish I could be there again, like 20 years ago in that place, from that song*'. Linking home to deceased parents makes Jihad's situation even trickier, especially as a Palestinian who cannot return to Palestine, but also as someone who does not feel at home in Jordan and cannot remain in Qatar forever.

This split highlights the ways in which nationhood and homeland are perceived: as tangible and imagined, as past and future, and as different states of affect. The Lebanese community, although happy in Qatar, mostly acknowledges living there to be '*temporary, because I want to go back*' *(Bianca).* The Lebanon Fairouz sings about, is their future, as well as their past and present. However, for those recipients who are facing political instability in their country, Fairouz brings them to the past, as they are uncertain about their future:

> *I have no, nothing, no concept, ya3ni, of home . . . I don't know what I consider home . . . Ya3ni, to me Kuwait is home, because I lived in it for 20 years, but after the . . . Gulf War . . . they kicked a lot of Palestinians out, and we sort of have this bitter feeling, and I never went back to Kuwait after I left.* (Lara, 50, Palestinian, Doha)

> *There is always the home you grew up in and experienced your childhood . . . when I say home I miss my departed parents.* (Jihad, 51, Palestinian/Jordanian, Doha)

> *[Fairouz] is reminiscent of home . . . home is where my family is.* (Rola, 29, Jordanian, Doha)

> *My country is my own. I carry my country with me and I interpret it the way I want. Whatever people do, they can't reach the country that I'm carrying in my mind. They are destroying Iraq and Beirut, they are ending lives, and they are changing the morals of people, but all this doesn't mean anything to me anymore.* (Hussain, 60, Iraqi, London)

> *And I'm still counting the days that we should leave London, I don't want to die here. I don't want to die in London. I love London very much, but I don't want to stay in Britain, definitely not, but I don't want to go back home. I have a problem because I'm married to a Frenchman, who finds Lebanon very challenging and tiring and the kids won't get the quality of life that we are getting here for less, as in education, medical [services] . . .. Because I have young kids, I'm gonna have to shut up and stay.* (Dina, 42, Lebanese, London)

> *Maybe it's an umbilical cord to a geographical location, but for me, because I'm not attached to nationalities and I feel that I'm very much kind of a global citizen, where everyone's equal and we should look after each other, no matter where we come from. Maybe it's not in the geographical sense. It's the fantasy, just the imagined who I am, and where I come from. This is where I come from; it's the umbilical cord to that. But it's not a location, that's the thing. It's like, (sighs) it's an imagined sense of belonging to something, if that doesn't sound too cynical.* (Maha, 35, Syrian/Lebanese, London)

It is here, at the interplay between the *micro-* and *meta-habitus*, participants' individual 'subject positions' and the subsequent mnemonic appropriating of Fairouz's 'aura' that the concept of home is understood. It is the point where past, present, future and the unknown converge to recreate and re-imagine a 'home' and 'belonging' that are at once personal and public. For Lara and Jihad, in Qatar, home is uncertain and in the past, whereas, for Rola, home is anchored through her parents and in the present. Lara's reference to living in Kuwait prior to the First Gulf War in 1991, and then subsequently being kicked out because she was Palestinian, is an indicator of how the *meta-* and *micro-habitus* intersect to create an image of home. For many respondents who lived in Doha or in the Gulf, 'belonging' and 'home' are vague, because of the potential for expulsion and thus the inability to be rooted in such places. In this way, home can be seen as a construct of the mnemonic, since it stems from a deep sense of personal loss. It is similar to Jihad's statement about his deceased parents and about not being able to feel a sense of home without their presence. Linking home to parents is also expressed by Rola, but since her *micro-habitual* situation differs from that of Jihad, in the sense that her parents are still around, 'home' is not in the past but is very much in the present.

Instigating the sense of home in her songs, Fairouz, through what Williams would call a 'structure of feeling' or a 'specific structure of particular linkages, particular emphases and suppressions',[80] taps into the individual and collective mnemonic imaginations, resulting in an amalgamation of the home. Manifesting in different forms, home, as a 'structure of feeling', is accommodated both *through* and *by* the music of Fairouz and her subsequent 'aura'. It is also something that can be mobilized and adapted, '*the idea, the home that you believe in, you will carry it with you, wherever you go*' (Jihad, 51, Palestinian/Jordanian, Doha); or it is mobilized and protected from the violence surrounding it, '*I carry my country with me and I interpret it the way I want. Whatever people do, they can't reach the country that I'm carrying in my mind*' (Hussain, 60, Iraqi, London). In this way, Fairouz travels with diasporic communities and is accessible to them wherever they go. She is at once the protector of home's memory and the trigger for it. Participants are thus able to keep home safe, revel in its recollection and grasp it in any way they want.

The idea of home is arguably affective. In the case of Lara who has '*no, nothing, no concept, ya3ni, of home*', affect lies in the absent 'home'. In order to claim its absence, Lara determines its lack of presence. However, this presence would have had to be understood, in order to recognize its absence, giving weight to the claim that 'home' is a 'structure of feeling', constructed through the *meta-* and *micro-habitus* and materialized through the mnemonic imagination. 'Home' is not necessarily a tangible place but is somewhere that 'particular linkages' are felt.[81] Affect thus not only works as '*in-between-ness*' to drive emotion but also straddles the gradients of absence and presence. Affect here inhibits a different form of '*in-between-ness*', one that falls between presence and absence, where Fairouz triggers the claim to the 'feeling', by tapping into the habitual aggregates which have positioned it.

For Dina and Maha, home is an unknown place they may be able to attain in the future. Even though both participants are married to non-Arabs, their perceptions of home differ drastically. While Dina does not '*want to die in London*', she does '*not want to go back home*'. Married '*to a Frenchman who finds Lebanon very challenging and tiring*, and as a mother to two young boys, Dina can no longer individually plan her way, as she has to consider what best suits her family. Maha, on the other hand, draws a very rich maternal image of what home means to her, separate from her husband and her original nationality. Although she is *'not attached to nationalities'*, Fairouz supplies an *'umbilical cord'* to the *'imagined who I am and where I come from'*. However, *'it's not a location, that's the thing . . . it's an imagined sense of belonging to something'*. Discussing the maternal images associated with Fairouz is significant, as it relates to the idea of homeland/ motherland. It is a sentiment echoed by Mariam, a Qatari living in London, who described Fairouz's music as *'nurturing, it's nurturing, it's soothing, like you hear her voice and you know it's healing . . . it's soothing, it is exactly like a mother's touch'*. The maternal warmth Fairouz supplies was often referenced in conversations, and she was, at times, described as a *'mother'* or *'grandmother'*. Respondents wanted to *'protect'* her or otherwise felt she *'protected'* them. While discussion on Fairouz as a maternal figure will be outlined later in the book,[82] it is important here to understand the results of these depictions in the framework of nationhood and belonging.

In her book *The Gendered Nation*, Neluka Silva argues that 'while feminised images . . . define the *iconography* of the nation, the *practice* of nationalism is reserved for the male'.[83] Although Silva tackles literal representations of nation and nationalism through feminist literature, for participants in this study, however, Fairouz embodies not just the passive 'aura' and 'iconicity' of a nation but also a universal and dynamic 'Arabized' form of nationalism. Through her poetic descriptions of village life and landscapes, of the uniting rivers that thread the mountains and the earth that anxiously awaits the seeds of its children, Fairouz literally houses the displaced in her songs, creating an *affective state*, with 'state' being understood as nationhood and homeland, but also as condition and circumstance. Fairouz simultaneously bestows upon her listeners an identity and a sense of belonging, away from actual borders or specific geographical locales:

She is the nationalistic Fairouz, the singer that reaches every heart, every brain, in every age. (Lara, 50, Palestinian, Doha)

[She reminds me of Palestine] but not because she sang about Palestine, because the way she speaks about Lebanon applies to any homeland in the world. (Jihad, 51, Palestinian/Jordanian, Doha)

She's Lebanon . . . I mean she's my mum's Lebanon and my grandmother's Lebanon. She's the Lebanon that does not exist, but I wish it did. (Maya, 46, Lebanese, Doha)

She represents our part of the world . . . we kind of hold her as a beacon, like this is where I'm from, not this. (Rola, 29, Jordanian, Doha)

I think I know every one of her songs and not like all the words of all the songs, but most of the words of most of the songs, and it's just beautiful to me, it's comforting, it's my, it's something that I feel absolute familiarity and love for, whereas I have been quite estranged and ostracized from quite a lot of things that I, you know, was sort of naturally born into, that I sort of separated slowly from, you know, and yes I was Westernized at a young age, because we actually lived in the States and I went to these British schools, you know, with only expat kids and stuff, mostly expat kids, then moving away, being in the UK for fifteen years, over fifteen years. That gap, and sort of that estrangement grew, but there's no estrangement with the music, and sometimes I even struggle to find words in Arabic when I'm with my family, like it doesn't not come, it just takes a few seconds or whatever, and I might end up using an English word and there's this feeling of: yeah, I don't know how to describe it, that I'm almost foreign, and that I feel them feeling me or experiencing me as foreign, but also experiencing me as totally family and more Qatari, and kind of shocked at my desire to be in the West, and horror, and none of them really want me to be here, but when I listen to the music, I am just Arabic through and through . . . there's no like, yeah, there's no separation, which is a great thing to have (Mariam, 32, Qatari, London)

It's just really you know . . . it's nostalgic really, like I remember my house, Sudan, all of us surrounded the TV you know. There was one TV in the whole house – watching a play, and everybody knew the play by heart . . . it just brings me to that, it brings me to, it takes me home, you know? (Nafie, 35, Sudanese, Doha)

These examples have multiple connotations. First, they defy what Silva alludes to in her notion of a male 'nationalism'. Through the female, Fairouz, participants feel *'patriotism' and 'nostalgia'* towards a felt homeland or *'the idea, the home that you believe in'*. In this way, Fairouz acts as a dynamic propagator in the dissemination of nationalism through her songs. She is not simply a silent symbol; she is an outspoken tool for 'Arabness' and *iltizam*. While in only one case presented earlier, this nationalism is placed in Lebanon, her songs also translate *'to any homeland in the world'*, thus giving credit to Stone's claim that Fairouz fell into the category of 'symbolic mothers of national families'.[84] However, Stone criticizes Fairouz's representation[85] as verging on the side of being a 'post-colonial, nation-building project'.[86] Using Fairouz and the Rahbanis' participation in the annual Ba'albeck International Festival in Lebanon as a point of analysis, Stone contends, this 'was not just a project that reflected a certain vision of Lebanese locality, but one that actively participated in producing it'.[87]

For Stone, Fairouz and the Rahbani brothers played a 'central, powerful and sometimes problematic role' in shaping a 'new "Lebanese" identity'[88] for a 'nascent state' slowly gaining independence from its French colonizers.[89] Tracing the rise of Fairouz and the Rahbani brothers against a historical and sociopolitical backdrop that 'coincided with the confluence of increasing migration both out of Lebanon and to its urban centers', Stone argues, 'the inclusion of the folkloric vignettes of the Rahbani musical-theatrical productions into an otherwise European dominated cultural agenda', such as the Ba'albeck International Festival, 'created a powerful nation-building combination'.[90] While there is strong evidence for Stone's thesis, and even though the intention of the creation of a 'Lebanese identity' may have been there, as mentioned before, tying Fairouz to a certain ideology, or time and place, limits the capability of her 'aura' to move beyond the borders of Lebanon to the dispersed fans of her music.

Through discussions with participants, Fairouz symbiotically symbolizes 'Palestine', 'Lebanon', 'Sudan', 'Iraq', the *'Lebanon that does not exist, but I wish it did'* and, in the instance of Shams, Fairouz is seen as an active symbol of *'all Arabs against Israelis'*. She is a reminder of *iltizam* and authenticity. She is an active agent and a leader in an 'us' and 'them' dichotomy, again paving the way for a sense of belonging. She is a desired, affective state that *'does not exist'* but *'I wish it did'*. So, as a 'figure', Fairouz is, in effect, post-national, but at the same time she is a *'beacon'* of defiance. Through their various 'subject positions', respondents are able to position themselves accordingly, in order to belong to Fairouz's post-national state. Patriotism here is thus not associated with one standardized place but occupies numerous community assimilations that are dependent on the 'mnemonic imagination', as well as on the intercontextual forms of *iltizam*. This gives evidence to the notion of an idealized 'Arabized' state, which moves beyond borders to incorporate a wider net of belonging while also maintaining certain cultural proximity in order for Fairouz's fans to find their way home. She is where the Westernized Mariam, who is *'ostracized'* by her conservative family, feels *'just Arabic through and through'*. By means of her lyrics, Mariam is no longer *'foreign'*; instead she is offered a safe haven, where she can combine different elements of her identity with *'no separation'* and *'no estrangement'*. For Nafie, this is different, as Fairouz brings him back to a time with his family in Sudan, where they would gather and listen to her songs or watch her plays. Fairouz is part of his mnemonic 'home', linked to specific people in a specific place, where he felt comfort and belonging. It is a different experience for Mariam, who was introduced to Fairouz through her mother, but then continued listening to Fairouz to seek out her own 'Arabness'. Putting these two statements in conversation highlights how Fairouz is able to accommodate a variety of ways in which 'home' and belonging are understood in different contextual situations in conjunction with the private sphere, but also very much driven by the *micro-* and *meta-habitus*.

Jihad's, 51, and Lara's, 50, accounts venture into the realm of the public sphere. For them, Fairouz is *'nationalistic'*, although this nationalism is not always linked to a particular nation. Jihad goes so far as to say she reminds him of Palestine, but not because she *'sang about'* it. Rather, her nationalism was able to amalgamate and transform through the mnemonic imagination. Many respondents brought up Palestine in reference to Fairouz, since many saw her as a force against injustice and occupation. As an active 'figure' of home and 'Arabized' nationhood, Fairouz embodies resistance and patriotism, which provides the very foundation of all forms of *iltizam*, whether participants saw it as a shared sentiment or whether they chose to define it on their own terms:

> *You know, Jamal Abdel Nasser and Yasser Arafat could come back from the dead and tell us Palestine would be free, and we wouldn't necessarily believe them. She goes up on that stage and sings one song and I believe her . . . I think that's . . . the amazing kind of power that she's got.* (Maya, 46, Lebanese, Doha)

There is also the political Fairouz. The songs she sang for Palestine, for resistance, and for Jerusalem. (Kareem, 36, Egyptian, London)

Even when she sang for Palestine, for Jerusalem, we were all ready to hold our guns and go there. . . . At that time, yes, I was ready to stand and fight for Fairouz. (Zuhair, 70, Lebanese, Doha)

I used to play her more serious songs, like 'Zahrat Al Mada'in'.[91] *This was during the First Gulf War, it gave me some kind of strength to move on with the day. I was really homesick, and wanted to get back to Doha, Doha is home for me, and I wanted to be with my parents. Although I am not Palestinian, the song always moved me and, in a way it made me happy, although it is not really a happy song.* (Clara, 44, Lebanese, Doha)

I also believe in resistance, but I don't consider myself Hezbollah. I can't limit resistance exclusively to Hezbollah. I am an Arab. I'm very proud of my language. I consider it a very strong language. I'm not very proud of our cultures. There are traditions I don't like in my culture. I'm very proud of our music. (Mounir, 37, Lebanese, London)

[Fairouz is] the only one that, if she dies, La Samah Allah,[92] *I'd go on the first plane to Lebanon for her funeral. It's her and another person, who is El-Sayyed Hassan Nasrallah,*[93] *these two I'd go to Lebanon for. I don't have a problem. Despite all the politics, but these two persons are a priority for me, they are Lebanon to me. These two may be so far away from each other and they are a contrast, but I am free. I can like anyone I want.* (Hisham, 42, Lebanese, London)

It is here that we understand the affective role Fairouz plays among her participants by generating an ideal of Arab nationalism that moves beyond Jamal Abdel Nasser's original vision. As a 'figure' of authentic 'Arabness', Fairouz represents 'resistance' and unification, away from the negative mediatized images broadcast from the Arab world or the racial rhetoric on Arabs transmitted by the West.

In Sara Ahmed's article 'Affective Economies', the author provides an alternative way of thinking about affect, which moves beyond the body to encapsulate discourse and context. While Ahmed focuses on the notions of fear and terrorism, her arguments can be translated to encompass other forms of affect. Ahmed states, 'affect does not reside in an object or sign, but is an affect of the circulation between objects and signs'.[94] For Ahmed, significations placed on 'objects' derive affect towards that 'object' through its collective 'circulation'. In this way, Fairouz, as a 'figure' who hosts a plethora of signs through her 'circulation', but also through the signs circulated by 'objects', is able to be revealed in different forms of affect. Affect is thus not contained within her, or her music, nor is it contained within her listeners, but affect is, instead, generated through 'the movement between signs'.[95] This highlights the importance of the *meta-* and *micro-habitus* in discussion of Fairouz and her fans, since, together, they capture the contextual and discursive structures working towards affect.

However, while Ahmed negates the agency and autonomy of the 'objects' and 'subjects' in the manifestation and intensity of affect, and focuses primarily on fear and hate, her work provides a strong framework through which to understand concepts discussed in this chapter, such as *hybridity* and *iltizam*. In an environment with a growing distrust of Arab leaders and continuous conflict among Arab states, Fairouz remains the pillar of resistance and unity. She is able to tap into the affective rationality of her listeners, reassuring them that '*Palestine would be free*' and mobilizing them '*to hold our guns and go there*'. This 'accumulation of affective value shapes the surfaces of bodies and worlds', opening up spaces for Fairouz to 'figure' as a representation of the Arab collective.[96] As mentioned previously, this is not a homogenous collective. Instead, *hybridity* and *iltizam* are both 'intercontextual' among members of the Arab diaspora. In addition, as the *meta-* and *micro-habitus* stipulate, these 'surfaces of bodies and world' are not stagnant but are alternatively dynamic. Affect, then, does not materialize unequivocally into resistance and nationalism but is complexly distributed according to both individual and social factors, and thus can also be seen as affectively 'intercontextual'.

To better outline this complexity, it is important to draw on Iris Jean-Klein, who discusses nationalism and resistance in the context of the Palestinian Intifada. The author highlights the differences between what she calls '*self-nationalization*' and nationalism. Her argument that 'the masses have nationalism projected onto or prescribed for them, by pervasive and persuasive (mis)representational actions of national(ist) elites and leaders' does not guarantee 'ordinary persons' exhibiting forms of '*self-nationalization*'.[97] Defining '*self-nationalization*' as a 'process wherein ordinary persons fashion *themselves* into nationalized subjects, using distinctive narrative actions and embodied practices that are woven into the practice of everyday life'. Jean-Klein calls for acknowledgement of 'these quotidian practices as influential' in the 'production of nationalist-*cum*-national subjectivities and communities'.[98] While Jean-Klein specifically frames '*self-nationalization*' within the realm of the Palestinian Intifada, her depiction of the term, and its reliance on everyday practices, is of particular interest, especially when looking at resistance as a form of 'everyday life'. At the same time, '*self-nationalization*' provides a framework through which to understand how resistance is an active display of identity and *iltizam*.

For the Arab diaspora in this study, Fairouz is a credible source of patriotism and a loyal voice against injustice. By intertwining Fairouz, 'Arabness' and resistance in their answers, respondents consciously catalyse mechanisms of '*self-nationalization*', which are both subjective and communal. The interchangeable implication of 'resistance' and 'Arab' expresses how '*self-nationalization*' among members of the Arab diaspora almost always translates into the struggle for Palestine. A foundational element of *iltizam*, the Palestinian cause is regularly a taken for granted point of commonality for most members of the Arab diaspora. While discussing the subject of Palestine moves beyond the parameters of this chapter, divorcing it from themes such as Arab belonging, identity, resistance and *iltizam* is detrimental, since often it is far too engrained within global, societal, national and individual level structures. As a site of resistance to occupation,

Palestine remains romanticized, mnemonic, affective and missed among the Arab diaspora, most of whom, in this study, were sympathetic to its cause. When brought up, many participants showed deep emotion and sadness at how Arab and foreign governments were divided on the subject of Palestine. Understanding resistance in this affective context thus allows 'us to get at the ways in which intersecting and often conflicting structures of power work together these days in communities that are gradually becoming more tied to multiple and non-local systems'.[99]

For Maya, Kareem and Zuhair, Fairouz not only fits into the structure of resistance, but she is the prime motivator of it. Viewed as more credible than any politician, she is a point of reference, a voice of activism and someone worth getting '*ready to stand and fight for*'. However, as Clara points out, being Palestinian is *not* an essential trait in appreciating, understanding and supporting the '*political Fairouz*'. It is a shared language and a right of passage towards 'Arabness'. Resistance to Palestinian oppression is almost innate. A performative mechanism towards 'doing Arab', it is a consequence of both the *meta-* and *micro-habitus*, which mould and shape its explanation and the method by which it is expressed. Although not all of the Arab diaspora share this enthusiasm for the cause, it is still inherited as a system of belief or socialized script. A refusal to align with the Palestinian struggle is raised by 'intra-diasporic subjectivities'.[100]

While no participant explicitly cited negative feelings or statements against the Palestinian cause, some chose not to mention it at all. Attitudes towards Palestinians, especially from Lebanese respondents, are quite polarized and dependent on religious, sectarian and political affiliations but, in this particular sample, there was no outward condemnation of Palestinians or their plight. Respondents either expressed sympathy with Palestine or ignored it completely. However, the notion of Arab 'resistance' was a point of contention at times, as evidenced in Mounir and Hisham's statements. While claiming to be an advocate of resistance, Mounir clarifies that he is not a supporter of Hezbollah, the Lebanese Shi'a political and military group who are staunch advocators of Palestinian sovereignty and have also played a huge military role in the Syrian conflict. Mounir's specific declaration that he '*believe[s] in resistance*' but does not '*consider myself Hezbollah*' is an illustrative example of 'intercontextual' *iltizam* and 'affective polarization'.[101] Believing in '*resistance*' is a form of Arab self-identity but, as a Sunni Muslim from Beirut, Mounir's intersectional qualities, coupled with his *meta-* and *micro-habitus*, position him at a point of difference with Hezbollah on the symbolic scale of 'resistance'. Iyengar, Sood and Lelkes argue this type of political difference should be considered 'affective' rather than 'ideological'. For them, social identity 'requires not only positive sentiment for one's own group, but also negative sentiment towards those identifying with opposing groups'.[102] Understanding political positioning in this way echoes Brian Massumi, who states 'affect holds a key to rethinking postmodern power after ideology'.[103] So, as an Arab who is '*very proud of my language*', Mounir is also '*not very proud of our culture*', as '*there are traditions I don't like in my culture*'. This 'dislike' is a key constituent to what Iyengar, Sood and Lelkes would call 'affective polarization'. Mounir's statement lies in contrast to Hisham, also from Beirut, but who equates

Fairouz to the Hezbollah Secretary General, Hassan Nassrallah, and states '*these two persons are a priority for me, they are Lebanon to me*'. Unlike Mounir, Hisham sees Hezbollah as a form of resistance he can believe in and trust, an instigator of hope for Lebanon and the Arab world, '*Fairouz . . . and the 'Moukawama'*[104] *and the living people. If it wasn't for them, I don't think that there will ever be hope*'.

These two examples show how the constant shifts in global structures, political ideologies and individual subjectivities within the multi-dimensional spectrum of 'resistance' causes *iltizam* to be affectively 'intercontextual'. It indicates the 'relationship between structure and agency as a dialectical articulation whose results are not preordained'.[105] While, in this case, 'resistance' was tied to affective ideas of nationalism and patriotism, it was clear from conversations and participant observations that 'resistance' moved beyond nationhood to encompass other forms of 'everyday life'.

Listening religiously

Charles cuts the hair of an older gentleman, but sporadically turns to me as I sit on the long leather couch of his unisex hair salon in West London. '*Fairouz*', he sighs, '*you've opened up something so dear to my heart*'. Charles looks at his client, '*Do you listen to Fairouz?*' he asks, as he carefully snips away at the white hairs. The gentleman smiles sheepishly and says, '*I used to listen to her a lot, but I don't listen to music anymore, it's more important to spend time with family*'. Charles finishes cutting the man's hair and once he leaves, Charles says loudly, shaking his head, '*you know why he stopped listening to music? Because in his opinion it's haram*'.[106]

Listening to Fairouz or *not* listening to Fairouz can also be understood through the framework of religion. The choice not to listen to her music – or any music, for that matter – shares the same religious implication of listening to her hymns during religious holidays. This form of self-representation brings to light key identifiers which move beyond borders of nationhood to encompass a more globalized structure and a stratified version of 'Arabness'. With religion comes newer ways of 'othering', and positionings, which often run on thin parallel lines. Through conversations with Arab-American youth in San Francisco, Nadine Naber discusses how 'Muslim First, Arab Second' self-classifications are 'a religious affiliation and a marker of the relationship between individuals and the divine' but also that it is 'a politics of identity, a politics of race, and a politics of gender'.[107] These 'new social identities' are constructed 'within discourses and practices specific to the socio-historical contexts' in which participants inhabit.[108] While Naber offers a different geo-historic backdrop and a different sampling field to the participants in this study, that is San Francisco, as opposed to Doha or London, and relatively soon after the 9/11 attacks, rather than more than a decade and a half later, her arguments prove significant in terms of the opposing ways in which respondents in this study listened to Fairouz/did not listen to Fairouz. In addition, the notion of 'Muslim First' was a 'strategic identity', in that it was 'multiple and shifting' according to various intersections of *iltizam* and was impacted upon heavily by both the *meta-* and *micro-habitus*, especially when conformity to environment was expected in order to attain a sense of belonging:

> *My mum loves Fairouz, she doesn't really listen to music anymore . . . yeah, so, she's conformed in ways . . . she's different to how she was when I was younger, she's had pressure from society and stuff, so, she's had to change her perspective and conform in order to sort of fit in and be happy . . . . Um, yeah, and so there's a lot less music around. She lives with my brother, for him music is bad . . . . My brother is married to a very religious cousin of ours. Her father's Salafi, and she kind of represents to him everything that our family wasn't, because we were the most liberal Qatari family, you know, and he has a bit of a complex with that, so the house has to all be with Qura'an and stuff like that, and so she doesn't really have the opportunity around that, and around us, to listen to music anymore. (Mariam, 32, Qatari, London)*

Mariam's excerpt is indicative of how religion, familial ties and *micro-habitual* situations can shape affective relationships with music. Fairouz was the point of commonality between Mariam and her mother and, as someone who grew up in a conservative society and then moved to London, Mariam was able to maintain her relationship with Fairouz. However, not leaving Qatar and having to live with her conservative son, Mariam's mother no longer listens to music, as it is seen as antireligious. While discussion on generational lineage and Fairouz will be outlined in Chapter 7, it is significant to look at how religion, identity and geography correlate to produce different forms of self-representation. The issue of religion arose explicitly or implicitly. Some respondents talked about religion in passing, while others were more overt in their conversation. Perhaps revealing of the era in which religion proves pivotal is best outlined by Tala, who states:

> *If you watch the news, all you are going to hear is, you know, revolution, post-revolution, religion, Daesh, war, blood, sectarianism, and it is really worrying, the thing with me, for a long time I didn't identify so much as an Arab. I just identified as me, and wanting to desperately fit in with my Western friends, you know. (Tala, 41, Libyan, London)*

The topical format of religion is of particular significance. As Tala mentions, religion is everywhere and carries with it a plethora of negative connotations. This again resonates with Sara Ahmed and her discussion on affective economies, when she writes, 'fear and anxiety create the very effect of "that which I am not", through the very affect of turning away from an object, which nevertheless threatens as it passes by or is displaced'.[109] Not wanting to align herself with Arabs and the implied Islam they represent, Tala shows this tension between '*wanting to desperately fit in with my Western friends*', but also 'the very affect of turning away' from Islam's negative mediatized representations around the world. As someone aware of her background and heritage, Tala maintains:

There is one role for religion, you would use it to help your spiritual development, but you know we have a language, and we have the cultural heritage, Arabic poetry, Arabic songs. Reclaiming our heritage, our cultural, artistic, archaeological, philosophical heritage, and not let this whole religion thing overcrowd and cover everything else. Maybe I sound a bit anti-religion, but I am not really, I am not. I just think, you know, my grandmother used to love Arabic poetry, she couldn't read or write, there is nothing wrong with that, but now it would be like haram and haram. The women's voice is Awrat,[110] *the women's voice is haram.* (Tala, 41, Libyan, London)

Here, Tala expresses a more gendered response to religion, which views women and their voices as seductive. She also traces a historical increase in a more fundamentalist perspective on religion through her grandmother, who *'used to love Arabic poetry',* but now *'it would be like haram and haram'.* The increase in religious fundamentalism splits the Arab diaspora into dichotomies of *haram* and acceptable, religious and not religious, affectively polarizing the two through the fear of appearing either.

Geographical and religious discrepancies among participants were key factors in playing Fairouz's music in the private and public spheres. Through her special hymns for Easter, or during Christmas, Fairouz adds a spiritual spin for those celebrating during those times of the year. However, the choice of where to enjoy her songs was significant. Illustrating this, Rola in Doha, and Toufic in London, listen to Fairouz at *'the most meaningful times'* in the year, showcasing the ways in which they are able to religiously identify with the singer. For both respondents, Fairouz enhances their religious experience, but the difference lies in where her songs are heard. Toufic plays her music in his bakery in central London, and does not care *'if the customer is happy'.* As a Christian, Toufic does not feel stigmatized in his environment and so playing Fairouz's music in public is no cause for concern, as it somewhat fits into the narrative in which he is placed. His religion allows for the sense of ownership he feels in the public sphere, one he does not need to hide. However, in a more conservative and Islamic environment, Rola listens to Fairouz's hymns in the private sphere of her home and in her discussions, her faith and environment remain two separate things, something which she does not feel she can share in the Qatari public sphere. These examples demonstrate the ways in which surroundings can position listeners on public and private tangents in the discussion of Fairouz and her music, but also, it provides indications of listening behaviours and how they can create a sense of belonging or 'non-belonging'. While the religion of listeners played a role in this conversation on identity, as a 'figure', Fairouz also brought in a number of signifiers:

I never knew that Fairouz was Christian, which is very wrong, like, why would you erase someone's difference? (Leila, 30, Moroccan, London)

This is going to be controversial. I'll tell you that, for me, I just get so upset by you know, all the religion and the oppression religion causes in the Middle East and the sexism that's imposed on women, and I know that Fairouz is a Christian person so she has a certain amount of freedom over Muslim women, and I get that's controversial. (Jana, 48, Palestinian/Syrian, London)

She doesn't have a label. If you've got Fairouz on, for instance, she's not, you're not labelling yourself as a South Lebanese, or as a Christian Lebanese, or a Muslim Lebanese, No . . . you are a Lebanese; and that is the gift she's giving to Lebanon. No division, no colour, you know. (Tarek, 36, Lebanese, London)

If anything, she unites religions. In a lot of her lyrics she refers to the prophets; to Mohammad to Issa,[111] to all of them. (Tala, 41, Libyan, London)

These four responses bring a number of issues to the surface. For Leila, not knowing *'Fairouz was Christian'* is something she disapproves of, because *'I think erasing differences is wrong so keeping those differences and uniting is possible'*. In her opinion, Fairouz's religion could be a uniting factor for Arab communities who feel disconnected from, and disconcerted by, other religions. Leila's call for the idealistic celebration of differences, hints at the discord between members of the Arab diaspora, especially in terms of their religious beliefs. Meanwhile, Jana's gendered response on Fairouz being *'a Christian person'* who *'has a certain amount of freedom over Muslim women'* puts into play the religious trajectories of Arab women and the spaces which they can occupy. For Jana, Fairouz represents the alternative to *'the oppression religion causes in the Middle East and the sexism that's imposed on women'*. Through Fairouz, perspectives on 'other' women in the diaspora are considered since, according to Jana, they lie in stark contrast to the singer and her capabilities as a *'Christian person'*.

Similarly, to the notion of embodying 'Arabness', discussed previously, Tarek and Tala see Fairouz as a religiously unifying tool, specifically for the Lebanese diaspora, but also generally *'to all of them'*. For Tarek, the various political and religious sects dividing Lebanon find common ground in the voice of Fairouz, as she has no *'label'*. At the same time, Tala's assertion of Fairouz's inclusivity mobilizes the singer beyond Lebanese borders to encompass a wider range of religious nationalities. It is through this appropriation and distancing of Fairouz, which reveals how religion and spirituality play crucial roles in self-identification. Either stripped of religious signifiers or branded by them, Fairouz appeals to the spiritual side of her listeners. By analysing religious references made by the Arab diaspora in relation to Fairouz and her music allowed for insight into deeper forms of identity creation that further put into play differences in the construction and understanding of 'Arabness' and intercontextual *iltizam*.

Performing parallel and intersecting identities

Fairouz and her music play a pivotal role in self-representation and identity formation within diasporic communities. Respondents are able to relate to her songs depending on their intersectional qualities, but also through the *micro-* and *meta-habitus*, which situates them. As a polysemic 'figure', Fairouz translates into different storylines and highlights the cross-sectional ways in which the Arab diaspora living in Doha and London process and relate to themes, which best fit their 'self-identity' in light of their 'social identity'.[112] The trajectories discussed here also show the ways in which affect materializes to position participants, individually and collectively, according to their *meta-* and *micro-habitus*. Widening the periphery for identification, Fairouz, as a permeable, *hybrid* space, allows for numerous affective entry points from which to self-align, creating, maintaining, reminding and opposing key identifiers for her listeners. In return, participants, through forms of 'intercontextual' hybridity, are able to negotiate and navigate within those spaces of *hybridity* to configure aspects of identity that they can understand and appropriate.

Claiming Fairouz as a 'figure' for 'Arabness' is justified, as long as 'Arabness' is seen as a flexible and malleable framework. Its attributes contribute to the 'front region' of Arab identity and assist in the performance of 'doing Arab'. A major component of 'Arabness' is *iltizam* and its subsequent connotations. The origins of *iltizam* are rooted in visions of a united Arab front, and so it is meant to heighten solidarity and 'authenticity' among Arabs. However, the 'new reality' of *iltizam* is its immersion in an era distinguished by fragmented audiences and confusing alliances. This evolved status of *iltizam*, which is defined as affectively 'intercontextual', illustrates the ways in which new *hybrid* identities, coupled with increasingly divisive factors among Arabs and the diaspora, have caused a shift in identity and representation. Through means of 'othering', 'intercontextual' *iltizam* is able to flourish, creating new sets of polarized identities primarily powered by affect. Moulded by sociopolitical, economic, religious and cultural alignments, 'intercontextual' *iltizam* and 'Arabness' are catalysts and products of a global system, which has seen a share of chaotic global positionings and microcosmic divisions.

Furthermore, it is through the lenses of *hybridity*, 'Arabness' and the 'intercontextual' *iltizam* that deeper levels of affective identity constructs, such as 'home', nationhood and religion, were analysed and discussed. Deeply dependent on their *meta-*and *micro-habitus*, participants were either confident or puzzled about the existence of 'home' and what they considered their 'home' to be. Accessed through their mnemonic imaginations, 'an active synthesis of remembering and imagining'[113] home was not always rooted to a place but was also expressed as a feeling or as a desired idea. In this way, 'home' and nationhood were not necessarily part of the same narrative, which made the links to patriotism and resistance even more interesting. While respondents attributed themes of patriotism and resistance to Fairouz and her music, trying to define them within a mnemonic perspective further shed light on the importance of affective 'intercontextuality' and the ways in which it shapes notions of *iltizam*, *hybridity* and 'Arabness'. Another key actor in this discourse was religion, which played a part in contextualizing self-identity in terms of social and environmental factors.

By considering Fairouz and her role in personifying a sense of home or nationhood, it appears Fairouz embodies a global and dynamic 'Arabized' form of nationalism, which participants access through their 'mnemonic imaginations', bestowing upon them an identity and a sense of belonging that is autonomous of confining borders and flexible enough for them to mould. The patriotism respondents thus claim to have by listening to her music is not particular to a specific state, but instead to an affective 'Arabized' structure dependent on factors such as habitual situations, intersectional qualities and consequential *iltizam*.

Dividing and aligning, including and excluding, participants in this chapter were able to express forms of identity construction through the songs of Fairouz. Subjective themes were analysed according to the *meta-* and *micro-habitus*, which allowed for a personal and public perspective that was dynamic and shifting. Trying to bind Fairouz, or the diaspora, to a constant unaltered state negates crucial dimensions that arise discursively and globally. Active agents in this process, the Arab diaspora work centripetally and centrifugally, internalizing and externalizing facets of their identity depending on the environment they inhabit. Through depictions of Fairouz, her songs and memories of when and where the songs were heard, the Arab diaspora in London and Doha articulated their experiences, giving deep insight into conscious choices made in trying to achieve a sense of identity, as well as conveying individual longings in the quest for social belonging. Essentially, in discussing Fairouz's music, participants in this study were able to provide a glimpse into the ways in which they formulated and connected, individually and collectively, in an unstable and obscure social, political and economic climate.

Chapter 4

FAIROUZ, AFFECTIVE SPACE AND THE DISPLACED

While the last chapter looked at the ways in which Fairouz provided members of the Arab diaspora, living in Doha and London, with various opportunities for self-representation and entry points for identification, whether they be individual or collective, nationalistic, regional or 'Arab', religion or gender-based, this chapter examines the spaces in which those occur. The space discussed here is, as Foucault writes, 'a heterogeneous space'.[1] An active and functioning 'heterogeneous' space, it contains, shapes and interacts. It is one of affect, a point of potentiality and '*in-between-ness*'. This space is political, gendered, cultured and social. Space plays a pivotal role in the discussion of Fairouz's music because of its relationship with 'personal' and 'public memory',[2] of home and the 'sheltered space' of the private sphere.[3] Space is where '*Al-ghurba*' occurs, an indicator and instigator of 'foreignness', or what Peter Blickle calls '*Entzweiung*' or the 'experience of alienation'.[4] It is a point at which one contemplates their presence in one space and absence in another.

Space links participants to Fairouz and her songs. It is reflective, allowing the relationship participants have with Fairouz and her music to be dynamic and affective. Evolving over time to encompass different parts of physical and psychological situations, space is individual and shared. It creates an environment in which emotions fluctuate and flourish. Space, as both place and concept, shapes and creates new ways of appropriating Fairouz's songs. Listening to Fairouz is a spatial activity, one that requires a register of its existence. Whether in cars, homes, workplaces or on portable devices, Fairouz travels through the ears and minds of the Arab diaspora, transporting them, rooting them to where they are and taking them away to where they want to be. Fairouz is, as Maha, a 35-year-old Syrian/ Lebanese social worker living in London, says, '*Dream-like, yet grounding; there's your tension. Dream-like, yet grounding*'. It is the journey of how the Arab diaspora navigate this tension of positioning themselves in regard to their environments, but also how they aspire, move and transcend space to occupy positions in which they find comfort, through Fairouz's music. It is this positioning and non-positioning, this 'territorialization' and 'deterritorialization', which is of importance here. It is, as Tarik Sabry writes, to 'dislocate' the discourse of the Arab diaspora from rigid temporal and spatial 'conjunctions' to, 'open up space that allows broader and less totalising articulations of Arab culture/identity to emerge'.[5] Through territorializing, or linking participants to individual and collective *meta-habitual* and *micro-habitual* contexts, it is important that those be analysed through forms of dynamic 'dislocation', which are in continuous flux and to not anchor them to essentializing, homogenizing and stagnant conversation and so giving them agency towards 'the creation of new and alternative discourses of becoming'.[6] However, it is important to note that members of the Arab diaspora are not the only elements in this study that require analysis through 'deterritorialization', but Fairouz does as well.

Fairouz: An affective space for interpretation

In the previous chapters, Fairouz was discussed as a 'figure' or a 'human simulacrum' of 'infinitely reproducible signifiers'.[7] Representative of 'Arabness' and *iltizam*, Fairouz, as both a singer and an individual, has often been criticized by music experts, journalists and fans as being distant and reserved. Conversations with participants showed how these traits provided spaces for appropriating and interpreting her songs. As someone who gives few interviews, Fairouz is able to keep the 'back region' of her persona secret, thus allowing for 'the capacity of a performance to express something beyond itself', to have the potential to be 'painstakingly fabricated'.[8] This gives way to strategically constructing Fairouz's enigmatic public persona into one which aligns with that of her music and the messages they convey:

> *She left us some space to imagine her the way we want.* (Helene, 52, Lebanese, London)

> *She represents emotions, music, love, success, the mysterious, magnificent personality, also on a personal level, it has nothing to do with her personality, but also she provokes you, she provokes you positively, what is this magic? Who is the person who is so far yet so close, she is far from the people, the media, her audience, you know, practically, but she is living in the hearts of people, no one knows anything about her, but she is so involved in our daily lives.* (Amar, 39, Lebanese, Doha)

> *I mean, and, of course, when you look at her history, I mean this is someone who has been consistent in her stances, consistent in maybe sharing so little of herself that we can draw whatever we want, but what we draw fits the music, it fits the stage character . . . so it kind of fits that integrity, that stance, you know what I mean? Um, and I think she's allowed us to continue building that character for her by not being public in anything else, so she never says anything for us to think the contrary. She never does anything, she barely interviews, so you can maintain that, idealistic, character.* (Maya, 46, Lebanese, Doha)

> *I would like for her not to speak as well. I prefer her not to speak. She is someone who shouldn't speak.* (Mona, 45, Lebanese, Doha)

On the personal level, she remained on the same path and in line with what was drawn for her. She maintained her big name among people and stayed away from all the gossip and the problems that singers deal with nowadays. That was a big plus for her. Even when she had problems, she never talked about them. She kept her personal life private, and this is something very nice about her. Her personal life shouldn't concern us, but it's much better for her to keep it private and only for herself, especially since she is a symbol for Lebanon. Several singers talk about their personal problems, which can impact their image. In the case of Fairouz, she maintained a good reputation in her personal life, and her reputation and position in music were also good. (Karam, 39, Lebanese, Doha)

She doesn't have a label. If you've got Fairouz on, for instance . . . you're not labelling yourself as a South Lebanese, or as a Christian Lebanese, or a Muslim Lebanese, No . . . you are a Lebanese; and that is the gift she's giving to Lebanon. No division, no colour . . . you're just Lebanese, under the Arzeh.[9] I mean, how many times has she sung about that? So, yes, she's a joy, she's a gift. (Tarek, 36, Lebanese, London)

No one can accuse her of taking sides with any political party, denomination or religious sect. . . . She is Lebanon. She is the Lebanon that we love, that we want to see, that we want. . . . She sang for Mecca, she sang for Jerusalem, she sang for Damascus, she sang for Beirut, ya3ni, she didn't choose sides on anything and no one can define her in that her politics are skewed this way or that, Lebanon, she is Lebanon, she is Lebanon. . . . It's so simple and beautiful. (Walid, 65, Lebanese, Doha)

I go where I wanna go, because it's, you know, she just fits in that place, you know, she puts you in that place, it's, uh, and then you're just free to go wherever, but it just . . . she just puts me in a certain surrounding, you know? (Nafie, Sudanese, Doha)

These excerpts indicate how the silencing of Fairouz's private life lays the foundation for respondents 'to imagine her the way we want'. For Amar, a Lebanese mother of twins, Fairouz's ability to 'provoke you positively' is magical and mysterious. Amar questions how Fairouz forms a key constituent of 'our daily lives', yet 'she is far from the people, the media, her audience'. The ability of Fairouz to transgress space and filter into the consciousness of the Arab diaspora while maintaining a measured distance is, in effect, affective. Fairouz is able to 'provoke', to provide 'joy' and to 'put you in that place'. As Sara Ahmed states, 'What moves us, what makes us feel, is also that which holds us in place, or gives us a dwelling place'.[10] The 'dwelling place' Fairouz provides is wide enough to accommodate multiple ways of connecting with her music affectively. By maintaining a distance from her fans, Fairouz is therefore able to incorporate the individual and shared space of her listeners within the 'dwelling' space of her songs, encouraging her fans to navigate, contest and interact through these spaces according to their *meta-* and *micro-habitus*. By being in diaspora, participants occupy different forms of social space, what Ahmed would call the 're-forming of bodily and social space'.[11]

In her article 'Home and Away: Narratives of Migration and Estrangement', Sara Ahmed looks at the interplay of bodies, space and affect in constructing a sense of 'home' and a subsequent belonging. For Ahmed 'migration narratives' encompass 'a spatial reconfiguration of an embodied self'.[12] This form of re-inhabiting space is of particular significance when looking at Arab diaspora in the context of Fairouz. Not only does it bring to the surface fluctuating 'bodily' and 'social' spaces, it sheds light on the ways in which the body itself, as an object, needs to 're-form', 're-habit' and 're-configure' accordingly both within and around such spaces. The Arab diaspora in this study who '*would like for [Fairouz] not to speak*' is thus essentially calling for a 'space which is pure, which is uncontaminated by movement, desire or difference, in order to call for a politics in which movement '*is always and already a movement away from home*'.[13] In this way, Fairouz's music embodies the familiarity associated with the 'home' of which Ahmed speaks. So, by the very means of her silence and a refrain from individualized political opinion,[14] Fairouz only offers her listeners the music, which they can then consume, appropriate and interpret in the various transformations of body and space. By maintaining her 'figure' as one that is in line with the music she produces, Fairouz remains the constant in a web of changes. She creates affectively autonomous areas for her listeners to '*draw whatever we want, but what we draw fits the music, it fits the stage character . . . so it kind of fits that integrity, that stance*'. Her silence thus confirms her position, her 'figure' and her representation, at both the individual and collective levels. Inhabiting a muted private space, Fairouz provides the suppleness through which her listeners are able to project and consume her music.

For her Lebanese fans specifically, she is able to neutralize her political position on internal politics, one which is, in fact, '*tainted*', '*contaminated*' and heavily '*divided*'. As Tarek, a butcher who has been living in London for over twenty years, says, '*She doesn't have a label. If you've got Fairouz on, for instance . . . you're not labelling yourself . . . you are a Lebanese. . . . No division, no colour*'. It is this sentiment of her standing as a unifying space, which is echoed by Walid, who states, '*No one can accuse her of taking sides with any political party, denomination or religious sect . . . she didn't choose sides on anything and no one can define her in that her politics are skewed this way or that, Lebanon, she is Lebanon*'. This idealized 'dwelling space' that Tarek and Walid describe is a result of the silent, and therefore non-partisan, 'figure' of Fairouz. Her refusal to publicly involve herself in domestic Lebanese politics gives her access to all religious denominations and political parties in the country. It is this lack of positioning which furthers her reach and bestows upon her listeners a sense of agency to appropriate her songs accordingly. Transcending the denotative space of incessant fighting, Fairouz nestles comfortably as a '*symbol for Lebanon*', with '*integrity*' and '*that stance*', which is at once reserved, but also very demonstrative of acceptance.

Fairouz: Omnipresent and definer of space

Ayman meets me by Westminster tube station on a warm July evening in London. After a hurried introduction, he raises his right leg, points towards his foot, and says, '*look what happened*'. The sole had detached from his white trainers and was flapping around apologetically. Shaking his head and smiling, he explains, '*I haven't worn these shoes in ages, but today, I was being stubborn and said I wanted to wear them*'. A 34-year-old Syrian refugee who moved to London in 2011, '*three days before everything kicked off*', Ayman and his worn-out shoes are symbolic of the limited, challenging and confining movement of the Arab diaspora and, namely, Arab refugees across streets, borders, oceans and continents. He is an embodiment of all forms of space: allowed, welcomed, sympathetic, negotiated, feared, hostile, forbidden, affective and mnemonic. Ayman's interview differed from all the others. It was mostly unstructured, at times a complex and personal monologue, which elucidated the role Fairouz, played in his life. Through Fairouz's music, Ayman described a clear divider of space and time, consciously creating a discrepancy of 'here' and 'there', 'then' and 'now', 'London' and 'Syria', the 'West' and the 'Arab world'. His eloquence in storytelling interweaved Fairouz in topics of politics, love, anger and frustration. For Ayman, Fairouz is a definer of familiar space, as she is '*related to me, being from Syria*' and '*from that part of the world*'. This sense of spatial familiarity will be discussed later on in the chapter, but here it is important to look at the ways in which Ayman and other participants attribute their recollection of such 'dwelling spaces' across trajectories of time and space. Trying to classify a timeframe or introduction of exactly when and how Fairouz came into the lives of participants was difficult. Often, Fairouz and her music were so deeply rooted in a spatio-temporal atmosphere that any attempt to disassociate her from that mnemonic space proved futile:

> *I don't think there is anyone from that part of the world that would know how Fairouz entered his or her lives. They would say that they are visitors in Fairouz's existence . . . I'm the one that intervened in Fairouz's existence; I'm a visitor. I came to Fairouz's era, rather than Fairouz coming to mine.* (Ayman, 34, Syrian, London)

> *I'll give you my experience about Fairouz in Lebanon and Syria. When we talk about Fairouz, we have to mention Syrians and Syria, because she is also really important to them. You asked me: when did Fairouz enter my life? Fairouz has been in all Lebanese homes for a very long time. She's part of all of us. She didn't enter my life, I was born into this world and she was present in it. Once you're born, you'll find that Fairouz is a part of each house, whether it was a house that admires music or that doesn't. Even if she wasn't present in her voice, the air in Lebanon contains Fairouz in it.* (Elie, 50, Lebanese, London)

> *I listened to Fairouz since I was a child. She was always around. If we weren't listening to Fairouz in the house, her songs would be playing at our neighbour's house, on the radio, and TV. She is always present. You have to listen to Fairouz. In Syria, they air a lot of songs for Fairouz on the TV. The radios also play Fairouz's songs. She was always there. Since I was young, I was basically raised on Fairouz.* (Maher, 44, Syrian, London)

> *Fairouz was in my life from the day I was born. She was present in my life from a very young age. My father listens to Fairouz, my grandmother listens to Fairouz.*

So, we'd wake up every morning and Fairouz's songs would be playing. When I took a taxi, Fairouz would be playing. When I entered a store, Fairouz would be playing. Even in school they played Fairouz in the morning. (Khaled, 38, Lebanese, London)

So Fairouz, and [her song] 'Da3 Shadi',[15] *specifically, is very present in our home. This is how Fairouz started, and we got used to Fairouz always being around. My mother really loved her, so we were raised to her songs, it was an essential part of our daily lives, like how when you wake up in the morning and you have to brush your teeth and your face, you had to also listen to Fairouz, it was as if it was something basic, something necessary in life, so we were raised that way and we continued.* (Amar, 39, Lebanese, Doha)

Yeah, so, I'm sure I've heard it a lot at home, and everywhere we went, you know, at cafes and . . . they always had Lebanese music, especially Fairouz, everywhere in Kuwait. Like, uh, any Lebanese restaurant, any Middle Eastern restaurant, Fairouz was in the background. (Lara, 50, Palestinian, Doha)

It [was] always in the background of every restaurant, every taxi ride, radio, even in . . .. I worked with a colleague as well in Abu Dhabi, she was very attached to Lebanon, and used to play it always in the background, while we were working; So, she's all over. She's all over, ya3ni, in all my memories Fairouz is there. She's everywhere. (Asma, 36, Syrian, London)

In this way, Fairouz is seen as omnipresent. She is '*always there*' and '*everywhere*'. An all-consuming force, her listeners are '*visitors in Fairouz's existence*'. Unable to pinpoint when Fairouz was introduced to them, these participants link the temporal with the spatial, since '*in all my memories, Fairouz is there*'. Trying to disentangle time and memory from space is no easy task. As de Certeau writes, 'space occurs as the effect produced by the operations that orient it, situate it, temporalize it, and make it function'.[16] Similarly, space here is not only about a certain period or a place in the mind, space here is one in which Fairouz has amalgamated temporality with the mnemonic, creating an 'aura' which simultaneously travels with participants, but also remains very firmly on the ground. Unlike the piece of artwork that Walter Benjamin argues needs to be appreciated in a certain temporal and spatial atmosphere to ensure its full 'aura' is attained, Fairouz herself produces this 'aura'. She is at once an experience to be appreciated and also one who enhances experience, '*even if she wasn't present in her voice, the air in Lebanon contains Fairouz in it*', she is both integrated into space and is the primary conductor of it. Fairouz is thus found in '*Syria*', '*Lebanon*', '*Kuwait*', '*Abu Dhabi*' and '*in the background of every restaurant, every taxi ride*'.

Fairouz is associated with home, with land, with countries and with a region. She is borderless, yet she simultaneously erects the mnemonic and affective borders of time and space. '*She's part of all of us*', an intrinsically specific, yet generally inclusive, form of identity, one which is determined in space and upbringing, since

'*Fairouz has been in all Lebanese homes for a very long time*', but also '*She's all over, ya3ni, in all my memories Fairouz is there. She's everywhere*'. Participants in these examples show how Fairouz not only provides the soundtrack to mnemonic space but also how she is embedded in the personal space of the individual and the collective.

For participants in this example, Fairouz takes on an immersive role. She is absorbed into space and time. She is a definer of both, yet cannot be defined. She exists, with or without participants, as Ayman states, '*I came to Fairouz's era rather than Fairouz coming to mine*', this is echoed by Elie, a musician living in London, who says, '*She didn't enter my life, I was born into this world, and she was present in it*'. Elie continues this thought by adding, '*Even if she wasn't present in her voice, the air in Lebanon contains Fairouz in it*'. This further enhances the notion of Fairouz's omnipresence and immortality among her listeners, and also shows how this omnipresence is tied in to being '*from that part of the world*' and '*once you're born*'. In essence, she is paradoxically 'dislocated' or 'deterritorialized', taking 'flight', yet she remains rooted and grounded through the mnemonic imagination of her listeners, effectively becoming 'reterritorialized', providing for a 'creative connectivity', which is simultaneously reminiscent of time and place, but also shifts to inhabit different 'planes' of 'self-reflection and creativity'.[17] Fairouz thus occupies a prenatal, parental and postnatal space, straddling the gap between childhood and adulthood. It is necessary here to draw on Abdelmalek Sayad who says:

> Immigration and its difficulties provide an opportunity to 'remember' and therefore to experience once more the frustration occasioned by the disappearance of the 'mothering' provided by both the 'mother-society', the nurturing land . . . and the actual mother, who is complacently described as being omnipotent and omnipresent, first in early childhood and then in the imaginary of the adult. (2004, p. 208)

For Sayad, the process of migration leads to the 'frustration' of being away from 'the nurturing land'. Through their recollection of Fairouz and her music, respondents are thus able to 'remember', and since '*in all my memories Fairouz is there*', the space associated with home life in their 'mother-society', which is in the past, in the 'nurturing land', and away from where they are in the present, becomes bound with that of Fairouz and her 'aura'. By being in the non-'mother-society', participants are effectively removed from this 'nurturing' space, one linked to being '*part of me*' and one that intertwines Fairouz and her music. Embedded within such space, Fairouz, through her 'aura', becomes its representation, the further removed she and her listeners are from it. Rather than relying on a spatio-temporal context to be appreciated in, Fairouz instead encompasses the two, almost becoming an aurally visualized 'simulacrum', since 'the real is no longer what it used to be' and so 'nostalgia assumes its full meaning'.[18]

While defining Fairouz as a simulacrum is both limiting and undermining to both her representation and her listeners' autonomy in appropriating her music, as well as to acknowledging the ways in which the two fluctuate according to different experiences and environments, what it does, is that it shows the ways in which affect, 'aura' and the mnemonic imagination come together to take on a new form of symbolic meaning, one which varies according to movement and temporality at both the individual and collective levels of understanding. For Keightley and Pickering, the 'mnemonic imagination generates movement between the horizons of experience, expectation and possibility. It brings the temporal tenses together and synthesises them productively in order to achieve new meaning in the present.'[19] Combining this temporal 'movement between the horizons of experience, expectation and possibility'[20] with the 're-forming of bodily and social space',[21] to accommodate the shifting individual and collective space of listeners, gives room for the 'synthesis' of Fairouz and her music to 'achieve new meaning in the present'.[22] 'New meaning' arises due to the 'effect of the movement between signs: the more they circulate, the more affective they become, and the more they appear to "contain" affect'.[23] So, movement, in all its forms, is a factor in generating 'new meaning' for listeners. However, it is also important to note how this 'dislocation from home'[24] is essentially an unravelling of the self, in which Fairouz is connected to the 'mothering-society', 'nurturing land' and the 'actual mother'.[25]

If we return to Sara Ahmed's discussion on migration, which she argues is 'a spatial reconfiguration of an embodied self', we see how Fairouz, who forms a *part of* the Arab diaspora, essentially travels with them, transmogrifying to take on different meanings and 'reconfigurations', but this change is also of the self.[26] Linked to family members, friends, habits, home and experiences, Fairouz automatically becomes a social, as well as an individual, experience, her 'aura' oscillating in 'the relationship between movement and attachment'.[27] As the body moves, so does Fairouz's 'aura'. Her music takes on different meanings as it morphs through migration in both space and time. This is best explained by participants who shed light on the ways in which listening to Fairouz's music changes according to the environment in which they are:

> *In England, it's completely different than here [Doha]. I think when you're in Europe, or away from Arab countries, and you listen to it, it feels more like she's talking to you, just you. Here, you lose a bit of the privileges, on the radio anyway. You still love it, but when you're by yourself in England, it's hitting you, just you and her, and a cold, icy road somewhere. Here, you open the window, you're playing the song, the car next to you, he's got a Fairouz song as well, it's not the same. It's a bit selfish, but it's different akeed.*[28] (Shams, 40, Iranian/Palestinian/Lebanese/ English, Doha)

> *It's like Ounsi Al Hajj [a Lebanese poet] says, he writes a lot about Fairouz, but he says, and I'm paraphrasing, 'there is no place for Fairouz, or Fairouz has no place, because everywhere is Fairouz'. She is everywhere, but she means a lot to me, because it's as if she is for me.* (Amar, 39, Lebanese, Doha)

> *Here, I intentionally make the effort to listen to her. I put her music on. In Lebanon, I see everyone listening to her. She's everywhere. But here, I make it a point to listen*

to her, I play her when I'm driving, or when I go to the shop, at home when I wake up. (Khaled, 38, Lebanese, London)

I actually only listen to Fairouz here. You're right; it's a very interesting insight. (Dina, 42, Lebanese, London)

For me, when I listen to Fairouz while abroad, I feel like I have an anchor holding me. (Helene, 52, Lebanese, London)

Once I moved away from Lebanon, nothing remained from Lebanon except the memories, and the things that Fairouz brought to us about Lebanon, and other artists as well, but she is the one that expresses what's in our hearts towards Lebanon the most, because she's inclusive. She covers everything. She covers patriotic feelings, feelings from the village, the feelings of love between people, the intimacy between people. You feel like she takes you back, she takes you back to a world of paradise. The paradise of Lebanon is Fairouz from the onset. Ya3ni, if you want to picture paradise in Lebanon, it has to come from Fairouz's songs, you can't do it without Fairouz's songs. (Walid, 65, Lebanese, Doha)

When we made Aallebnene [29] *and we were at the principal's office in school, I told him that, for the dignity of my husband's tears, Aallebnene should happen, there is an empty space when we live abroad . . . Fairouz fills it. Fairouz fills this empty space that we are living with when we are abroad. She fills it and it's enough. I don't need to smell fresh air to feel [like I'm] in Lebanon. Her voice gives me the lovely weather that we as Arabs living in the Gulf, those Arabs living in Canada may not make this point, but for us as Arabs living in the Gulf, we need to . . . the butterfly, we don't see a butterfly here, but when I listen to a song by Fairouz, I feel it, I feel like this light movement, ya3ni, listen to Fairouz and walk, you feel like you are flying off the ground. You are walking with more ease, and me, let me talk about myself, I walk with greater ease when I listen to her.* (Mona, 45, Lebanese, Doha)

When I travelled to Czechoslovakia, it was the first time I left Lebanon. I lived in Czechoslovakia for two years, and I was really attached to Lebanon. I was very sad that I wasn't able to visit Lebanon during these two years; therefore, Fairouz was the ambassador between us. In Czechoslovakia I got really attached to Fairouz. During that time, she sang a very nice song about. . . . I forgot what's its name. . . . I even remember asking someone to buy it for me and he sent it to Czechoslovakia. It talks about immigrants. I really forgot its name. . . . It was a wonderful song that mostly talks about Lebanon, immigration, and the immigrants. During that phase, my connection and attachment to Fairouz increased. (Marwan, 73, Lebanese, Doha)

I love nature, so I love to drive my car in some nice places, where I can admire nature while listening to Fairouz. I feel like I'm living her songs, especially the ones about Lebanon, like I'm part of the experience. But here, no, of course not, it hurts me to hear it here. In Lebanon, its different, I feel happy, and I enjoy her songs, because I know that I'm a part of that, where I belong. I feel like what Fairouz is singing about, I'm a part of, I'm enjoying it, she sings about the sky in Lebanon, I can see it. But here, sometimes I'm uncomfortable, when I listen to her a lot, I feel very homesick that I would even book a ticket the next day to go back to Lebanon. Yeah, that's how much she triggers the feelings inside of me. It's different really. (Bianca, 37, Lebanese, Doha)

This is why if I am in a place and they are playing cards and listening to Fairouz it is not the same, I won't enjoy it. I switch it off . . . when Fairouz is playing you want to hear her words, you want to hear what she is saying. She is different. She takes a person in a trance, she makes them see and feel what she is singing. (Yassine, 70, Egyptian, Doha)

They're relaxing, very relaxing, because London is very visual, and when I'm on the bus, I always sit on the top, so I feel like I'm on the top, so I put my headphones and it's moving, Trafalgar, and Piccadilly, and you look at people and you're listening to something totally different than what you're looking at, and it just makes sense. (Dina, 42, Lebanese, London)

The spaces and places in which Fairouz is heard are an important feature in the behaviour, understanding and appreciation of her music. Shams, a 40-year-old man who grew up in Doha, but who has since then also lived in England and Dubai, before moving back to Doha, loses some of the '*privileges*' associated with listening to Fairouz in '*Arab countries*'. In England, he feels as though she is '*talking to you, just you*', but in Doha, '*you open the window, you're playing the song, the car next to you he's got a Fairouz song as well, it's not the same*'. It is important here to bring back the concepts of the *meta-* and *micro-habitus* to best explain how the 'aura' of Fairouz absorbs and disseminates contexts. For Shams, the *micro-habitus* of living in different parts of the world plays a part in the ways in which Fairouz is heard. Being a minority, that is an Arabic speaker in England, Shams feels a special closeness to Fairouz that is unique and exclusive, whereas, in Qatar, his privileged status is compromised, thus altering the experience of listening to her songs. His *micro-habitus* is thus determined by the *meta-habitus*. Space forms a key constituent of the *meta-habitus*, especially, in its relationship to the *micro-habitus*.

It is also interesting to note how the awareness of his position as a member of the diaspora differs for Shams between England and Doha. There is a level of familiarity in his non-'*privileged*' status in Doha, whereas '*when you're by yourself in England, it's hitting you, just you and her and a cold, icy road somewhere*'. For Shams, England is '*not home. You miss the language, um, family. . . . The music . . . some, some of them laugh at us*'. Although he is not a Qatari citizen, and it is very unlikely he will ever be able to obtain citizenship there, he is more at ease than in England, where he holds a British passport and is married to a British woman. This distinction is explained through Fairouz's music, although Shams is not necessarily a minority in listening to Fairouz's music in Doha, he links the space of Qatar to '*family and language*', whereas, in England, '*it's hitting you, just you and her*'. Not only does Fairouz thus become associated with a certain space and region, but also with a sentiment of somewhere holding an affective familiarity.

For Amar, who also lives in Doha, Fairouz occupies a special place, even if she is everywhere, since '*it's as if she is for me*'. Amar's '*for me*' is similar to Shams's '*just you*'. Both respondents describe a private, individual experience of Fairouz in the midst of a different spatial context. While Amar feels this '*for me*', '*everywhere*', Shams is specific in that the private experience of '*just you*', is found in England, and '*away from Arab countries*'. In both Qatar and in England, Shams identifies with being a member of the Arab diaspora, however, this is more prominent in England, indicating more of a disconnect with the surrounding space. Ironically, Shams has been a British passport holder since 2011, which puts into play the 'dialectical relationship . . . between immigration . . . and the nation – in other words at base, between immigration and naturalization'.[30]

For Sayad, 'Naturalization feeds upon immigration and, once the eventuality of a definitive return has been ruled out, immigration is dissolved into and by means of naturalization'.[31] While Sayad is talking about a specific form of immigration, namely that of Algerian migration to Paris, and while, for Shams, 'the eventuality of a definitive return' has actually been transformed into another migration elsewhere, the 'dialectical relationship', which Sayad refers to, is of particular interest. Essentially, this 'relationship' is one of 'body' and 'space' of being 'dissolved into' or of being incongruously impermeable. It is necessary here to come back to Sara Ahmed's work on 'home' and 'migration', especially looking at her discussion of 'a spatial reconfiguration of an embodied self: a transformation in the very skin through which the body is embodied'.[32] For Shams, the disparity between England and Qatar, of '*not home*' and '*home*', of '*just you*' and losing '*some of the privileges*', is the result of the body's interaction with the surrounding space. Space, here, is one of affective potentiality; 'the individual subject comes into being through its very alignment with the collective. *It is the very failure of affect to be located in a subject or object that allows it to generate the surfaces of collective bodies.*'[33] Space is therefore not the harbinger of affect but instead creates an opportunity for affect '*to generate*' in the meeting of the individual with the collective. Through Fairouz's music, and the affective spaces of '*home*' and '*not home*', the individual is thus 'reconfigured' in position to the collective.

Space is also a significant factor for Khaled, a hair stylist, and Dina, a filmmaker, who both live in London. For these two participants, listening to Fairouz is a conscious decision, since '*in Lebanon, I see everyone listening to her, she's everywhere*', but in London, '*I make it a point to listen to her*'. In a way, this ties in to Shams's discussion, as it sheds light on the unique experience of listening to Fairouz, as opposed to her being '*everywhere*'. Linking this to the idea of 'a spatial reconfiguration of an embodied self'[34] shows how the 'body' can 'dissolve into' the music of Fairouz to create a space within another space, but also how Fairouz plays a part in that 'reconfiguration'. For Khaled and Dina, London is where '*I put her music on*', whereas, in Lebanon, there is no need, since '*she's everywhere*'. The individual act of listening, here, is thus to combat the public forum of non-listening. Space is thus 'reconfigured' to accommodate the 'body' through the act of '*put[ting] her music on*'. Khaled plays Fairouz '*when I'm driving, or when I go to the shop, at home . . .*'. In this way, Fairouz is present in every space Khaled occupies in London. Another London inhabitant, Helene, compares Fairouz to '*an anchor holding me*' when she listens to her '*while abroad*'. Rather than 'reconfiguring' in space, Fairouz strengthens the position of Helene's 'body' within it. Travelling with respondents, Fairouz not only creates an affective space with her music, but her 'aura' is one, which grounds her listeners as well.

This grounding is also found with Walid, who found a deeper appreciation for Fairouz and her music when he moved to the United States, since '*nothing was left of Lebanon, except the memories and the things Fairouz brings us from Lebanon*'. For Walid, the affective potentiality found within Fairouz's songs is attributed to her being '*inclusive. She covers everything*', but also it is the mnemonic imagination within space that allows 'past experiences to be schematised and organised in meaningful ways'.[35] Movement from one space to another combined with a re-engagement of the *micro-* and *meta-habitus* not only catalyses the composition of the mnemonic imagination but also forms key contributions towards its composition. For Walid, therefore, '*if you want to picture paradise in Lebanon, they have to come from Fairouz's songs, you can't do it without Fairouz's songs*'. Via her music, Fairouz transports the 'aura' of '*paradise in Lebanon*', through the mnemonic imagination, which works in tandem with the movement of the 'body' through space to acquire new forms of 'reconfigurations'. Fairouz '*takes you back*' and is able to supply Walid with the imagery of '*paradise*', one that is 'schematised and organised' through the mnemonic imagination and linked to a space away from the present.[36] It is the fusion of temporality with the spatial, which assists in the organization and schematization of the mnemonic imagination. Similarly, Marwan '*got really attached to Fairouz*', when he moved from Lebanon to Czechoslovakia, since '*it was the first time I leave Lebanon*'. For Marwan, Fairouz was the '*ambassador*' between the two countries, comforting him during this '*phase*' of migration. Hence, 'space' and temporality again surface as key contingents of the '*connection and attachment to Fairouz*', but also the mnemonic imagination can act as a conducer of 'space' in another 'space'.

Mona, who, like Walid and Marwan, lives in Doha, shares this visualization of space through the mnemonic imagination. For Mona, '*there is an empty space when we live abroad*', which '*Fairouz fills*'. Through her music, Fairouz bridges the gap between spaces geographically, but also spaces within the 'self'. Space, here, is not seen as being separate to the 'self', instead, it is a need, one Fairouz '*fills*' and '*it's enough*'. Fairouz's 'aura' is able to travel affectively and bring Mona into contact with '*fresh air*', the '*butterfly*' and the ability to '*walk with greater ease*'. These elements of nature are linked to a specific place (Lebanon) and lie in contrast to a specific space (the Gulf). Mona alludes to the climatic and landscape differences between Lebanon and Qatar, but also she simultaneously describes a non-completion of the 'self' when '*we are abroad*'. This 'self' is very much linked to place and the components associated with it. It is as Ahmed would describe 'The intrusion of an unexpected space into the body', which 'suggests that the experience of a new home involves a partial shedding of the skin'.[37] The 'shedding of the skin' is symbolic of the 'empty space' found within Mona. In this way, Fairouz becomes interchangeable with place, space and the complete self. The activation of the mnemonic imagination here is thus not only about 'reconfiguring' space, but also about 'reconfiguring' the self. When Mona listens to Fairouz, she feels *'like you are flying off the ground'*. The reconnection of place within space is one of affect, especially as it is linked to the reconnection of the 'self'. In addition to their discussion of individual forms of remembering, Keightley and Pickering also look at the ways in which 'memories are organised, used and refashioned' based on the 'various social groups and environments in which people move during the course of their lives'.[38] So, the 're-inhabiting' of space, which Sara Ahmed talks about, can be linked here to the mnemonic imagination, which 'helps us construct our sense of narrative self by grasping together the disparate elements of experience in our lives'.[39] While Keightley and Pickering discuss temporal 'experience', it is also difficult to divorce it from spatial experience, especially in the context of the Arab diaspora. Mona's connection to space, both via the affective 'self' and the mnemonic imagination, is deepened and satisfied through the process of listening to Fairouz and her music, *'her voice'* is *'enough'* to *'fill this empty space that we are living in when we are abroad'*. However, Mona's interaction with space and Fairouz differs greatly from that of Bianca, who also lives in Doha. For Bianca, Fairouz amplifies the feeling of being in nature when she is in Lebanon, *'I'm part of the experience'*. However, in Doha *'it hurts me to hear it'*, making her *'uncomfortable'* and *'homesick'*. This contrast in affect brings us back to Ahmed, who argues 'the relationship between movement and attachment is contingent', suggesting 'that movement may affect different others differently'.[40] Even though Bianca and Mona share the same *meta-habitus*, as they both live in Doha, with the same environmental climate and topography, Mona, through the music of Fairouz, is able to transport herself and feels *'this light movement'*. Bianca, on the other hand, is pushed to *'book a ticket the next day to go back to Lebanon'*. This shows how it is not only 'space' that determines the response to Fairouz and her music, but the relationship within that space and the 'intersectional' qualities of participants, as well as their *micro-habitus*. Although both Mona and Bianca acknowledge the discrepancy between listening to Fairouz's music in Lebanon and Doha, Mona is able to accommodate the 'aura' of Fairouz as a supplement to feeling *'empty'*. Alternatively, Bianca is more content with listening to Fairouz in the spatio-temporal context, which she absorbs and disseminates in the lyrics of her songs. Space, as a dynamic force, brings together the individual with the collective, but their relationship to it, and with each other, is determined by, and in turn 'reconfigures', according to affect.

Arguably, 'space' itself can be 'reconfigured', thus giving autonomy to both the individual and the collective within the framework of affect. Taking an active stance in trying to create a culturally collective space to share with others, Mona and Walid initiated a project called 'Aallebnene' as a collaborative complement to the education at the Lebanese School in Doha. Featuring activities and events revolving around the theme of Lebanon, such as screenings of Fairouz's films, or playing marbles in the park without any technology, or the opportunity to learn the traditional *dabke*, a folk dance that is typically practised in the countries of the Levant, Aallabnene's objective is to introduce the younger generation of Arab, and mostly Lebanese, diaspora to cultural and traditional pursuits pertaining to Lebanon. One of the projects spearheaded by Aallebnene was broadcasting Fairouz's songs on the loudspeakers of the recess areas at the Lebanese school during drop-off times in the morning. Engulfing students, parents and teachers with the music of Fairouz is a form of 'reconfiguring' space, which is significant, especially in the context of affect and the mnemonic imagination:

> *If Fairouz sang to us in the morning as we come in [to school], this calmness that she gives us, that we've gotten accustomed to, the mornings of Lebanon, the mornings we used to experience. The nicest thing I had was the voice of Fairouz in the morning.* (Walid, 65, Lebanese, Doha)

> *[Shows me a video of Fairouz playing on the loudspeakers as children are being dropped off to school] See how he's dancing? Now people will pass by singing the song . . . Walid agreed because he knew the positive impact it would have. He wanted us parents, all teachers and students to start with this wonderful morning with Fairouz. . . . Almost a year ago, there were political tensions in Lebanon, and as I was dropping off my kids to school here, I heard a man threatening another man [because of their political affiliation], and I thought to myself, ouf, if they really listen to Fairouz in the morning, they would be ashamed of what they are saying, and from there the idea popped up. I am not waiting for the father, or the parents, to teach the kids. The school has a great impact on the development and musical feel and respect towards our country.* (Mona, 45, Lebanese, Doha)

Even though this example was tackled in the last chapter with regard to identity and belonging, it is also important to look at it from the perspective of space. As Ahmed argues, 'Migration is not only felt at the level of lived embodiment. Migration is also a matter of generational acts of storytelling about prior histories of movement and dislocation.'[41] In this way, Mona and Walid's determination to create 'Aallebnene' feeds into the desire for a reconnection not only of the 'self' but also as a form of collective 'storytelling' to pass on to Lebanese parents and children living in the diaspora. In this space, *'political tensions'* cease to exist and are replaced with *'respect towards our country'*, something Mona is not expecting from parents of the children who, according to her, are still stuck on old political ideologies. For Mona and Walid, it is the resurrection of place within space, *'the mornings of Lebanon, the mornings we used to experience'*. It is the 'body' within the 'reconfiguration' of space, which gives *'this calmness'*.

In his discussion on spaces and places, de Certeau differentiates between the two, stating, 'places are fragmentary and inward-turning histories, pasts that others are not allowed to read, accumulated times that can be unfolded . . . symbolizations encysted in the pain or pleasure of the body',[42] while 'space is composed of intersections of mobile elements. It is in a sense actuated by the ensemble of movements deployed within it'.[43] In effect, by thus putting into play 'space' and 'place', de Certeau brings up variants in matters of temporality, of 'past', 'present' and 'future', of movement and stagnation, of agency and compliance and of affect. For de Certeau, 'place' is affective since it holds 'symbolizations encysted in the pain or pleasure of the body'.[44] 'Space', however, also holds the potentiality of affect, this 'in-between-ness' mentioned by Gregg and Seigworth,[45] since 'space' can easily be transformed to 'place', or even act as a reminder that such 'space' exists in stark contrast to a 'place'. Stemming from this, it can be argued that a 'space' such as the Lebanese school is something Mona and Walid transformed into an affective 'place' by broadcasting Fairouz's music in the morning. However, it is an idealized representation of Lebanese 'space' and 'place', divergent from segregating politics, active and stagnant, past and present, encompassing the *'wonderful' 'calmness that [Fairouz] gives us'.* Within this 'reformed' and 'reconfigured' 'space', Fairouz narrates new forms of 'storytelling', and 'stories' of both Sara Ahmed's 'migrants' and de Certeau's 'place', to correspondingly 'reconfigure' and 'reform'.

This 'reforming' and 'reconfiguring' of places and spaces are also relevant to Dina, a Lebanese filmmaker in London, and Yassine, an Egyptian man who recently retired in Doha, although not in the same way. On public transport, Dina listens to Fairouz atop London's double-decker buses, traversing its streets and landmarks, *'you look at people and you're listening to something totally different and it just makes sense'.* The acoustic and visual merging of Fairouz's music amidst London's landscape is a form of mediated hybridity, altering 'place' to *'just make sense'.* Conversely, for Yassine, Fairouz needs to be heard in specific places with no distractions, otherwise, *'I won't enjoy it'.* At social occasions, where, *'they are playing cards and listening to Fairouz',* Yassine feels removed from the music and unable to enjoy it as he would if he were in a more private setting. Essentially, Yassine describes a space without the potentiality of affect, one in which he is unable to *'hear what she is saying'.* Even though, *'[Fairouz] makes them see and feel what she is singing',* Yassine requires a contextual space in which affect can flourish, rather than one clouded with a card-playing collective. These two examples show how, in some cases, participants are active in their selection of places to listen to her music in order for them to be better engaged, to be able to fully appreciate her 'aura', but also it indicates how Fairouz can 'reform' and 'reconfigure' space to create an 'aura' of her own. This auditory mobility through 'space', which generates an affective 'space' of its own – a 'space' of affect within a 'space' of potentiality – is of great interest, especially when such 'space' is remembered as shared 'place' through the mnemonic imagination.

Riding in cars with Fairouz

Recounting stories of driving on the 401 Highway from Michigan to Toronto, or during morning rides with parents in cars, Fairouz provides participants with a soundtrack and a narrative. By way of her songs, Fairouz is able to mobilize through 'space' to create a parallel 'space', which participants tap into through their mnemonic imagination. Combining spatio-temporal elements with the individuality and commonality of listening to Fairouz in cars highlights the ways in which families, friends and feelings connect:

Every time I think of Fairouz, actually there's a particular time . . . that I remember very, very well . . . it's basically going driving to school with my mother in Abu Dhabi, and this was probably my teen years when I was actually not talking to my mum very much, but on . . . on the radio would be Fairouz. And Fairouz for a while was our only kind of common ground . . . and for that period of time, as we were driving listening to Fairouz, it was un-contentious, and my mum was human. (Maya, 46, Lebanese, Doha)

It's more personal, honestly, because, so far, it's been very personal, with the music and my kids, my parents, not so much social, me driving in the car, heik, like that . . . but not like partying with Fairouz, no. It's very personal, and I think her music is very personal, to be honest, it's nice on a personal level; it is not commercial, not like hip-hop. (Asma, 36, Syrian, London)

As a kid, I loved 'Nihna wil Qamar Jiran',[46] *my mother and father sang the song in the car when we were kids. It was also one of the first songs that I taught myself to play on the piano.* (Clara, 44, Lebanese, Doha)

So, we divide ourselves, so the men will sing along with Nasri Shames El Dinne and us girls will sing with Fairouz. It's really rare now to see a family like ours, I mean look at the people in cars, they don't have any expressions. They don't have smiles on their faces; they're not unhappy, but they are just like robots. So, when you see a car where everyone is happy, you look at them as if they are crazy. She's put a little craziness in our family, which I really like. (Nora, 37, Lebanese, Doha)

We travel more in Europe and the USA, and wherever we travel we take a CD for Fairouz in our suitcase, like the other time we rented a car from Italy and went south to Monaco, Nice, and we have Fairouz's CD. We were in France and listening to Fairouz, so you can say we are in trouble. (Ghassan, 45, Lebanese, Doha)

The best thing in the car would be our friend who would play one of Fairouz's tapes. We used to play it while we were on the 401 Highway from Windsor to Toronto. I couldn't get enough, ya3ni, I wouldn't even feel how long the drive was, because, the weather would be nice and the roads were empty, and trees all around us, and she would sing these things. It was as if I moved and lived in Lebanon, in that car's environment. (Walid, 65, Lebanese, Doha)

Me and my brother, we went through a phase of, we were in his car, so you don't touch his radio, so we have to listen to what he does, Fairouz, Fairouz, Fairouz, like it or not, we have to listen to it. (Shams, 40, Iranian/Lebanese/English, Doha)

It is within these small moving spaces that Fairouz builds emotional, social and familial bonds. A shared experience in a shared environment, but also a memory and a reminder, Fairouz, through her 'aura', traverses space and time, to affectively evolve through the mnemonic imagination. Fairouz's 'aura' stimulates the mnemonic imagination resulting in affect. However, affect also travels to take on different meanings in different spaces and contexts to shape the mnemonic imagination. For the participants mentioned earlier, the memory of being in the car, with Fairouz and their family members, instigates a sense of happiness, but the experiences are dependent on both their *meta-* and *micro-habitus*. With Maya, a programme manager for an NGO, Fairouz humanizes her mother, during a period in which they lacked '*common ground*'. During her teenage years, when Maya '*was actually not talking to [her] mum very much*', Fairouz acted as a substitute for conversation.

For Asma, a single mother of two boys, Fairouz symbolizes personal relationships, '*with me and the music, my kids, my parents, not so much social, driving in the car*'. This private, intimate sharing of Fairouz within space is also expressed by Clara who remembers listening to Fairouz with her parents during long drives. For Nora, an architect who lives in Doha with her husband and three children, Fairouz offers the opportunity to '*put a little craziness in our family*'. Describing a fun, interactive atmosphere, for Nora and her family, car rides with Fairouz are an opportunity to let loose, providing a contrast to other drivers on the road, who are '*just like robots*'. Even though they occupy different geographical 'places' than those Fairouz sings about, Ghassan and Walid, through her songs, keep the singer close to them on long drives in the private 'spaces' of their cars. In this way, 'place' and 'space' fuse together to create an experience, which is symbiotically diverse yet familiar. Sonically juxtaposing Fairouz in 'space' 'reconfigures' 'place'. So, the link Fairouz supplies here allows for the dissolution of 'place' into 'space'. It is through her 'aura' that Fairouz shifts spatio-temporal continuums to take on deeper meanings for her listeners. Fairouz ingests and disseminates her 'aura', to accommodate spatial contexts and affectively triggers the mnemonic imagination.

While other participants imply compliance with listening to Fairouz in the car with their parents or children, Shams, a 40-year-old man living in Doha, alludes to a sense of control and ownership of car 'space' by his father, forcing him to listen to her music, '*like it or not*'. However, Shams later recounts how, after his father's death, the memories of those car rides triggered an unexpected emotional response:

> *Anyway, what happened is . . . I didn't cry until a year and a half . . . we moved to Dubai, I had some of my boxes from England shipped, so I had my CDs there . . . so I found . . . one of my Fairouz ones, stick it in, going to work, 'Nassam 3aleyna al Hawa'*[47] *comes on, and I just exploded by myself like an idiot . . . That was the only time . . . Because it reminded me of him playing the music in the car.* (Shams, 40, Iranian/Lebanese/English, Doha)

Shams's example highlights how by listening to Fairouz with his dad transforms her 'aura' into one that becomes associated with him and his subsequent absence. According to Brian Massumi, 'the body doesn't just absorb pulses or discrete stimulations; it infolds *contexts*, it infolds volitions and cognitions that are nothing if not situated'.[48] Unable to cry '*until a year and a half*' after his father's death, the 'infolding' of '*contexts*' when listening to Fairouz in the car brought on an emotional release. Amalgamating through 'space' and the mnemonic imagination, '*contexts*' are acknowledged affectively in the distinction between presence and absence. Affect does not remain unchanged in the '*context*' of both. While Fairouz and her 'aura' were very much in the present of the car rides that Shams experienced with his father, that 'aura' has since transformed into a substitute for his absence. 'Absence' and 'presence', the occupying of 'space' and that which becomes memory, thus not only alter the relationship with Fairouz and her 'aura' but also instigate different forms of affect. This interplay between absence and presence is significant in the discussion on Fairouz and 'space', especially within the framework of the Arab diaspora, and this will be discussed at length in the next chapter.

Affective spaces and mnemonic places

In his book *Postmodern Geographies*, Soja calls for a theoretical discussion on what he calls 'the spatiality of social life', studies involving the 'social being actively emplaced in space *and* time in an explicitly historical *and* geographical contextualisation'.[49] Geography and space, Soja argues, should be given the same weight and consideration as history and time when observing social phenomena. It is evident in this chapter how important it is to observe and engage with space, especially in the context of the Arab diaspora and the music of Fairouz. Drawing on Foucault, Soja contends that space 'still tends to be treated as fixed, dead, undialectical'.[50] However, as outlined here, space is an essential structure through which to assess not only the positions and situations of the diaspora but also their relationships to the self and others through Fairouz's music. Dynamic and affective, space works in shaping experience, but also it is shaped by it. From the ways in which participants view and connect with Fairouz to the way in which they understand their own personal journeys and concepts of 'home' and 'self', space proves to be the common thread.

Beginning with the premise of Sara Ahmed that 'the organization of social and bodily space creates a border that is transformed into an object, as an effect of this intensification of feeling'[51] already indicates how space acts as both potential and inducer of affect. Adding the music of Fairouz to the mix, it becomes clear how 'bodily space' and 'social space' can work together to create new forms of consumption and understanding. It is not only the relationship of the music of Fairouz, which is revealed, but also participants are able to chart their own positionings within 'bodily space' and 'social space'. It is important to note how Fairouz, as an artist, provides room with which participants can 'creatively connect' and circumnavigate these private and public spaces through her 'aura'.

The spatial and metaphorical distance that Fairouz maintains from her listeners allows a safe 'dwelling place', something that 'moves us . . . makes us feel . . . that which holds us in place',[52] but also she becomes available for appropriation. The absence of polarizing signs positions the singer as one for the people. Her persona is maintained through her music, and she does not deviate from the values she sings about. As an omnipresent figure, Fairouz is embedded within space and time. Participants are unable to dissociate her from memories of home, family and past experience. In this way, Fairouz not only possesses 'aura', but she also creates it through recollections of such memories via the mnemonic imagination, a definer of space, one, which is personalized and individualized, Fairouz is thus able to transport her listeners to places associated with the memory of hearing her songs. A constant reminder of existence, many respondents could not recall when they first heard her songs, showcasing not just the longevity of the singer but also the rooted depth of Fairouz spatially and temporally. Fairouz is reminiscent not only of space and time but also of family and shared experience, affectively replacing both in their absence.

Chapter 5

MUSIC, MIGRANCY, PRESENCE AND ABSENCE

In his article 'Of Other Spaces', Michel Foucault argues, 'the present epoch will perhaps be above all the epoch of space'.[1] Through his analysis of what he terms 'utopia' and 'heterotopia', Foucault demonstrates the different ways in which 'heterogeneous' space can transgress and take on meaning. Defining 'utopias' as 'fundamentally unreal spaces' and 'heterotopias' as 'places that do exist and that are formed in the very founding of society', Foucault uses the mirror to highlight his point.[2] Through the mirror, Foucault puts into play absence and presence, of being in one place and in another, 'I am over there, there where I am not, a sort of shadow that gives my own visibility to myself, that enables me to see myself, there where I am absent'.[3] It is 'from the standpoint of the mirror I discover my absence from the place where I am, since I see myself over there'.[4]

Perhaps neither as complex nor as philosophical, the allegory of the mirror reflects the in-between spaces of the diaspora and their positioning in both geographical and mnemonic space. Simultaneously, a 'placeless place', and thus 'utopic', as well as a 'heterotopia', in that 'the mirror does exist in reality, where it exerts a sort of contradiction on the position I occupy', the mirror is 'at once absolutely real, connected with all the space that surrounds it, and absolutely unreal, since in order to be perceived it has to pass through this virtual point, which is over there'.[5] Arguably, the diasporic space resembles the trifecta analogy of the mirror and its creation of utopia and 'heterotopia', as it provides a dialogue between presence and absence. Conflating space and time, the diasporic space through the proxy of the mnemonic imagination – which can be seen as a mirror of sorts – puts into perspective the 'here' and 'there' of diasporic experience. It is the point where past, present and future meet, contorting phantasmically between actuality and idealism to create a new form of heterotopia, which is illusory and yet very real, social but deeply personal, thus catalysing and situating concepts such as lived experience, imagination, and the 'aura', public and private space, the notion of grounding and deterritorialization, of 'roots' and 'seeds', of movement and stillness, of acceptance and rejection, and, finally, of integration and alienation.

Through their subsequent positioning, participants are able to navigate these spaces with the manifestation of the mnemonic imagination as their guide. More importantly, it is Fairouz's music which drives this awareness towards destinations 'absolutely real' but also 'absolutely unreal'. It is important here to look at the notions of absence and presence in its different manifestations before discussing the terms further in the context of Fairouz. In Mahmoud Darwish's *In the Presence of Absence*, translator Sinan Antoon describes the renowned Palestinian poet's book as a 'space where presence and absence, prose and poetry, and many other opposites converse and converge'.[6] Exploring concepts such as exile and return, death and life, past and present, memory and reality, Darwish integrates the politics with the personal. Absence and presence take on different meanings according to the contexts in which he refers to them, 'an itinerant crisscrossing the fusion of the "here" with the "there"'.[7] It is a more political and migratory absence and presence than Foucault's, an acknowledgement of 'lack', since 'everything here is proof of loss and lack. Everything here is a painful reminder of what has once been there'.[8] So while Foucault discusses absence and presence as a reflection of self in space, Darwish's exploration of the terms is saturated with the political violence and subsequent exile of a personal experience he has endured. Essentially, for Darwish, presence connotes 'lack' and 'loss', an absence of 'what has once been there'. It is both a material and 'metaphorical' loss, since 'metaphors . . . teach beings the play of words. Metaphors that form a geography from a shadow'.[9] While Foucault's usage of 'shadow' is a way to illustrate one's 'own visibility', for Darwish, the 'shadow' is the illusiveness of borders and nations, a 'presence' of space in its 'absence'.

In his book *The Suffering of the Immigrant*, Abdelmalek Sayad relates presence and absence in his conceptual examination of immigration and emigration. Sayad argues:

> immigration results in a presence, and emigration finds expression in an absence. A presence makes itself felt; an absence is noted, and that is all. A presence can be adjusted, regulated, controlled and managed. An absence is masked, compensated for and denied. These differences in status determine the differences in the discourses that can be applied to both presence (immigration), which is amenable to discourse, and absence (emigration), of which there is nothing to be said except that it has to be supplemented. Immigration, or the presence of immigrants as foreign bodies (foreign to society or the nation), is the object of a problematic that might be said to be totally imposed, or external to the object it discusses. (2004, p. 120)

While Sayad is talking about migration from the perspective of the communities in which the migrant is both received and released, his discussion on absence, presence and 'foreign bodies' is significant in discussions on Fairouz and her music. Through conversations with the Arab diaspora in this study, an awareness and consciousness of both their presence and absence were expressed. Via Fairouz's music, respondents were able to vocalize their situations between the two states, as well as explain their position as a 'foreign body':

The meanings of her songs are deeper and more appealing to someone abroad. In Lebanon, the songs won't have the same impact because I'm in the comfort of my own country and I'm not nostalgic to it. So, the emotions that the songs bring are stronger here. Since I'm separated from my home country, her songs provoke more feelings here. (Helene, 52, Lebanese, London)

But, here we felt it more because we have been away from Lebanon and [Fairouz] reminds us of the emotions, childhood, Lebanon, happiness and all the nice stuff. All the nice stuff, because we love Lebanon a lot, but unfortunately we can't live there, we can't enjoy Lebanon. Because when you live in a country and you can't go out and enjoy with your family, siblings or parents. . . . Seeing all the people go out and enjoy [themselves], and you can't do that because you cannot afford it, because you are living in Lebanon and you know the average salaries and rates are low. You can't afford going to downtown once a week to have a dinner or lunch, right? (Hisham, 39, Lebanese, London)

I also have some cousins here, and my siblings are here. So, I don't feel very far away from my family and country. However, I'll always be nostalgic to the general atmosphere of my country and to its vibes . . . I'm happy in London because I'm working. As long as I'm working, I'll be happy, because I'll be achieving something. However, if we want to consider everything else, I prefer my own country. (Khaled, 38, Lebanese, London)

Really, Fairouz is our most beautiful dream. She is the dream I adhere to, that prevents us from reaching desperation. I was just telling you that I don't feel like a stranger here in London. This is not a positive feeling; people should have a sense of belonging to their homeland. It's not good to cut all your connections with your homeland and to say that anything that happens in your country doesn't concern you. It is the build-up of frustrations and disappointments that led me to say that my country is here in London. However, there still remain these small dreams that are imposed on us more than we're attached to them. Fairouz is one of these dreams, and she's the most beautiful one of them. (Hussain, 60, Iraqi, London)

Fairouz takes your imagination to different places and not one specific place or one specific location. You swim with the music. You reach a place that you are dreaming of, but it does not necessarily have to be the sea of Lebanon or the mountains of Lebanon. (Yassine, 70, Egyptian, Doha)

I've been here for 25 years, so you know home for me is always a question, Where? How? It's like it's always somewhere else, you know. So, yeah, she takes me where . . . where I didn't have to ask these questions, I think that's why you know it clears my mind kind of. (Nafie, 35, Sudanese, Doha)

The place, the place, because there isn't a time I listen to it where I don't cry, the ancient roads of Jerusalem, we lived there, now I don't know if it was a happy part of my life that time, I don't remember if it was happy or sad, but it's like I said, it reminds me of how we were, the roads of Jerusalem, the churches, how our life was, I don't even remember her making me happy, I don't remember, it's true, it's always, not sad, maybe, any person who listens to the songs of Jerusalem and stuff, might not feel sad . . . but for us it is (Carmen, 70, Palestinian/Jordanian, Doha)

Fairouz taught us that, no matter how far we went, and no matter how far we've been out of our homeland, we'll always remember our past, our family, our people and everything. So, that's why our days are full with Fairouz, every day in the morning that in our life in London Fairouz is with us. (Amin, 27, Palestinian, London)

I remember our old house before moving to our new house, riding bicycles, returning back home, Fairouz's songs resonating in our house or at the neighbours' house, I remember the house, the timeframe, how we looked like, how we used to enter the house, the discussion with my father's neighbour in the store, he talked about Fairouz. (Ferial, 46, Palestinian, London)

When you are abroad and far away from home, what connects you to your country? Is it the problems that happen in it? People in it? The things that happen? New singers? On the contrary, music is very essential in a person's life. No matter how strong he is, any person should feel his heart beating inside, so I feel that Fairouz is the best way to allow a person to change their feelings of pride to the feeling of the Earth, to his country's feelings and emotions that she gives. (Ghassan, 45, Lebanese, Doha)

In dark days, 2006, it was always Fairouz. Anything war, and anything that reminds you of Lebanon, and bombing, I see myself put Fairouz, maybe because it will make my tears go down faster because 'Ya Allah,[10] *they're bombing Beirut.' And I remember 2006 was a very big Fairouz time for me, because we would be sitting, I'd feel paralyzed, I'd wish I was in the war, inside, because sitting outside with my mum and brother there, you get that fear of not knowing what's happening, you really don't know. And even if I was watching Arabic TV, I'd even install the satellite for the war, there's a war, we're going to go live. So I started watching it systematically almost 19 hours a day, and I remember it was one of the toughest times in my relationship with my husband. He was like: 'You brought the war here.' It was New TV, they had installed cameras on rooftops and I would just put it and go cook, and you would just hear Beirut, and the noise of the bombs, and there was no anchor, they would leave the camera from 2.00 am to 11.00 am, and I would be awake because I wanted to see the war behind Julien [Julien's back]. When Julien is around me I try to keep it quiet, but when he goes to sleep, I live the war in the lounge. So I played Fairouz then, a lot.* (Dina, 42, Lebanese, London)

When you told me [that] you're working on Fairouz and her symbolism to the diaspora, I thought about it for a while. I sort of discovered that I didn't really like Fairouz's songs about the village. I mean the things from her plays. I always found the plays the hardest to connect to for me, because they were always sort of local Lebanese things about the village and mountains. Therefore, it was sort of hard for me to connect to them. As a city kid, I didn't have any longing to the village. However, since I moved to London these songs took another meaning as I listen to them here. Now I have some place to long for, to look back to, to hope to go back to, and to contrast with my new hometown. So, that was one revelation that came out of thinking about my relationship to Fairouz. As I told you, the relationship with her grows with you, and throughout stages [in life] her songs take different meanings. The songs function differently in your life. (Kareem, 36, Egyptian, London)

And when I came here it was nice, you know, like mornings, sometimes when I'm studying. When I miss the Middle East, like she, she just . . . she was that face of the Middle East. Oh! Like I've never, I mean I know that I've never thought of her as Lebanese per se. To me, she was just Middle Eastern, so like she could possibly be Moroccan, it wouldn't you know, like I didn't, you know, link her to a nationality, but when I visited Lebanon, then Lebanon made sense, like Lebanon looks like her. You know what I mean? (Leila, 30, Moroccan, London)

What I'm trying to say is, I don't have to love her music, I don't have to love Fairouz's music, and, in fact, I'm not sure that I do love her music, you know? I feel a need to listen to it when I need to be grounded, when I feel like I need to ground myself. Because London is a place of anonymity, which is a blessing and a curse. It's great, in the sense that nobody is after your business, but it's not so great, in the sense that you can feel like you're losing yourself. And me, where I come from is very important to me, the fact that I am from an Arab background and my parents are Lebanese-Syrian, so there are these layers of identity that are important for our self-image and your construction of self. So, in that sense, Fairouz provides that. She's like a bit of a pillar, so when I listen to her on a Sunday morning, it's almost because I need to rebuild myself. This is my rebuilding time, and it's not because I particularly crave . . . no! No! I take that back! I crave her music. I do crave her music. And it's not because I love it, it's because I need it, and it's very strange that way. I don't love her music, I can live without it, but I need it, you know? (Maha, 35, Syrian/Lebanese, London)

This is Fairouz, you know? She's everything that contradicts the desert culture, the desert thought, the desert relation. The cities of salt? These are cities of salt. Even the relations. You might think that we have the best relations with the Qataris, and at a certain point of time, he turns the table, he throws the glove in your face, because they were raised as such, unlike us. They were raised, in their culture, that all the non-Qataris are here to serve us. It's a culture, maybe 99%, 1% don't have it. But the majority has it, so that's why. It's not you. It will never be, and that's why you will always belong to Fairouz and to her culture. (Jihad, 51, Palestinian/Jordanian, Doha)

All of a sudden, you want to listen to the Arabic music . . . you want to go and smoke shisha,[11] and you want to make mloukhieh[12] at home, and you know it's the nostalgia of home that gets to you, um, so I used to listen to her a lot over there [in Australia], and a lot of just Arabic music in general. (Rola, 29, Jordanian, Doha)

Yes, of course she does. And more than that, she keeps this flame inside of me that makes me miss Lebanon even more. I constantly think about Lebanon and I'm very much attached to it, even though I'm very happy in Doha. You know, if somehow Lebanon weren't on my mind, well Fairouz would pinch me and remind me of it. I feel as if I'm missing all the beauty, this patriotism she sings about, it's all happening now, even though she sang it before, it's happening without me. (Bianca, 37, Lebanese, Doha)

You live it with more depth when you're abroad, it's more profound, you're more focused, when you're abroad, you live it more. I told you, it's because she calms the haneen that you have. Haneen, you know? It invades you more when you're away, you listen to Fairouz, and it's as if you've taken medicine, she sedates you, it sedates you, it takes away this pain of missing, it makes you feel like you're home again, it compensates for being away, it's enough, it's like she's medicine for Al-ghurba that makes you feel like you're back in Lebanon. This is how I connect it. (Amar, 39, Lebanese, Doha)

From these excerpts it is evident that Fairouz reminds participants of where they are, but also where they are not. 'Presence' and 'absence' delineate listeners' positions in space and show how affect and the mnemonic imagination work in tandem with their intersectional qualities and their *micro-* and *meta-habitus* to produce different implications for consumption and interpretation. The potentiality of affect in space is also strengthened, since it occurs in both 'presence' and 'absence'. Helene, who lives in London, initially laments that when she listens to Fairouz, she feels '*Far from the Lebanon that I know*', positioning her absence from a 'place'. She later conveys how '*The meanings of her songs are deeper and more appealing to someone abroad*', marking the discrepancy between listening to Fairouz in spaces of 'presence' and of 'absence'. This further stresses the argument that Fairouz's 'aura' is more powerful and 'appealing' the further away she moves from the spatio-temporal context with which she is attributed. Similarly, Hisham, who also lives in London, '*feels*' Fairouz's songs, '*more because we have been away from Lebanon and [Fairouz] reminds us of the emotions, childhood, Lebanon, happiness and all the nice stuff*'.

However, Hisham is quick to justify both his 'presence' and 'absence' in 'place', by rationalizing 'space'. For Hisham, '*when you live in*' Lebanon, '*you can't enjoy it*', because '*the average salaries*' are low, and '*you cannot afford it*'. Hisham is unable to mobilize within Lebanon, because it is too expensive and salaries are low, '*you can't afford going to downtown once a week to have a dinner or lunch*'. Hence, his economic situation limits movement there. Fairouz, for him, presents '*all the nice stuff*' of Lebanon, but he acknowledges that it is because '*we have been away*' from that environment. The reality of Hisham's financial situation cements his positioning, and while he recognizes his 'absence' in 'place', he is able to justify it, which is similar to Khaled, who is '*happy in London because I'm working*', but, '*if we want to consider everything else I prefer my own country*'. Although Hisham concedes the difference between listening to Fairouz abroad and in Lebanon, he also understands how space, distance and proximity work together to romanticize or vindicate the '*happiness and all the nice stuff*' Fairouz sings about. This differs from Khaled, who still prefers Lebanon, regardless of its faults. While Hisham, Khaled and Helene contrast 'presence' and 'absence' with a lived 'place', which is 'absolutely real', in that it is 'connected with all the space that surrounds it', Hussain, an Iraqi artist living in London, makes the connection of 'place' to one, which is 'absolutely unreal'.[13]

Hussain does not '*feel like a stranger here in London*', which he argues is '*not a positive feeling*' because '*people should have a sense of belonging to their homeland*'. Being too comfortable in London indicates a shortage of '*connections with your homeland*', implying a lack of both 'absence' and 'presence'. For Hussain, '*Fairouz is our most beautiful dream*', offering a glimpse into the '*sense of belonging*', which he seeks. However, contrary to Helene, Khaled and Hisham, this '*belonging*' is not tied to a specific place. Rather, it is a '*dream*', an affective state with no set geographical boundaries. In this way, Hussain challenges the notions of 'absence' and 'presence', unravelling them from the tapestries of 'space'. Hussain, who came to London from Iraq '*on vacation*', days before the First Gulf War erupted in 1990, was unable to go back to Iraq because of the conflict, and so he found a job in London and has lived there ever since. It is necessary here to highlight how *meta-* and *micro-habitus* play a role in the notions of 'presence' and 'absence', and also how they determine their existence. Visiting Iraq '*only once*' since he moved to London, Hussain '*felt like a stranger there*'. For the Iraqi artist, Fairouz is the '*only thing left from our past*'. In this way, Fairouz remains the constant, the in-between; she is both 'presence' and 'absence', since she is able to reflect both. Incapable of feeling belonging in the Arab world, Hussain recognizes 'absence' of place within Fairouz's music, but instead finds 'presence' in the space of her songs. In her book *Space, Place and Gender*, Doreen Massey criticizes the notion 'that places have single, essential identities' or that 'the sense of place' is 'constructed out of an introverted, inward-looking history'.[14] Instead, she calls for a more 'extroverted' way of looking at place, one 'which includes a consciousness of its links with the wider world'.[15] The *meta-* and *micro-habitus* are thus useful in examining the 'sense of place' Massey talks about, since they are about connection and 'links with the wider world'. In this case, Iraq, as a 'place', does not remain inert. It is a product of geopolitical events, which have changed – and continue to change – its social, political and cultural dynamics. This altered 'place' is where Hussain feels '*like a stranger*', but it is important to note that Iraq is not the only thing that has changed. Hussain himself is also a product of his *meta-* and *micro-habitus*, which positions 'place' as not only a geographical concept but also one reliant on 'social relations',[16] as well as subjective and collective interactions. Yassine, who lives in Doha, echoes the sentiment of Hussain in that Fairouz provides '*a place that you are dreaming of*', but that 'place' does not necessarily have to be tangible or real. For Nafie, a political cartoonist, 'home' is the eternal question. Having lived in Doha for '*25 years*', 'home' is '*always somewhere else*'. However, he finds solace in Fairouz's songs, since '*she takes me where I [don't] have to ask these questions*'. Fairouz, who offers a sonic place of belonging, comforts the eternal 'absence of' home for Nafie. Here, Fairouz charts not only the 'absence' or 'presence' of participants but also space and place.

For Carmen, Amin and Ferial, three Palestinian participants, 'absence' and 'presence' take on a very different meaning, as do notions of 'place' and 'space'. Carmen, in Doha, is reminded of 'place' through Fairouz's songs. During an emotional interview at a Doha coffee shop, Carmen recalls listening to Fairouz's songs about Jerusalem, and '*there isn't a time I listen to it when I don't cry*'. Fairouz brings her back to '*the roads of Jerusalem, the churches, how our life was*', to a 'place' active in her mnemonic imagination. Carmen's emotional response to place is one she feels is specific to her and other Palestinians, since '*any person who listens to the songs of Jerusalem and stuff, might not feel sad . . . but for us it is . . .* ' Here, affect is manifested in absence, but it is absence not only of the individual but of the 'place' itself. Carmen's '*us*' is inclusive of those who feel that 'absence' and displacement. With the Israeli occupation of Palestinian land, the continuous demolition of homes, physical and emotional violence, and Israeli settlers moving into Palestinian properties, Carmen is unable to return to Palestine. As 'place', it will remain confined to Fairouz's songs and the images found in her mnemonic imagination. Its present and future 'absence' is made even more affective by its past 'presence'. Similarly, Ferial is also able to link Fairouz to 'place' through her mnemonic imagination with '*Fairouz's songs resonating in our house or at the neighbours house*'. Fairouz thus plays a part in that construction of 'place', but also she is a reminder of Ferial's absence within it. Although remembering is usually associated with temporality, these two examples highlight the role of space in remembering, especially in the context of 'absence' and 'presence'. To remember, here, is to be absent from a 'place' one was once present in. For Amin, in London, Fairouz is precisely that reminder of place, '*no matter how far we went, and no matter how far we've been out of our homeland*'. To compensate for his physical absence in space, '*our days are full with Fairouz*'. In this way, Fairouz travels with participants, providing a 'presence' of 'place' in its 'absence', a reminder of past, but also a substitute for present and future.

Ghassan, in Doha, and Dina, in London, both see Fairouz as connecting 'presence' to 'absence'. For Ghassan, it is the '*music*' that '*connects you to your country*' when '*you are abroad and far away from home*'. Specifically, it is Fairouz who transports Ghassan '*to his country's feelings*'. In this way, Fairouz is able to affectively connect place to place in the in-between space of 'presence' and 'absence'. Dina's recounting of the 2006 war in Lebanon is especially relevant in the discussion of Fairouz as a connector of 'presence' to 'absence'. Feeling '*paralyzed*' at being far away from her '*mum and brother*' during the conflict, '*2006 was a very big Fairouz time for me*'. Affective, '*it will make my tears go down faster*', Fairouz was able to bridge the distance between Dina's 'absence' from her parents and from Beirut, with her 'presence' of living '*the war in the lounge*' of her London home. This affective connection which Fairouz provides to Dina in a way soothes her 'absence', when '*you get that fear of not knowing what's happening*', and wishing '*I was in the war, inside*'. Corresponding to the violent conflict in Lebanon, Dina was experiencing not only a conflict of 'absence' and 'presence' but also conflict with her French husband, who accuses her of bringing '*the war here*'. During her husband's 'presence', Dina tries '*to keep it quiet*', however, in his 'absence', she continues to '*live the war in the lounge*'. Expression of affect is suppressed in this social space and in the 'presence' of Dina's husband. This parallel living of the war puts into play 'absence' and 'presence', within the framework of the *meta-* and *micro-habitus,* showing how Fairouz can act as an affective connector of 'space' and 'place'. Recreating 'place' (Beirut) within 'space' (Dina's London flat), Dina tries to overcome her 'absence' during a tense time in which she regrets being far away. As soundscape, Dina's London flat is where *'you would just hear Beirut, and the noise of the bombs',* juxtaposed with Fairouz's music. An acoustic representation of the 2006 war, Dina's example highlights how Fairouz contributes to recreating 'presence' in a time of 'absence'. Her role is not only one of affect but is strategic in 'reforming' 'space' to occupy the feeling of 'place'.

Kareem and Leila, in London, vocalize an altered relationship with Fairouz in the binary of 'presence' and 'absence' and in the change of 'place'. There is a change in perspective with Kareem, who *'didn't really like Fairouz's songs about the village'* when he lived in Egypt. As a *'city kid',* who grew up in Cairo, songs about the village were *'the hardest to connect to'.* Kareem even went so far as to link the songs to a particular place, *'for me . . . they were always sort of local Lebanese things about the village and mountains'.* Describing not just an alien landscape but also a place with confined borders. However, since moving to London, *'these songs took another meaning as I listen to them here'.* In the 'absence' of the familiar environment of Egypt, those same songs represent, *'some place to long for, to look back to, to hope to go back to, and to contrast with my new hometown'.* This shift, in accordance with Kareem's 'presence' in London, is significant, since it is the same songs that *'take different meanings'* and *'function differently in your life'.* It is both Kareem's 'presence' and 'absence' which result in this longing for the 'place' Fairouz sings about. While, in Egypt, this 'place' was adamantly Lebanon, for Kareem it has since changed to being *'some place to long for, to look back to'* and a *'contrast'* to London. This shows the ways in which Fairouz transgresses space to occupy an affective state in the realm of 'absence' and 'presence', but also how, through the *meta-* and *micro-habitus* of participants, this state morphs to take on *'different meanings'* and *'functions'.* 'Place' here is thus not the 'fragmentary and inward-turning histories' of de Certeau,[17] but is rather a malleable, reflective and porous 'progressive sense of place', which is 'constructed by linking that place to places beyond'.[18] Contributing to the capability of 'place' to be cognitively transformed is the mnemonic imagination, which does this by allowing for both 'continuity with the past' and 'the accumulation of new experience'.[19] In this way, Fairouz moves on from her past role to one in the present, but also one Kareem hopes *'to go back to'* in the future. The mnemonic imagination, here, is at the intersection of temporality and spatiality, producing new affective forms of understanding and consumption of Fairouz's music. For Leila, this process worked somewhat in reverse. When moving to London from Morocco, Fairouz occupied a more regional space for the young academic; she *'was that face of the Middle East'.* However, when Leila visited Lebanon, *'Lebanon made sense',* since *'Lebanon looks like her'.* Here, Fairouz reverts to a specific 'place' after the 'accumulation of new experience' of Leila visiting Lebanon and associating the singer with the environment about which she speaks.

This identity of 'place' and 'space' is an important factor in the context of 'presence' and 'absence', especially in discussions around positioning the individual among the collective. Maha, a social worker in London, listens to Fairouz *'when*

I feel like I need to ground myself. Describing London as a *'place of anonymity'*, something she sees as both a *'blessing'* and a *'curse'*, in that *'nobody is after your business'* but also *'you can feel like you're losing yourself*. Part of the 'self' Maha mentions is that associated with her *'Arab background'*. Maha's 'presence' in London thus threatens the 'self' linked to 'place'. Essentially, Maha's fear of losing 'place' is actually concerned with losing the 'self'. Fairouz rescues this absence of 'place' within the 'self' by helping Maha *'rebuild'* these *'layers of identity that are important for our self-image and your construction of self*. As a key constituent of Maha's identity, Fairouz here pacifies the subsequent 'absence' felt within the 'presence'. It is 'a spatial reconfiguration of an embodied self', a 'self' that has been invaded by 'an unexpected space'.[20] The affective process of having to *'rebuild myself'* on a *'Sunday morning'* by listening to Fairouz is thus a 'reconfiguring' of the body to ensure the 'self' is not lost in this 'unexpected space', an attempt to 'rebuild' place within 'space'. Further justifying her 'need' to 'rebuild' herself, Maha exalts, *'and it's not because I love it, it's because I need it, and it's very strange that way. I don't love her music, I can live without it, but I need it, you know?'* In this way, the 'self' – one associated with Maha's *'Arab background'* – becomes interchangeable with Fairouz and her music, not only is Fairouz a representation of that 'self', but she is an integral component of it. In addition, space, as affective potentiality, drives Maha to adamantly seek 'place' in its absence.

Jihad and Rola in Doha also make the distinction between 'self' and space. For Jihad, Fairouz *'is everything that contradicts the desert culture'*, something he links with *'the desert relation'* and the *'cities of salt'*, what he sees as superficial and opportunistic interpersonal relationships, which are based on financial expectations, since *'all the non-Qataris are here to serve [the Qataris]'*. The *meta-* and *micro-habitus* play a key role in the interpretation of space in this example. As a *'non-Qatari'*, Jihad knows his time in Doha is limited and is dependent on his skills in the workforce. In *The Suffering of the Immigrant*, Sayad argues, 'The immigrant is no more than his body. . . . Away from work and other circumstances that concern and address the immigrant only insofar as he is a body, the immigrant remains a *minor'*.[21] While Sayad is talking about a specific immigrant – the 'Maghrebin immigrant or one originating from a third world country' – in a specific 'space' (France), this notion of being viewed as a 'body', or a 'working body' in the case of Jihad, is significant in the context of Qatari 'space'. As mentioned previously, to live in Qatar means you have to be working in Qatar. Occupying any 'non-working' status often indicates you have to leave the country (unless you can find a new working status),[22] and the acquiring of citizenship is close to impossible. What Jihad alludes to is thus the migrant 'body' being positioned as one, which needs to *'serve'*. It is a 'serving' body, ripe with significations of power. It is a 'serving' body, since it cannot exist as anything else within such 'space'. It is within 'space', where the 'body' therefore maintains its status as a 'working' and 'serving' one. In addition, it is Fairouz who *'contradicts'* this culture, which Jihad dubs *'the desert culture'*. Jihad *'will always belong to Fairouz and to her culture'*, something which he lacks in the 'presence' of being a 'working body' in Qatari 'space'. Here, the distinction between 'presence' and 'absence' is heavily linked to the *meta-* and *micro-habitus*, which operate together to position the 'body' within 'space'. The 'absence' of being seen as anything but a 'working body' is precisely due to 'presence' in a certain 'space', and the power dynamics bracketed by the *meta-* and *micro-habitus*.

Micro-habitual situations, such as gender or familial circumstances, may also affect relationships with 'space'. For Rola, moving to Australia during her university years brought a different perspective from living in Doha. Rola grew up in Qatar, moving there with her family when she was five years old. Her relationship with the Gulf Peninsula *is 'probably the closest thing I have to home'*. During her upbringing, Rola was a typical *'Third Culture Kid'*, listening to Western bands, like Destiny's Child, attending British schools and socializing with an eclectic group of friends from all over the world. Even though her mother played Fairouz in the house for years, Rola first *'started listening to [Fairouz] on [her] own'* at the age of fourteen/fifteen, because she *'was trying to find a connection with her family'*, whom she sensed *'had this kind of dissatisfaction with how we were turning out to be'*, since *'we were very disconnected from the culture'* from which they came. However, it was not until she left home to pursue her higher education that her relationship with Fairouz and her music grew. For her university years, Rola moved to Australia, and *'all of a sudden, you're in the middle of this brand new culture . . . even though it wasn't that new, I mean we've been going and coming to Australia for many years, but as an adult, by myself away from home'*. It was during that time, experiencing the 'absence' of being away from her family and home environment, when she felt, *'you want to listen to the Arabic music . . . you want to go and smoke shisha, and you want to make mloukhieh at home'*. Her 'presence' in this *'brand new culture'* called for a reassertion of what Aly would call 'doing Arab', a performance of ethnicity, 'through acts, enunciations, objects, spaces, bodies and settings'.[23] Although 'doing Arab' was not the case for Rola in Doha, her 'presence' in Australia brings a different dynamic of 'body' and 'space', which instigates the desire to *'listen to the Arabic music'* and perform other attributes associated with 'Arabness'. This 'absence' of being in a familiar place, what Rola calls *'the nostalgia of home'*, is an affective state by which she needs to 'reconfigure' her 'Arabness' and identity to adapt to her new surroundings. Again, Fairouz allows Rola to strengthen her Arab 'presence' in a space of 'absence'.

For Amar and Bianca, two Lebanese participants living in Doha, Fairouz is a jarring cue of both 'presence' and 'absence'. She is an active catalyst in making the participants feel as if they were *'back in Lebanon'*, but she is also an affective prompt *'pinch[ing] me and remind[ing] me of it'*, even if *'somehow, Lebanon weren't on my mind'*. When listening to Fairouz, Bianca is reminded of what she is *'missing'* and how *'it's happening without me'*. Bianca's description of the ways in which Fairouz actively affects her during her 'presence' in Doha is linked directly to her 'absence' *in* Lebanon. Even though Bianca is *'very happy in Doha'*, her 'absence' from Lebanon is difficult, since she is *'very much attached to it'*. In this way, Fairouz transports the 'aura' of place, which, in turn, *'keeps this flame inside of me that makes me miss Lebanon even more'*, enhancing her position of 'absence'. While Fairouz summons Bianca and *'reminds'* her of her 'absence', with Amar, Fairouz is a calming force, one which, *'sedates you'*, and *'takes away this pain of missing'*. For

Amar, listening to Fairouz is '*enough*', a '*medicine*', she '*compensates for being away*'. Fairouz fills the 'absence' of being in '*Al-ghurba*' and calms the '*haneen*', which '*invades you more when you're away*'. It is interesting to note the ways in which '*Al-ghurba*', '*haneen*' and '*being away*' are described as ailments, which Fairouz is able to heal, '*sedate*' and '*calm*' with her music. Bringing together notions of 'space' and 'place', 'absence' and 'presence', Amar's excerpt also introduces two important spatio-temporal concepts, '*haneen*' and '*Al-ghurba*', which will be discussed in the following section.

Haneen and Al-ghurba: Constant cravings and migration

Presence and absence, space and place, are key collaborators of the terms '*Al-ghurba*' and '*haneen*'. At times symbiotic, while at others mutually exclusive, the relationships between the concepts build and feed, intercept and repel. '*Haneen*' is an affective circumstance, but it is not an essential consequence of '*Al-ghurba*'. Being in '*Al-ghurba*' does not necessarily lead to '*haneen*' and, similarly, expressing '*haneen*' does not mean one is in '*Al-ghurba*'. However, participants in this study tended to use the two together, expressing their '*haneen*' in view of being in '*Al-ghurba*'. To better explain these terms, it is necessary to draw on Peter Blickle, whose exploration of Heimat, the German notion of homeland, puts into discussion notions of belonging from the perspective of space. In order to be able to position this belonging, there needs to be an acknowledgement of non-belonging, or *Entfremdung*, roughly translated from German to mean 'alienation', which, according to Blickle, 'already has a spatial aspect'.[24] The same could be said about the Arabic term '*Al-ghurba*', which translates as expatriation, or '*absence from one's country*', and also has a 'spatial aspect' to it. To live in '*Al-ghurba*' means to live away from a geographical location that is familiar to you, to live 'abroad'. It is a spatial shift. It is 'absence' from 'presence', and a movement to 'space' from 'place'. '*Gharaba*' means 'to depart, to go away, to leave'. It is a movement in space 'away' from something. To say that someone had '*gharaba*' is to say that they left or departed, from the point of 'presence' to one of 'absence', from 'place' to 'space', from 'here' to 'there' or 'somewhere'. '*Al-gharb*' in Arabic can be translated to mean the West, and '*Tagharaba*' means to emigrate or immigrate, while '*Gharrab*' means to go West, or to the Occident. '*Al-Mughtarib*' or '*Mughtaribeen*' describes someone or a group of people who live in '*Al-ghurba*', who have emigrated. In some cases, '*Mughtaribeen*' classifies the Arab diaspora. '*Al-ghurba*' can also be translated as 'alienation', '*ghurba*' or '*ghareeb*' translates as 'foreignness' or 'strangeness', and '*ghurbiyé*' means foreigners. This lexical discussion on '*Al-ghurba*' helps to understand the way the term shapes and moulds and is significant in the discussion of Fairouz and the Arab diaspora, since to live in '*Al-ghurba*' has connotations of 'alienation', 'foreignness' and even 'strangeness'. '*Al-ghurba*' is always an arrival from a point of departure.

In discussions with participants, many referred to '*baytuna*'/'*bayti*', our/my home, or '*baladna*'/'*baladi*', our/my country, or '*watanna*'/'*watani*', our/my nation, or even '*dayi'tna*'/'*day'ti*', our/my village. Those were mainly talked about in the past tense, '*kan*', from the perspective of living in '*Al-ghurba*'. Positioning themselves this way thus demonstrates a spatial difference from '*bayti*', '*baladi*', '*watani*' and '*day'ti*', which not only defines participants spatially but also temporally, since they are launching from the point of '*Al-ghurba*' and from the present. In this way, '*Al-ghurba*' becomes an affective space, one in which self-reflection and contemplation occur with the assistance of the mnemonic imagination. It is an examination not only of space but also of the 'self', as Blickle contends, 'The interrelationship between a sense of self and the perception of one's world is a central aspect in the formation of a sense of Heimat.'[25] While there will be a deeper discussion on Heimat in the next chapter, it is the conversation between the 'self' and 'the perception of one's world' which is significant here. More specifically, it is the positioning of the 'self' within the space of '*Al-ghurba*'.

In *The Suffering of the Immigrant*, Sayad provides a key discussion on the term '*elghorba*' and the trajectories that form its existence. The spelling of '*elghorba*' and '*Al-ghurba*' differs here because of the Arabic dialect in which it is pronounced; however, the two forms have the same meaning and are to be taken as interchangeable. While Sayad focuses primarily on Algerian migration to France, tracing the political, economic and sociological implications of emigrants/ immigrants, his book provides insight into ways in which migration needs to be examined. His explanation of '*elghorba*' is especially important. For Sayad, 'The entire discourse of the emigrant is organized around the triple truth of *elghorba*'.[26] Traditionally:

> *Elghorba* is associated with 'sunset' and 'darkness', with going away and isolation (amongst foreigners, and therefore exposed to their hostility and scorn), with exile and fear (the fear inspired by night and the fact of getting lost in a forest or a hostile natural environment), with being lost (because you have lost your sense of direction). . . . In the idealized vision of emigration as a source of wealth and a decisive act of emancipation, *elghorba*, intentionally denied in its traditional meaning, tends (without completely succeeding in doing so) to bear another truth which identifies it, rather with happiness, light, joy, confidence, etc. The experience of the reality of emigration dispels the illusion and re-establishes *elghorba* in its original truth. It is the entire experience of the emigrant that oscillates between these two contradictory images of *elghorba*. (Sayad, 2004, p. 26; emphasis in original)

'*Al-ghurba*' can thus be seen as situational, dependent on the background and contexts of participants and, more specifically, on their *meta-* and *micro-habitual* conditions. As Mahmoud Darwish writes, 'Homeland is not always daylight and exile is not night.'[27] Incorporating both negative and positive attributes, it can be argued that '*Al-ghurba*' occupies a range of meanings. It is a state of affect, especially when coupled with the affective state of '*haneen*'. It is a point by which one reflects on their presence in one space and their absence in another. '*Al-ghurba*' is a mediation station, hostile towards an essentialist binary, as it is not just a physical state but also a spectrum of sensations. Through Fairouz's music, participants can situate themselves on this spectrum accordingly, consciously aware of transgressing set boundaries and also, at times, feeling bound by them. However, it is not only these intersections *across* spaces, which are important, but also *within* space, in private dwellings and domestic shelters. An active concept, 'space takes for us the form of relations among sites'.[28] It is idealized, revered and sought, imagined, created and desired. Space is one of the reasons for 'haneen', nostalgia, and craving, longing and yearning. It is *within* space that 'haneen' occurs, but it is also *through* space that it travels. It is important to note here that a key constituent of this research required the translation of texts and interviews, a task that was challenging on a number of levels. Translation is a contextual process, a 'bridging of the gap between meaning and being',[29] where fluency in language plays little part in its manifestation. To be able to translate thoughts and insights in a number of dialects requires knowledge of the cultural and social discourses surrounding the 'pre-thinking' and the 'temporality that precedes the thinking process'.[30] This is especially applicable in the cases of '*Al-ghurba*' and '*haneen*', which are not only difficult to translate, since they can mean so many things, but also rely on the *meta-habitus* and *micro-habitus* to contextualize both the 'pre-thinking' and the translation aspects of respondents' answers. Initially, the terms '*Al-ghurba*' and '*haneen*' (and their derivatives) were translated. However, for this section they will be kept in the excerpts as they illustrate how they can be shaped and moulded according to different settings:

> *Yes, it is bitter. I wish that, if we had a government, if all the Lebanese people there, all of them, are made to live in Al-ghurba, if they were just thrown into Al-ghurba in every country around the world, to taste its bitterness for a few years, so they can appreciate their lives in Lebanon, and see what it's like to be in Al-ghurba.*
> (Charles, 49, Lebanese, London)

> *In actual fact, most Palestinians I know . . . they like [Fairouz] not because of that Quds, Jerusalem, song, it's actually a bit funny because she, even when she says: 'Ya Tayr Ya Tayr Fo2 Traf el Dene',[31] they're out in the West, they've got families in their homes, so her songs, don't just. . . . We look at it as our songs, as Lebanese, but in actual fact, no; it is not. It is for all of us whose travelled. 3aysheen bel ghurbeh,[32] if you want, who suffered being away from their families, and what's important.*
> (Tarek, 36, Lebanese, London)

> *For the Mughtaribeen . . . [33][Fairouz] may give them haneen for their country, or she may reunite them. . . . When we used to sing in America, people would come to her and you would find them crying, telling her you brought back our haneen, you brought us back to our childhood, to when we were kids in our village. She reminds them of all these things, of course. People used to come and cry after our concert, we would finish our concerts and find people crying. When she sang to them live, people would lose control; even Americans came, not only Arabs, and all Arabs would come, from all religions and sects. Even at the Abu Dhabi concert, there were a lot of Lebanese, of course, but there were also a lot of Arabs who were living*

there, you would find her concerts, like wow, it just resonated so much with them.
(Viviane, 56, Lebanese, London)

Al-Mughtarib has an immediate haneen for Lebanon when they hear Fairouz. You have to think of her as though she was one of Lebanon's cedars. It makes you feel that you went back with your thoughts to Lebanon directly, back to family, friends, back to everything. (Rodger, 38, Lebanese, Doha)

When you're in Al-ghurba, you feel haneen for your country. So, you get more emotional when you listen to Fairouz's songs than if you were in Lebanon. It will affect you more because you are in Al-ghurba. The songs will mean more, it makes your heart bihanen[34] more; your emotions will duplicate when you are away from your country, it duplicates. (Karam, 39, Lebanese, Doha)

Fairouz means so, so, so much more to you, when you're in ightirab,[35] there's a secret, I don't know what it is. As much as I listen to Fairouz, when I'm in Lebanon, one or two days may pass when I don't listen to her, but when I'm abroad, even if I were on a trip, or vacation, or something, you feel like it is your duty, or it's a need, an emotional need, she is like a prayer. When I pray, I relax she is like a prayer. It's an emotional need for me to listen to Fairouz, in all my senses, so that I can rest, so that it puts out this haneen, this haneen for your country. (Amar, 39, Lebanese, Doha)

Sometimes, when you feel haneen, as I told you, a song for Fairouz reverts you back to your country, in that sense also, when you listen to her, you feel her, you feel your own emotions, you feel like this song targets your feelings, therefore, everything that addresses you becomes a part of you, and you become part of it, this is in general but, sometimes, the same song takes you to your country, it means that it's both ways, not just that it is only a means to remember your country, or your feelings of haneen, no, no, that's really important if this song reminds you of a certain event, a certain place, the smell of a certain place, like the odour of the coffee. These songs remind you of them, but sometimes you, as an Arab person, you feel like this song is sung for you, not for a certain event, but you react with the song, and the song reacts with you, so you are part of the song and the song becomes part of you. Sometimes you go and listen to Fairouz, you venture yourself into that place, in that song that is an entity, you subject yourself to it, you live it, you can feel the hunger of that bubble. This is one thing, and also it reminds you of your country. It reminds you of the haneen and everything. Those two things: in that sense, she's an arena of confusion. (Ferial, 46, Palestinian, London)

Yes. When we consider the separation factor and living in Al-ghurba, because I'll be missing my country, and my home in Lebanon. Sometimes, I also tear up if I listen to her songs in Lebanon, because I'm used to linking them with being in Al-ghurba. They carry the symbol of separation. So, even if I visit Lebanon for a month or two, and listen to Fairouz's songs there, she'll still evoke the feelings that I feel when I'm in diaspora. The meanings of her songs are very nice, but they are saddening for someone living abroad. I've been in London for 24 years, so I listened to Fairouz here more than I listened to her when I was in Lebanon. (Helene, 52, Lebanese, London)

When you listen to her in Al-ghurba, you get back the old feelings, the family feelings. You get back a feeling of haneen. Even though we go to Lebanon every year, but I don't stay in Lebanon more than a week or ten days in a year. (Ghassan, 45, Lebanese, Doha)

Listening to Fairouz in '*Al-ghurba*' '*means so so so much more to you*'. It is a '*more emotional*' experience, often resulting in '*haneen*'. Similar to the Welsh word 'hiraeth', roughly translated as 'homesickness' or 'nostalgia', or to a 'state of missing/craving/yearning', '*haneen*' is a difficult word to translate and explain in English, because there is no English equivalent. It is a porous term that continues to absorb socio-historical, political, economic and cultural elements in order to take on a subjective yet collective meaning. In this way, '*haneen*' is dependent not only on the *meta-* and *micro-habitus* but also on the position of participants within '*Al-ghurba*'.

In her chapter 'Worlding Refrains', Kathleen Stewart discusses the concept of bloom spaces, which she describes as 'all forms of attending to what's happening, sensing out, accreting attachments and detachments, differences and indifferences, losses and proliferating possibilities'.[36] This is a space in which there is expectation and potentiality, where affect can flourish in a variety of opportunities. In this way '*Al-ghurba*' and '*haneen*' can be seen as bloom spaces. Spectra within which vectors of individual and collective *micro-* and *meta-habitus*, subject positions and mnemonic imaginations intersect, '*Al-ghurba*' and '*haneen*' each occupy a bloom space of their own. As space and as feeling, '*Al-ghurba*' is '*bitter*', a place where respondents '*suffer from being away from their families*', but also it is within '*Al-ghurba*' that they are '*reunited*', able to make their living and, at times, to escape from political or economic strife. A space of security, but also one where '*I'll be missing my country and my home*', the Arab diasporan is 'unable to resolve the contradiction in which he [*sic*] is trapped'.[37] These bloom spaces are thus also contradictory spaces, '*haneen*' is something which can be happily '*brought back*' in the recounting of a Fairouz concert, but also it is an ailment, something which needs to be '*put out*' so '*that I can rest*'. Fairouz glides across these bloom spaces, evoking and comforting, arousing the mnemonic imagination and transporting participants both temporally and spatially. Fairouz thus stands as the opposite of '*Al-ghurba*', she is the familiar 'place' found within the bloom spaces of '*haneen*'.

Angry with his fellow compatriots, Charles, a hair stylist living in London, wishes the '*bitterness*' of '*Al-ghurba*' on them, blaming Lebanon and its government for his own status: living in '*Al-ghurba*'. A curse, '*Al-ghurba*' is the remedy Charles asserts to make '*all Lebanese people*' living in Lebanon '*appreciate their lives*'. For Tarek, a butcher who has lived in London for over twenty years, '*all of us who have travelled*' and who are living in '*Al-ghurba*' share the same common consequence of having '*suffered being away from their families*'. It is not only the Lebanese who appreciate Fairouz and her music, Tarek argues, it is also the Palestinians and '*all of us who have travelled*'. Tarek thus conjures a more forgiving and united collective. '*Al-ghurba*' becomes a state of being, one shared, regardless of nationality but as a result of movement through space. Viviane echoes this sentiment of communality. Describing a time when she used to perform and travel with Fairouz in concert, as part of the choir, Viviane describes the emotional response they would receive from the '*mughtaribeen*'. A uniting force, Fairouz and '*Al-ghurba*' would see '*all Arabs*' '*from all religions and sects*' come together. In this way, '*Al-ghurba*' does not distinguish between individuals but instead grasps them all. However, it is Fairouz within the space of '*Al-ghurba*', who gives audiences '*haneen*', something they cherish and for which they are grateful. This might be translated into nostalgia, or longing for '*country*', '*our childhood*', or '*when we were kids in our village*'. As bloom space, '*haneen*' provides an affective range, allowing participants to position themselves on multiple shelves of its active archive. For Amar, '*haneen*' is something she wants to '*put out*', something unwanted and uncomfortable, a consequence of '*Al-ghurba*'. It is something felt, which Fairouz is able to '*soothe*'. By listening to Fairouz, Ferial also '*feels*' '*haneen*' in a number of ways. '*Haneen*' is subjective, '*everything that addresses you becomes a part of you, and you become part of it*', and it is sensual '*the smell of a certain place, like the odour of the coffee*', temporal, '*a certain event*', and spatial, '*a certain place*'. Weaving her way through these elements, Fairouz opens up vents for memories, senses and emotions through which respondents '*venture . . . into that place*'. While Ferial is talking about a private and individual experience of '*haneen*', she is doing so *within* the very public and collective state of '*Al-ghurba*'. So, '*Al-ghurba*' and '*haneen*' merge here, bringing to the surface '*the hunger of that bubble*' which Ferial finds in Fairouz's songs. Ferial's journey through Fairouz's songs thus '*becomes a part of you, and you become part of it*'. The singer allows for an internal as well as an external '*venture*' of the 'self' in which Ferial is able to travel through the tunnels of '*Al-ghurba*', finding '*haneen*' on the way. The 'self' is thus linked to both '*Al-ghurba*' and '*haneen*'. For Helene, who also lives in London, listening to Fairouz, even when she is in '*my home in Lebanon*', may also lead her to '*tear up*', since '*I'm used to linking them with being in Al-ghurba*'. So even if she does not physically occupy the space of '*Al-ghurba*', she is still occupied by its state, since 'no matter how near you come, you will remain distant'.[38] It is not only participants who move *across* space, who are in '*Al-ghurba*', but it is thus also '*Al-ghurba*' which moves *within* them. Space then shifts beyond the borders of surroundings or the positioning of the 'body' within such surroundings. Instead, it is an etching of the self, a cognitive process and an affective state. This internalization of space into the self is also found with the notion of time. Ghassan, who visits '*Lebanon every year*', feels '*haneen*' when he listens to Fairouz in '*Al-ghurba*'. Technically able to freely move geographically and regularly, time, in Ghassan's case, is also a non-determinant of '*Al-ghurba*' and '*haneen*'. Being away for short or long periods of time does not affect '*Al-ghurba*' or '*haneen*', but, like Helene, it is the concept of being in '*Al-ghurba*' in the first place. '*Al-ghurba*' and '*haneen*' thus connect through the mnemonic imaginations of participants to compare and contrast, and to reflect, on spaces of 'absence' and 'presence'.

Space, affect and the unbearable state of 'Al-ghurba'

A spatial positioner and a point of reflection, Fairouz and her music allow for a contemplative journey through the relationships of place to space, absence to presence and 'Al-ghurba' to 'haneen'. Reinforcing the importance of space in discussions of the Arab diaspora and their relationship with Fairouz and her music, similarly to the mirror's functions in Foucault's analogy, Fairouz demarks participants' positions of where they are, but also where they are not. Bringing together notions of the 'body', 'self', 'place' and 'space', absence and presence, Fairouz is the crossroads at which the elements interconnect. However, these are not only physical standpoints but also cognitive and psychological ones. Affect and the mnemonic imagination collaborate with the intersectional qualities of the Arab diaspora, incorporating *micro-* and *meta-habitual* situations, to unravel the ways in which 'absence' and 'presence' function within the framework of Fairouz and the Arab diaspora. It is also in the individualized and collective deliberation of 'space' and 'place', 'absence' and 'presence' that 'Al-ghurba' and 'haneen' come into play. As both a spatial shift and a 'structure of feeling', 'Al-ghurba' and 'haneen' are affective states that find solace in Fairouz's songs. 'Al-ghurba', expatriation, is a movement away from somewhere familiar. It is a point from which one reflects on their presence in one space and their absence in another. 'Al-ghurba' is a mediation station, hostile towards an essentialist binary, as it is not just a physical state but also a spectrum of sensations. Through Fairouz's music, participants are able to situate themselves on this spectrum accordingly, consciously aware of transgressing set boundaries and also, at times, feeling bound by them. However, it is not only these intersections *across* spaces, which are of importance, but also *within* space, in private dwellings and domestic shelters. Space is an active concept. It is idealized, revered and sought, imagined, created and desired. Space is one of the reasons for 'haneen', nostalgia, and craving, longing and yearning. It is *within* space that 'haneen' occurs, but it is also *through* space that it travels. However, 'Al-ghurba' and 'haneen' are not clean-cut categories, they need to be seen as 'bloom spaces', or spaces with 'proliferating possibilities'.[39] They are both spaces of expectation and potentiality, where affect can flourish in a variety of opportunities. Fairouz glides across these bloom spaces, evoking and comforting, arousing the mnemonic imagination and transporting participants temporally and spatially. In this way, Fairouz stands as the opposite of 'Al-ghurba', she is the familiar 'place' found within the bloom spaces of 'haneen'. A source of comfort and familiarity within the 'bloom spaces' of the two states, Fairouz travels by way of the mnemonic imagination, catering to the emotions of her listeners, transporting them through space, but also anchoring them firmly within place.

'Dislocated' from the temporal and spatial boundaries with which she is associated, Fairouz's 'aura' becomes more affective and powerful. She forms a reflective space, providing the acoustics of belonging. For Palestinian participants, Fairouz transforms memory from a temporal experience to a spatial one. A reminder of a lost homeland, a 'proof of loss and lack'[40] her songs house past, present and future. She is able to recreate 'presence' in a time of 'absence', as well as provide 'place' within 'space'. Her affective connection with the 'body' allows for a 'reconfiguration' in space, one which is contemplative and mnemonic. She is both instigator and cure for '*haneen*', which is, paradoxically, mutually exclusive, but also deeply symbiotic with being in a state of '*Al-ghurba*'.

Chapter 6

VISUALIZING AN ARAB HOMELAND, NATURALIZATION, MOBILITY AND 'POWER GEOMETRIES'

While Chapter 3 of this book looked at impressions of homeland and nationhood in terms of identity and self-reflection, this section will look at homeland as a spatial and visual concept. In his book, Peter Blickle discusses the academic and social conundrum of trying to explain the term 'Heimat', the German notion of homeland. Outlining previous philosophical, sociological and literary work on the term, Blickle positions Heimat as 'a crucial aspect in German self-perceptions . . . it is the idealization of the postmodern within the modern; it unites geographic and imaginary conceptions of space; it is a provincializing, but disalienating, part of German bourgeois culture'.[1]

The closest Arabic equivalent to the term 'Heimat' would be *Al-Watan*. However, most research surrounding the notion of *Al-Watan* focuses on its political and religious history, rather than the way it is understood socially and culturally. Definitions of *Al-Watan* in academia do not bring out the sociocultural nuances of the word, nor do they showcase how it can differ among Arabic speakers from various religious and ethnic backgrounds. Depending on one's political positioning and ideology, *Al-Watan* may be replaced with *Al-Umma*, *Mawtani* or even *Al-Balad*. The term itself can be limiting in terms of expression and understanding, but through conversations with participants, this chapter will show how dynamic and discursive opinions of *Al-Watan* can free it from pre-existing notions that are rigid and inert.

In his comprehensive chapter 'Al-Watan and Al-Umma in Contemporary Arab Use', Said Bensaid traces the evolution of the terms *Al-Watan* and *Al-Umma* in ancient and contemporary political philosophy. In English *Al-Umma* translates to 'nation', 'people' or 'body politic', whereas *Al-Watan* translates to 'homeland', 'fatherland', '(home) country', 'native country' 'native land' or 'home'.[2] Referencing Arab thinkers and philosophers of the time, Bensaid writes that there are eight different ways, in which *Al-Umma* is used, from its religious connotations to one in which it defines a group of individuals. Whereas '*Al-Watan*' has a 'semantic field' that is 'much narrower' and is 'less frequently' used in 'ancient Arabic literature'.[3] Launching from Ibn Manzur's definition of *Al-Watan*, in which Ibn Manzur defines the term as 'the house in which you live, one's residence or native place; the home of sheep and cattle; the places where these animals lie down to rest', Bensaid highlights the use of term linguistically as an identifier of place for humans or animals.[4]

However, Bensaid argues that there is a major difference between the ways *Al-Watan* was used during Ibn Manzour's time and more recent uses of the term and its by-product *Wataniyya*, meaning patriotism. Contemporary uses are seen as more affective and imply 'the existence of linguistic, racial and cultural ties between different groups and individuals living in the same geographic area'.[5] According to Bensaid, this is especially true in cases of resistance against Ottoman rule, where Arab countries viewed the *Watan* as something to fight for and liberate. This is in line with Spinoza's notion of nation that seeks to overthrow 'monarchic power'.[6] Bensaid argues the Western understanding of the nation is rooted in ideas of revolution while its political discourse is linked to meanings like 'fatherland' and 'citizen'.[7]

Bensaid divides concepts of *Al-Watan* into three influential categories derived from political systems over time: nationalism, pan-Arabism and pan-Islamism. According to the author, these three movements shaped understandings of *Al-Watan* and showcased the way its meaning transformed historically and ideologically. A key contributor to the nationalistic perspectives of *Al-Watan* was Rifa'a at-Tahtawi, an Azhari scholar who witnessed the events of the nineteenth-century French Revolution. The *Watan* at-Tahtawi writes about is related to the 'home one was born and brought up [in]', but also he furthers the concept of *Watan* with 'many new notions, such as fatherland, fellow-countrymen citizen, patriotism etc'.[8] So although at-Tahtawi like Ibn Manzour links *Watan* to home and family as well as to 'land', 'soil', 'food' and 'air', he brings to surface new concepts that unite countrymen through language and common leadership. From here, the meaning of *Al-Watan* shifts to connote the need for protection and is also 'connected to nationalism and patriotism'.[9] In addition, notions of citizenship, identity and freedom are introduced, 'where one can live with dignity and respect'.[10]

With regard to the pan-Arab model, *Al-Watan* is trumped by *Al-Umma*.[11] So, while the nationalist perspective refers to *Watan* as 'a specific geographical area that constitutes the homeland of citizens bound to each other by legal and emotional ties',[12] the pan-Arab definition focuses on the ideas of 'league' or 'union',[13] and a 'dream of a single Arab state or Arab unity'.[14] This is a more conceptual version, the Arab '*Umma*' which hosts a 'group of provinces that share the same boundaries'.[15] Citing one of the biggest promoters of pan-Arabism, Jamal Abdel Nasser, Bensaid observes that Al-*Watan* plays a much smaller and less significant role to the much larger and prominent Arab nation. *Al-Watan* in this pan-Arab context is a tiny piece, a 'small fatherland' compared to the 'great fatherland'[16] or an Arab '*Umma*'.

According to Bensaid, the Islamic fundamentalist model focuses on comparisons between Western and Arab governance. Bensaid notes that thinkers and writers of this movement tend to view Occidental politics as superior to Arab politics. For Islamic fundamentalist thinkers, the West is progressive in its equal treatment of citizens as opposed to the more dictator-type rule of the Arab world. Bensaid notes that there is a more positive attitude towards Western forms of government in this model than those following a more pan-Arab path. He argues that Islamic thinkers believe European notions of democracy as being in line with and stemming from Islamic thought, especially in decisions related to 'progress and justice'.[17]

Bensaid's informative discussion of *Al-Watan* brings to surface semantic differences in meanings and understandings and how they have evolved over time. However, the discussion is positioned from a more political and historical perspective. The term *Al-Watan* here needs to move beyond its political meaning to take on a new role. Many authors have explored or described conceptions of *Al-Watan* in Arabic poetry and prose[18], but in this chapter we will see how members of the Arab diaspora visualize and understand the notion of *Al-Watan* through the lyrics of Fairouz. By linking perceptions of *Al-Watan* to those of Heimat, newer ideas on how the *Al-Watan* has transpired over time and space will be brought to light.

While Heimat is indisputably a German concept, with a host of sociopolitical connotations, Blickle's discussions on space, belonging and self-perception are extremely relevant in looking at ways in which homeland and motherland are understood among the Arab diaspora in this study. It is also a lens through which to contextualize *Al-Watan* and view the various ways in which its derivatives such as home, homeland, nationhood and motherland have meaning among members of the Arab diaspora. Even though Chapter 3 tackled the ways in which respondents perceived home in relation to the 'self' and linked it to constructions of self-identity, this chapter attempts to unpack the spatial associations attributed to 'home'. Blickle explains that German speakers 'tend to acknowledge at once that there is more than one Heimat', and while it is challenging to define the term precisely, they tend to associate Heimat with 'such terms as *self, I, love, need, body* or *longing*'.[19]

The perspective of Heimat as part of the body and the 'self' resonates with the affective angle from which 'home' was recognized by participants in this study, reminiscent of Sara Ahmed's discussion, in that 'the home is not exterior to a self, but implicated in it'.[20] Here, the internalization of 'home' is a link with understanding its presence in constructions of self. However, in this chapter, home takes on a more spatial meaning. Blickle explains Heimat is geographically dependent and can take on 'the form of the house where one was born and grew up', or 'one's literal native town' or even 'the country where one has grown up or at least lived for an extended period'.[21] These descriptions are similar to the ways in which Bensaid describes nationalist descriptions of *Al-Watan*.

The discrepancies in meaning show the complexity of trying to streamline the definitions of Heimat, similar to attempts at defining 'home' or *Al-Watan* among the Arab diaspora. However, 'home' can be seen as both an affective state and a tangible place. Portrayals of 'home' are not dependent on the term itself, 'home' cannot assign itself meaning, but rather, meaning lies in its projection through the active synthesis of the *meta-* and *micro-habitus*, aided by the mnemonic imagination. 'Home' is thus 'both a spiritualized province (a mental state turned inside out) and a provincial spirituality (a spatially perceived world turned outside in)'.[22] Through discussions with the Arab diaspora on the music of Fairouz, it became apparent that ideas of 'home', 'homeland' and 'motherland' did not fall into one category. Some participants expressed confusion about where their home was, others took ownership of the term and stated that 'home' was within them, something they carried around and could access whenever they wanted; and some respondents were sure of their 'home', they could define it geographically. It was either a place to which they wanted to return someday or somewhere they never wanted to live in again. Essentially, trying to divorce 'home' from the context of the participants is ineffective, especially among those in the Arab diaspora, who hail from diverse historical, cultural and socio-economic environments.

While I agree with Bickle that the 'idea of Heimat is emotional, irrational, subjective, social, political and communal',[23] I also want to add that this is not the case for all 'subjects'. This idealization or 'irrational wish-fulfilment' of 'home'[24] is a common staple among the Arab diaspora but not the only one. The 'shelterdness and harmony', Heimat and home provide, Blickle argues, are a contrast to 'modern experiences, such as alienating city life'.[25] Blickle draws on a number of philosophers and social theorists, for example Hegel and Giddens, to position Heimat as a response to modernization. For Blickle, it is a 'longing' for the 'pre-modern state', where 'anxieties about reason and the self, essence and appearance, thought and being did not yet exist'.[26] While Blickle discusses Heimat in relation to both pre-modernity (the desired) and modernity (the catalyst for desire), I would argue that post-modernity brings in an even deeper 'longing' for this 'pre-modern' state.

Defining 'familiar modern experiences' as 'urban alienation, the industrial workplace, the technologized mode of existence, mass politics and the nation state', which Blickle argues 'Heimat stands in contrast to', allows for an explanation into the appeal of Fairouz's songs.[27] In a post-modern era, defined primarily by globalization, mediatization and migrancy, reverting to Heimat is again a return to the pre-modern state. In this way, Fairouz provides the Arab diaspora with a link to the pre-modern through her lyrics. The lyrics of her songs also allow for sociocultural perspectives on *Al-Watan*. At times these perspectives were similar to the pre-modern Heimat and at other times, they showed specific attributes to a conceptualized *Watan*. Since a textual analysis of Fairouz's songs require translation through a contextual and symbolic lens, and are far too complex, the following excerpts from participants provide a significant perspective on the songs and lyrics which resonate with them the most:

> *I feel like she takes me back, she takes me back to my home, to my country, ya3ni my roots. For example, in one of her plays, she says . . . yay, this is the right answer to your question . . . there is a play called, Al-Mahata,*[28] *where there are two personas of Fairouz, talking to each other, one wants to leave and one wants to stay. The one that wants to stay says, 'Rja3eh 3a Baytik Rja3eh',*[29] *then Fairouz, who wants to leave, says, 'Leh ta Irja3, Ana Bayti Ma3i, Bayti Ma3i'.*[30] *This is in a song [she begins to sing]. And I think that's why I listen to Fairouz, I feel like my home is still present, it's still present, I feel like I don't have to go to Lebanon to feel this belongingness. My home is with me this is the feeling.* (Mona, 45, Lebanese, Doha)

I think of my mother's uncle, how he used to bring us birds to eat . . . they would go down and clean them and cook them. That drunkard who used to always drink Arak, like that, it took me, the mountains, the people, the way they used to talk. It always took me somewhere where I wanted to be, and where I wasn't. When I was in Jordan, it used to take me, all of us, even my father, for him, he knew the life of the village, the life of Lebanon. No matter where you are, she takes you without you feeling it, to the atmosphere, which makes you satisfied, and content, nostalgia maybe. (Carmen, 70, Palestinian/Jordanian, Doha)

Fairouz drives me crazy, because I am forbidden to see my parents. Fairouz – what do I want to tell you, Fairouz is the tannour bread, Fairouz is the village, Fairouz is Mom and Dad, Fairouz is when I pass by and the letters fall out the windows before I go to the army at midnight. You know what I mean. The days of love and childhood, I lived them with Fairouz. So this reminds you of everything. (Akram, 37, Syrian, London)

Whereas Fairouz sings about everything, she talks about roses, the sea, the moon, the waves, the thunder and lightning, about the village, a lot of things, Fairouz did mini operas and stories. She doesn't just sing about one topic. She takes me to the place she wants to take me to, or the song wants to take me. (Yassine, 70, Egyptian, Doha)

Fairouz embodies all these emotions, all these feelings that we have, and our faith in Lebanon, past and present. There's nothing about Lebanon that she did not cover, whether it was about the nature of Lebanon, the climate in Lebanon, the beautiful scenery, they all feature in her songs, the village life, we're talking about the values, 'Sini 3an Sini',[31] *when she sings this, 'Khidni w Zra3ni bi Ard Libnan',*[32] *'Ya Qamar Mashghara,*[33]*' this song is very important to me. When she sang it in Detroit, I'm from Mashghara!* (Walid, 65, Lebanese, Doha)

When I listen to 'Aatini El Nay Wa Ghanni'[34] *I get directly transferred to a different location, as if I'm sitting on a riverbed in Iraq. Fairouz is genuine, she has been a shelter. She is also the sounds of nature; the rustling leaves, the chirping birds, and the running water. Fairouz allows you to live a certain situation.* (Ali, 64, Iraqi, London)

For example, 'Li Beirut'[35] *makes me cry big time it's really saddening. It kills me . . . It makes me cry, because Beirut, for me, there is no distinction between Beirut and Palestine. I have Lebanese and Palestinian friends, for me, Beirut is an Arab city wrecked and ruined, although not like Baghdad and Damascus, but it is ruined several times, it's under the ash. When she says 'Ya Ramadi',*[36] *it's really sad what happened to our Arab world, and Beirut is a specimen of what happened to all the Arab cities, people still have the desire to live and love life, that's fine, but there's huge destruction, like the song says, exactly, the lyrics, the rhythms, the performance, everything. She also got a song translated from a foreign song called 'the morning after the carnival', I forgot its name in Arabic, when Fairouz sings that song, it's really heart breaking, Fairouz has really sad songs, but they do not depress you.* (Ferial, 46, Palestinian, London)

'Li Beirut': the reason I love that song so much is because it is the dream of what Beirut can be. It's the fantasy of what Beirut was, whether Beirut was that or not, it's a different matter. It's our fantasy. It's our fantasy of home, our dream of Lebanon reaching its full potential, and so these kinds of songs hold that for me. And then you have 'Yekhreb Bayt 3younik ya Alia Shou Helwin',[37] the reason is that this kind of hedonistic, gypsy reinterpretation of Ziad El-Rahbani just lets you feel this limitless possibility of wildness that the Lebanese can have, and I absolutely love the madness of that song. It's literally mad! When it launches, I just feel like this incredible kind of, letting go of anything constricting, whether it's a bra, or a belt, or pants, or shoes, you know? It all goes off; it's like this imagination of, a wild naked body leaping wildly. (Maha, 35, Syrian/Lebanese, London)

Even though she sang about the war, but if she didn't sing, the war was still happening on the ground, but in our heads, it was done. I was one of the people where Fairouz's war songs really allowed me to overcome the war. [She sings] 'Li Beirut men Albe Salamon li Beirut'.[38] She never swore, she never destroyed the image of Lebanon. Even in the midst of war she kept on engraving the beautiful images. 'Kubalon lil Ba7ri'.[39] She keeps this sincerity always. Sure, there are bad memories, but her songs really saved the war, which could have been much worse for our wellbeing. She was the hope. (Mona, 45, Lebanese, Doha)

I want to say that, again, it's the context she sang, of course songs about Jerusalem, which were beautiful and very moving in that context with those people, but even once in Beit Eddine, she just came up and sang 'Jeyi Ma3 el Sha3b el Meskin'[40] and I couldn't stop crying, because here is this woman speaking to us, you know? Just, standing there and just knowing what we were going through, and feeling what we were going through, and saying: I'm here for you, and she has no power. She has no influence, you know, she's nothing but just that, that empathy, that that was coming through, I mean. So, there's a lot of heke,[41] there's a magic to her live performance. (Maya, 46, Lebanese, Doha)

A lot of her songs 'Sanarja3ou Yawman',[42] 'Raji3oun',[43] and so on, which are, which are, well, of course, about Palestine. I'm not Palestinian, but it's somehow, it's about a lost homeland, which I feel I have lost in Lebanon, and so, and so they make me sad, ya3ni, generally speaking it's a mixture of pride, but sadness, it's not like pride that I would have liberated, it's actually quite the opposite. It's pride and surrender, but I have to also tell you that to surrender to sadness has been more recent in my forties, as I realized that there's so little we can do. In my thirties it was, a lot of 3enfouwan,[44] it was heke. I don't know how to translate that. There was more of a pushing forward and wanting to do something and, you know, we can overcome, and we can do it, so on. Um, but, I don't, no, I mean, I don't feel as much of that now. I feel more that I'm celebrating, a time that is paradise lost forever, and I'm grateful that I have something to document it in her songs, because I think that, that it is lost. (Maya, 46, Lebanese, Doha)

For me, Lebanon, it is my home. You know the song 'Watani'?[45] Yeah, this is it for me. Not just because I was born there, but also because it's my home. Wherever I'll go in the world, it's temporary, but Lebanon will always be the place where I belong and will go back to. When she sings 'Sanarja3ou Yawman ila Hayena'[46] I feel, yeah, I want to go back, or 'Watani Shou Bene Aam Ikbar wa Tekbar bi Albe',[47] yeah, it's true. The things I feel, I long for going back and staying in Lebanon. I feel like I'm living for the day that I will go back and live in Lebanon. I'm fine, I'm not stressed, but I live for the thought that one day, maybe tomorrow, a year after, or maybe ten, I am going to live in Lebanon, to be in my permanent home. She nourishes this feeling inside of me, that's true. (Bianca, 37, Lebanese, Doha)

I mean, she sang a lot about Al-Watan,[48] ya3ni, not necessarily Lebanon, but Al Watan in general, yeah, very, very. Zahrat Al Mada'in?[49] Is just amazing this song. Everything she sang to every country, which is beautiful. (Lara, 50, Palestinian, Doha)

She takes you to many places, back to your childhood, teenage years, love, betrayal, like this song about the village, 'Bayi Sakar il Bouwabeh wa Ana Natteyt Min Alshebbak',[50] for example, families from the village who know about these things, she draws the village for you, and the idea, it makes you imagine the scene and smile, it's something. It's of the highest standard, the highest level, 'sahl al momtane3'.[51] (Amar, 39, Lebanese, Doha)

'Kan il Zaman w Kan [Hanna il Sikran], fi Dukani bil Hay',[52] there was a sikran [drunk] guy in our old neighbourhood, he wasn't named Hanna, but I don't recall his name, but it really was like that, like a nice comfestive, where he was always drunk and where, there was like, that little shop, where the elders of the neighbourhood used to sit there, between the afternoon and evening prayers, joke with this drunkard and it literally takes me there. Yeah, Hanna il Sikran, it's amazing. (Jihad, 51, Palestinian/Jordanian, Doha)

Recently, now I listen to Fairouz and I would analyse the lyrics. I would say: 'What is she singing? Is it possible with this simplicity, she could have taken us, stolen us?' I mean, if you listen to the lyrics, her words are really simple, you feel like it's a diary. Someone wrote a diary and she sang it as songs. That simply, she stole our hearts. Maybe because of how simple it is, she captured us. Maybe because we are living with her, I mean how, I don't know, how everything in Fairouz's songs you feel like you are present in it. Like, yeah, you were sitting on a bench and the days pass by and the papers became yellow. And, yeah, this is what we are living now, and you fell in love with the neighbour's son and you stayed together in the house alone. She waited for him to get her a gift, and he got her a scarf, a ring. I mean, really very simple things, but we can't really talk about it like the Rahbani's did. So, maybe this simplicity that we reminisce about, that we miss, is what makes us more attached to Fairouz. (Nora, 37, Lebanese, Doha)

The imagery expressed in the lyrics mentioned earlier is similar to those used by Blickle in his discussion of the visualization of the pre-modern Heimat, 'alpine meadows; a rushing brook and a field in flower; the mill and its millwheel . . . with the miller's beautiful wife standing by; a grazing deer in the morning sun in a clearing in the woods'.[53] However, the *Watan* takes on a slightly different form. Images of the pastoral, of the 'villages', the '*mountains*', are juxtaposed with the '*sea*' and the '*moon*', a depiction of the Mediterranean landscape, which contrasts with that in Germany. The 'mill' is replaced by the '*tannour*', the 'chirping birds' replace the 'grazing deer' and the '*moon*' replaces the 'morning sun'. Perhaps symbolic of the '*moon's*' tempestuousness, these images of nature, coupled with images of resistance, are particular to the Arab world and its idealized homeland or *Watan*. What remains common 'is the longing for a specific, differentiated sheltering space'.[54] Whatever the differences in their perceptions of their *Watan*, participants make a distinction between it and the space they occupy in diaspora. Whether it is the desert landscape of Doha, or the cityscape of London, Fairouz offers her listeners '*shelter*', '*our fantasy of home*', making '*you satisfied, and content*'.

An example of how *Watan* is not always an idealization or 'irrational wish-fulfilment' of 'home', Mona, who lives in Doha, equates the subject of 'home' with the 'self'.[55] Through Fairouz's music, Mona is transported '*back to my home, to my country . . . my roots*'. However, using a scene from the play, *Al-Mahata*, in which Fairouz performs a monologue on the notion of 'home', Mona relates to the position of feeling '*like my home is still present, it's still present, I feel like I don't have to go to Lebanon to feel this belongingness, my home is with me*'. For Mona, 'home' forms a part of the 'self', and is identified through the music of Fairouz. Even though, temporally, Fairouz takes Mona '*back*', '*home is still present*', since '*my home is with me*'. Spatially, the inner belonging Mona feels is elevated through the music of Fairouz, but it still exists without it. Resonating with Sara Ahmed's discussion in that, 'the home is not exterior to a self, but implicated in it',[56] Mona in this instance does not feel the loss of 'home' or the 'discomfort of inhabiting a migrant body, a body which feels out of place, which feels uncomfortable in this place'.[57] Instead, she is able to rationalize 'place' to determine its existence within the 'body' and also to situate her own position within that self. In this way, *Watan* can be seen as linked to the body. It is something that is able to travel with participants and take on new meanings.

For Carmen, Fairouz occupies a different role, since she '*always took me somewhere where I wanted to be and where I wasn't*'. It is this conversation between 'absence' and 'presence' that differentiates Carmen from Mona. Carmen views herself within space, comparing where she was with '*where I wanted to be*'. It is this association 'with an inner emotional capacity to attach oneself with personalized memories of experiences to a place, a family, a specific landscape', which is characteristic of Heimat.[58] From her descriptions, Carmen alludes to a pre-modern *Watan*, complete with '*mountains*', '*the village*', the '*atmosphere, which makes you satisfied, and content*', and memories of her '*mother's uncle*'. The imagery of this Arabized, pre-modern *Watan* is broadcast through Fairouz's lyrics but is acknowledged through the mnemonic imagination. It is important to note that while individual experience may drive the mnemonic imagination, these images of the *Watan* are shared.

For Akram, in London, '*Fairouz is the tannour bread, Fairouz is the village, Fairouz is Mom and Dad, Fairouz is when I pass by and the letters fall out the windows before I go to the army at midnight'*. Again, through these examples, it is clear how this *Watan* can be seen as individual and collective. It houses family members and loved ones. It is a simple time, before technology, when secret letters would '*fall out the windows'*. It is an affective state of longing. A place that is deeply personal, but also reassuringly communal. This *Watan* is constructed centrifugally, through the familiar images Fairouz projects in the lyrics of her songs, to which the Arab diaspora is able to connect with, as well as centripetally, through the mnemonic imagination, which selects, links, filters and merges experience with landscape, loved ones and cherished moments.

The *meta-* and *micro-habitus* are key to both processes of construction, since they shape experience and determine association. Yassine's excerpt is less specific than Akram, Carmen and Mona's, in that he describes elements not specific to a certain place or space, but his reference to nature and landscape is one connected to simplicity and the pre-modern. It is Fairouz who drives Yassine. Relinquishing his own agency, Fairouz takes him '*to the place she wants to take me to, or the song wants to take me'*. While Yassine does not correlate the '*village'*, the '*waves'* and the '*moon'* to a specific place, Walid is deliberate in his descriptions. For him, Fairouz '*embodies'* the '*climate'*, the '*nature'* and the '*values'* of '*Lebanon'*. Walid's is an indisputable image of *Watan*, one he associates with '*Mashghara'* the village he is from. For Ali, in London, Fairouz transports him to '*a riverbed in Iraq'*. She personifies the pre-modern elements of nature, '*the rustling leaves, the chirping birds, and the running water'*. He describes the singer as a '*shelter'*, and as '*genuine'*. Ali brings back this notion of being genuine and authentic, something previously expressed by participants within the framework of identity, 'Arabness' and *iltizam*.[59] It is thus difficult to disassociate the sociopolitical climate of the *Watan*, since Fairouz's appeal is not only limited to one specific nation. This *Watan* comprises the romanticism of *iltizam*, but also the realism of its intercontextuality. Welcoming, yet resilient, peaceful, yet war-torn, hopeful, yet sad, this *Watan* is a contradictory 'sheltering space'[60] constructed through Fairouz's music and recognized by her listeners.

Best exemplified by the similarities and discrepancies found in the excerpts of Ferial and Maha, in London, and Mona, Lara and Bianca, in Doha, intercontextual *iltizam* is a component of *Al-Watan*, engrained in its mnemonic soil, connoting strength and power amidst the carnage and destruction. Each participant expresses a separate and affective understanding of Fairouz's songs pertaining to wartime, resilience and the '*Watan'*, which is intercontextual and established by both the *meta-* and *micro-habitus*. Ferial, a Palestinian journalist living in London, makes '*no distinction between Beirut and Palestine'*, and so Fairouz's song '*Li Beirut'* '*makes me cry big time'*. As '*an Arab city wrecked and ruined'*, it is '*a specimen of what happened to all the Arab cities'*, a reminder of the destruction in the region, this *Watan* bears the grim realities of war and violence, but also it is a contradictory backdrop to the '*people'* who '*still have the desire to live and love life'*. For Maha, a Syrian/Lebanese social worker, who also lives in London, '*Li Beirut'* is '*the dream of what Beirut can be'*. It is a '*fantasy of home'* and the '*dream of Lebanon reaching its full potential'*. A song released during the Lebanese civil war,

'*Li Beirut*' is a visually poetic piece about the beauty and consequent destruction of Beirut, lyrically patriotic, maternal and filled with detailed imagery, it is a song about perseverance, loyalty and overcoming devastation. As a '*fantasy of home*' Maha alludes not just to the beauty of landscape but also to the ability, and the '*full potential*', of coming together to rebuild and restore.

Al-Watan is about nationalism and resistance, but also about community and unity. Maha further describes the affective state of *Al-Watan* by highlighting the '*limitless possibility of wildness that the Lebanese can have*', one that is unrestricted and confining, '*this imagination of a wild naked body leaping wildly*'. Amidst the sadness, *Al-Watan* harbours '*limitless*' joy and the capacity for '*letting go*'. In addition to showing the potentiality of the Arab world to move on and persist, Fairouz plays a role in maintaining the '*beautiful images*' of landscape for her listeners. Mona, in Doha, explains how, even through the ugliness of the war, Fairouz '*never destroyed the image of Lebanon*'. A forgiving figure, who '*keeps this sincerity always*', Fairouz '*was the hope*', which allowed Mona '*to overcome the war*'. By not tainting '*the image of Lebanon*', Fairouz was not only able to preserve it but was also able to project it in its ideal, affective form, '*sav[ing] the war*', and, in parallel, '*our wellbeing*'.

Fairouz's '*sincerity*', expressed by Mona, was also something Maya touched upon. Maya, who has seen Fairouz live in concert on more than one occasion, and has '*never been able to make it through a whole concert without crying at some point*' for '*different reasons*', explains how the context of hearing the music of Fairouz in diverse spaces is significant in producing various forms of affect. An example she gave was watching Fairouz in Amman, '*years ago*' when it was '*the first time . . . after the Palestinians of 1948 could come*'. Attending the concert with Palestinian friends, Maya '*was soaring with pride*'. Hearing '*songs about Jerusalem*' in '*that context with those people*' was '*very moving*'. Indicating the inclusivity and *iltizam* of this *Watan*, and further highlighting its position in relation to the Palestinian cause. The second example Maya gives demonstrates the '*empathy*' of this communal state. During a rendition of '*Jeyi ma3 el Sha3b el Meskin*'[61] by Fairouz in Beit Eddine, Maya '*couldn't stop crying*'. Moved by the lyrics, but also by the stance of '*this woman speaking to us*', Maya describes Fairouz as a voice for those who have suffered, and continue to suffer, but also as someone who remains loyal and compassionate throughout hardships, even though '*she has no power*' to change anything. It is this consistency among the turbulence of the region that connects Maya to Fairouz, one enveloping those who suffer and also those who resist. Maya does not allude to only one nationality for whom this is the case, but, rather, she is more comprehensive of those who fall under the category of '*Sha3b el Meskin*'. It is an all-encompassing idea of *iltizam* and *Watan*, which transgresses the borders of nations to incorporate a regional form of solidarity. However, this is not a shared sentiment and, as previously mentioned, *iltizam* among participants has been more '*intercontextual*', dependent on the *meta-* and *micro-habitus*, and the intersectional qualities of the Arab diaspora in this study. It is therefore necessary to discuss Maya's second excerpt, with that of Bianca's, to show how the interpretation of the song '*Sanarja3ou yawman*' – we will return one day – positions the respondents in terms of '*Al-Watan*', but also brings back to the surface *iltizam* and its intercontextuality.

For Maya, '*Sanarja3ou yawman*' is '*of course about Palestine*'. Even though Maya is '*not Palestinian*', the song resonates with her because it is '*about a lost homeland*', which she feels she has '*lost in Lebanon*'. Maya's relationship with the song has changed between her thirties and her forties, from a '*pushing forward and wanting to do something*' to '*surrendering to sadness*'. It is through this '*surrender*' in which Maya '*celebrates*' a '*paradise lost forever*', feeling '*grateful*', since she has '*something to document it in her songs*'. *Al-Watan*, here, is '*lost forever*', but still lives within Fairouz's songs. The singer can thus be seen to '*document*' the existence of such a place, where Maya can find solace and '*surrender to sadness*'. Maya's intertwining of Lebanon and Palestine is significant, as it highlights how *Al-Watan* internalizes a regional sense of loss, but also a '*grateful [ness]*' at having existed, and continuing to exist, in Fairouz's songs.

Bianca's interpretation of the song shows a narrower and more individualized form of homeland, which is very much linked to boundaries and a specific *Watan*. Bianca's relationship with '*Sanarja3ou Yawman*' is reflective of the '*long[ing] for going back and staying in Lebanon*'. It is a hopeful projection of the future, but also it highlights how the song is understood by Bianca to be about a specific '*Watan*' – Lebanon – and does not possess the regional inclusivity described by Maya. Bianca is certain of her '*home*' and '*Watan*'. It is a point of return for her, '*where I belong and will go back to*'. Fairouz thus '*nourishes this feeling inside of me*', one that promises '*to live in Lebanon, to be in my permanent home*', and so connects Bianca to a specific place. It can be argued that this lack of *iltizam* beyond the borders of '*Al-Watan*' is a result of the perception of the *Watan* and how subjective experiences can dictate perceptions and identifications. It is, however, also dependent on factors arising from the *meta-* and *micro-habitus*. Lara, who also lives in Doha, strengthens this argument, since in her mind, the '*Watan*' Fairouz sings about is '*not necessarily Lebanon*'. Intercontextual *iltizam* is thus also something, which affects and is affected by the concept of *Al-Watan*, to position participants in both space and place.

This centripetal and centrifugal consumption and projection of Heimat by Blickle is relevant to the conversations of Amar, Jihad and Nora, but it is important to add the role of the mnemonic imagination in generating a 'spiritualized province' and a 'provincial spirituality'.[62] Through personal and popular memory, participants are able to vocalize elements of an Arabized Heimat or *Watan*, which they have accumulated through both 'individual and social elements of experience',[63] those which they have lived through themselves, and also those which have been told to them. Amar relates Fairouz to her past, since she '*takes you to many places, back to your childhood, teenage years, love, betrayal*'. Fairouz triggers the lived experience of this *Watan*, but also creates an idealized environment, '*she draws the village for you, and the idea, it makes you imagine the scene and smile*'. It is this double mechanism through which Fairouz is able to draw on the 'personal memory' of participants, as well as conjuring scenes of a more 'popular memory' to build an individualized and communal notion of *Al-Watan*. Similarly, Jihad remembers elements of his '*old neighbourhood*', with a '*drunk guy*', and '*that little shop, where the elders of the neighbourhood used to sit there, between the afternoon and evening prayers, joke with this drunkard, and it literally takes me there*'.

By narrating the scene, Fairouz is able to visually project images Jihad recognizes and to which he can relate, images he has seen in his past, but also scenes particular to Fairouz and her songs. It is this familiarity that Fairouz provides, a malleable space in which both 'personal' and 'popular memory' coalesce and are reconstructed to form a *Watan* that respondents access through their mnemonic imagination, but also long for to exist. Nora defines the lyrics of Fairouz as '*simple*' and like a '*diary*', private and social, Fairouz allows her listeners to be the actors against the backdrop she provides: '*everything in Fairouz's songs you feel like you are present in it*'. It is this '*simplicity that we reminisce about, that we miss, is what makes us more attached to Fairouz*'.

A pre-modern *Watan*, which is both familiar and desired, Fairouz broadcasts imagery associated with 'home' and consequently the 'self', transporting her listeners to a place they acknowledge through their mnemonic imagination, but also one in which they will always aspire to live. Fairouz stands with participants in recognizing the advancement of the *Watan* into the post-modern, she is temporally there to reflect on a past and on a pre-modern state. Through her songs, Fairouz provides conversations on *Al-Watan* that move beyond its political and historical definitions to incorporate individual and social narratives. *Al-Watan* is somewhere and nowhere, it is the fictional and the real, it is violence and beauty, it is inclusivity and exclusivity, it is surrender and resistance, and it is a contradiction of the lived and the imagined.

Fairouz as a gendered 'figure': Temporal mobility

The women in this study offered a wide trajectory of ways they connected to Fairouz and her music. Examining the role Fairouz played among respondents, without focusing on gendered implications surrounding her position as an artist or through the consumption of her music, would thus be to ignore an essential aspect of the singer's place among them. Through her music, Fairouz gives a peek into the gendered public and private lives of the Arab diaspora living in London and Doha. Interweaving with their various intersectional qualities, Fairouz allows for a more comprehensive understanding of gendered experience, highlighting differences and similarities between participants, and offering a socio-historical context in which to understand them:

I think she's a stateswoman, she is an ambassador, she's elegant, she's proud, she's talented, she is beautiful, she has a stunning voice, she commands respect in her music because she has been playing for so long, she's somebody that I'm proud of, she's a role model for me. She's a talented, educated, enigmatic woman. She commands the respect of people and I think she's a good role model for women from the Middle East. This is going to be controversial. I'll tell you that for me I just get so upset by, you know, all the religion and the oppression [that] religion causes in the Middle East, and the sexism that's imposed on women, and I know that Fairouz is a Christian person, so she has a certain amount of freedom over Muslim women, and I get that's controversial. But I think she's a wonderful role model, and she makes me . . . she's one of the few people that makes me proud because she's such an amazing role model. She is focused on her music. She is very serious about her music . . . she hasn't had to sell her body like, say, Haifa Wehbe.[64] *I think that Haifa has sold her soul to the devil and that to her what's important is the way she looks.* (Jana, 48, Palestinian/Syrian, London)

This woman [Fairouz] is just a symbol of patience, a symbol of nationalism and of good motherhood, and as much as I would say, there are many people who are appreciated, but I think, I think she is underappreciated, because people, when they listen to her songs, they don't go into, they don't discover her, and I think that's so important. (Tania, 20, Palestinian, Doha)

She's a strong woman. As a woman, as an Arab woman, with such a powerful talent, powerful; and that's always it, isn't it? As for little girls growing up, she was a role model, the role model of doing art, but at the same time being modest and humble. I've, never seen Fairouz dressed up in a normal outfit, you know, she's always very slightly formal. Yeah, maybe for some people she is maybe slightly boring, I do not know, or just too serious; she is very serious. Her voice, my God, like, look at this woman. (Tala, 41, Libyan, London)

Essentially, the attributes given to Fairouz by the women are associated with her strength and commitment to her art, but they also specifically highlight her virtue and lack of hyper-sexualization. Complementing these qualities, Tania, a medical student living in Doha, asserts Fairouz is also a '*symbol*' of '*good motherhood*'. This falls in line with Christopher Stone's observations when he describes Fairouz as having the 'qualities of Virgin Mary-like chastity onstage and domestic maternity offstage'.[65] However, while Stone argues this persona bestowed upon Fairouz is in line with 'the role of women in postcolonial nationalist projects',[66] in this study, respondents classified the singer as a '*stateswoman*' and '*an ambassador*', someone they felt ideally represented Arab women. To interject Stone's argument is important here, since Stone tries to bind Fairouz to a certain space and time, absolving her of agency and keeping her locked in a 'post-colonial nationalist' vacuum, away from geopolitical and social vicissitudes. Fairouz as a 'figure' of 'embodied histories and politics' is subject to change.[67] Fairouz, as a 'figure', allows her audience to embed meanings unto her and, as previously discussed, her silent public life gives room for her listeners to '*imagine her the way we want*'. She is also able, as a 'figure', to 'take up positions', but these do not remain stagnant, she evolves to encompass a plethora of contexts at both the individual and collective levels. Her comprehensive appeal may lie in her dedication and somewhat conservative nature, but it is not the only reason. For Jana, Fairouz is situated as '*a Christian person*' who has '*a certain amount of freedom over Muslim women*' via her gender, Fairouz thus provides insight into differences among the women recruited for this study, highlighting the various positions they occupy within space and the *'freedom'* they are allocated within it. Through difference, Fairouz creates a discourse of 'othering'. One that lies in contrast to *'the oppression religion causes in the Middle East, and the sexism that's imposed on women'*. She becomes an admired 'other', associated with 'respect and engagement'[68] rather than one aimed at 'creat[ing] boundaries'.[69]

In her discussion on *Space, Place and Gender*, Doreen Massey contends that examining 'geographical variations' allows for an analysis of 'differences among women (and, indeed, among men)', showing their 'construction as gendered people' and also 'the way in which they relate to particular struggles, including those around gender itself'.[70] For Massey, ignoring gender in discussions of space provides an inaccurate and curtailed conversation, and neglects key perspectives on 'the ways in which gender is constructed and understood in the societies in which we live'.[71] However, comparing genders in any given geographical space without analysing participants' intersectional qualities and the contexts surrounding them is equally unproductive. The 'othering' of Fairouz, in this instance, thus highlights not only the 'differences among women' but also 'the way in which they relate to particular struggles, including those around gender itself'.[72] It is this heterogeneity among participants, their 'particular struggles', which surface in discussions of Fairouz as a female artist. There is also a temporal element within space, which is difficult to eradicate. Even though, in the excerpts mentioned earlier, Jana, who lives in London, brings up Fairouz's religion as a factor in her *'freedom'*, or movement in space and in other parts of her interview, Tala, who also lives in London, shows how Fairouz charts women's situations during a certain time in a certain place:

[Fairouz] creates this, again it's the nostalgia, and maybe of the time when there was hope for the Arab world, you know, maybe a time when we were a modern culture. Now, go to Syria, go to Jordan, but Lebanon is still in touch with a modern-ish, a bit more liberal, world. Um, but now you have people saying it is haram[73] to listen to music.

We used to sing and dance religious songs, now that is all haram. It is all haram. And how can you live in a world where you want to silence people singing, and you want to silence people from playing a musical instrument, or silence them not to write poetry, or cover up a woman and not let her have a right to work or to travel on her own. . . . Every Libyan woman my age has had an education. We cannot say thanks to Gaddafi, but now, post-Gaddafi, if I walk down the streets in Libya, they are all going to be checking my boobies. I am covered everywhere else, but my hair is not covered, so I become a target for rude remarks or harassment; and they are now stopping Libyan girls at the airport, 'Who is your wali?'[74] 'Where is your permission to travel?' It is disturbing, very disturbing. (Tala, 41, Libyan, London)

Tala's excerpts detail an increasingly religious atmosphere in Libya, where women's movements across space are policed and monitored, something she links with those who '*want to silence people singing, and you want to silence people from playing a musical instrument, or silence them not to write poetry*'. For Tala, Fairouz acts as a historical continuum of women, chronicling how their role within Libyan, or Arab, society has changed, and offers a '*nostalgic*' glimpse of a time '*when we were a modern culture*', one which was neither dictated by extreme religion nor oppressive to women. This again raises the concepts of the *meta-* and *micro-habitus*, and their importance in providing a dynamic geo-historical framework within which to analyse and assess collective and subjective diasporic experience. Through Fairouz and her music, Tala is able to trace the journey of women in Libya and other parts of the Arab world affected by religious fundamentalism, and its repercussions for their mobility and development, where they now '*cover up a woman, and not let her have a right to work or to travel on her own*'. Essentially, Fairouz is able to highlight issues as a result of the *meta-habitus*, through discussions of the *micro-habitus*, showing how fluctuations in the *meta-habitus*, such as changes in government regimes, or an increase in Islamic fundamentalism, can impact on those of the *micro-habitus*, like the position of women and their ability to navigate their new environment. Tala's example also sheds light on the ways in which movements across geographical locations are dependent on the *meta-* and *micro-habitus*. For example, in Qatar, female participants interviewed for this study were all there because either their husbands or their fathers had migrated for economic or political reasons. This does not mean, though, that the women did not go on to pursue careers for themselves, but that their movement and placement across geographical space was orchestrated by male family members or spouses.[75]

In London, the situation of female respondents was evenly divided. Of the twelve women recruited, half had come to the English capital to continue their higher education, or for job opportunities, while the other half also travelled with husbands or fathers. Migration, movement *across* spaces, can thus be seen as a gendered phenomenon. As Doreen Massey contends, 'space and place, spaces and places, and our senses of them (and such related things as our degrees of mobility) are gendered through and through'.[76] However, while the concepts of mobility and movement are extremely important in discussions of gender and the Arab diaspora, especially in the context of naturalization, mobility is not a topic that is only reserved for women, but also for men. As David Morley contends, 'borders mean very different things, depending which side of them you stand and how easily you can cross them'.[77] The following excerpts bring to the surface further notions of mobility and naturalization, and the ways in which borders, gender and citizenship blend in discussions on Fairouz:

> But my ticket to freedom is my passport, I go back [to Qatar] for big funerals and big weddings, but it sort of ends up, almost once a year sometimes. Now you know it's going to be. . . . If I don't go this Christmas, it's going to be two years [that I haven't been back]. (Mariam, 32, Qatari, London)

> I never had, like, the dream of migrating, having a new passport and stuff like that. So, I've never struggled with it, to a certain extent, but I didn't have it as, like, a

dream, like 'ouf, ouf' I'm gonna change my passport, 'this is gonna be great'. If it happens, it happens, it's a good thing. If it doesn't, I don't think . . . I don't think I'm keen, like, in the sense that everybody would want to have a new passport. It would ease my life. (Leila, 30, Moroccan, London)

Yeah, so it felt strange getting a British passport at the time, all of a sudden. Well, all of a sudden, I was formally a British citizen after formally being an Iraqi citizen for such a long time. Um, and that felt a bit strange. I didn't really enjoy it until I went to the US. Then I got a taste for travelling and freedom of movement . . . it's different when you get that passport, when you get a citizenship. You know you can just relax. You can move, and know you can come back. (Ahmad, 35, Iraqi, London)

So, every time I come here, I have fun with the immigration officers because they ask me questions. . . . As, why were you in Barcelona? However, we both got used to it because. . . . Yes, what can I do, I'm a Syrian refugee, and I'm legally staying here, but still they need to ask all these questions and I need to answer them. So, I've stopped being nervous about this matter. . . . I was always nervous about it, and they're always respectful and nice. I'm waiting for September of 2017. A year from now I'll be able to claim citizenship here. (Ayman, 34, Syrian, London)

I heard Fairouz when I was in Palestine. I visited Palestine using my British passport. I was visiting a friend of mine in Bethlehem. She's a widow, and her life is very hard. I was sleeping at her house. Every day she plays Fairouz's songs, while doing the dishes, on a small transistor that she places by the window. Her life is filled with sorrow and misfortune. Their situation is really hopeless, but Fairouz gives them hope. One day, when I was there, I woke up and a song for Fairouz was playing. I started crying so much, because I never heard her songs in that way and manner. Her songs meant more to me when I was in Palestine. They felt more powerful. I felt that her songs are for Palestine more than Lebanon. (Helene, 52, Lebanese, London)

I'll start university in September, but I still don't have the passport. The Home Office, they are not giving me the passport. [I've been here] for six years. . . . I applied for citizenship and I gave them my passport since 2014 and they haven't given it back to me yet. My brother got his passport back in seven days. My stepmother also got her passport back. My passport didn't come back, so I'm having to fill loads of applications, therefore, when listening to Fairouz, I'll have the 'whatever' attitude. I won't care about the rest of my problems. I'll want only, to live my life. That's why I listen to music, because if I don't listen, I'll keep thinking over and over again. Therefore, when I sometimes listen to her music in the morning, I get all these positive emotions. It will change my mood. I'll feel that it's a good day. (Kathem, 23, Iraqi, London)

I've been in Qatar for 40 years. In these 40 years, I left only for four years to Canada to acquire the Canadian citizenship. Fairouz accompanied me on all these trips. Fairouz left a great impact on me. From the day I started listening to music in my life; Fairouz has always been on the top of my list. (Marwan, 73, Lebanese, Doha)

While not all of the excerpts presented earlier are directly linked to Fairouz and her music, they are able to show the differences in movement through space of members of the Arab diaspora, whether male or female, and the ways in which citizenship plays into that motion. Essentially, these examples aim to highlight discrepancies between respondents to better understand the ways mobility among the Arab diaspora is dependent on *micro-* and *meta-habitual* factors. But also, they reflect the flexibility of occupying positions within space between Fairouz, who is seen to have '*a certain amount of freedom*', and her listeners. Two female respondents living in London, Mariam and Leila, offer different perspectives in terms of acquiring a British passport. For Mariam, a Qatari who holds a British passport, describes it as her, '*ticket to freedom*'. Being an '*unmarried Qatari woman*', Mariam's British passport is a method through which she is able to move unrestrictedly and to live and work without her family in the UK, even though '*it's not acceptable in [Qatari] society*'. While, for Leila, a British passport, '*would ease my life*', her current citizenship and status, as a single woman, does not hinder her movements across space. The experiences of the two women here should be put into discussion with Sayad, who devotes a whole chapter in *The Suffering of the Immigrant*, to the notion of 'naturalization', something he argues is 'tantamount to denouncing and renouncing one's nationality'.[78] Sayad's stance on 'naturalization' resonates with the notion of *iltizam* or as Mona Mikhail calls it, 'commitment as a test for authenticity'.[79] Sayad describes experiences of 'naturalization' as a form of 'double betrayal' among the Algerian migrants in his research, one which he describes as 'social and political', since, 'he has betrayed both his immigrant condition and his status as a national (i.e. his nationality)'[80] and is thus a shift away from the 'authenticity' found in definitions of *iltizam*.

In this study, 'naturalization' highlights the 'intercontextuality' of *iltizam* and the way it is manifested across the intersections of gender and citizenship. Although providing an insightful outline of 'a sociology of emigration and immigration', namely, that of Algerian migration to France, Sayad fails to recognize gender as a key 'trajectory' in attempting to 'understand the complete system of determinations, which having acted prior to their emigration and continuing to act . . . in the process of emigration, to their current point of arrival'.[81] This could be mainly because the migration he focuses on is that in which men travelled and the women followed. Sayad contends, 'women are not directly affected by naturalization'.[82]

The author goes on to position women's attitudes to 'naturalization' and nationality, mostly in relation to men and the private/public sphere, arguing 'the nationality of origin, or the nationality into which he [*sic*] was born, which he had left behind and rejected, used to be the concern of men, it now concerns women'.[83] Sayad categorizes this 'nationality of origin' as a 'female nationality', one which he describes as pertaining to 'the nationality of private and domestic life', whereas, the 'nationality that requires [immigrants] to take steps, either boldly and triumphantly or hesitatingly and in resignation, is becoming a male nationality'.[84] Although Sayad does mention women with 'masculine preoccupations, tasks and roles (either of necessity, as is the case with widows or women living alone without the support of any family or close male relatives, or as a result of an education that has led them to break with traditional socialization)' as being 'less opposed than men to their own naturalization',[85] emphasis or analysis is not placed on these 'preoccupations', nor on the 'freedoms' associated with naturalization across spaces. Bringing to light Sayad's argument in reference to the concept of intercontextual *iltizam* and the Arab diaspora in this study is important, and so it is necessary to place Sayad's thesis into a contextual framework, to allow for a stronger foundation from which to explain differences in migratory, diasporic and citizenship experiences.

Sayad's 'beginning' is very different to the 'beginnings' discussed in this study. By 'beginning', I refer to Tarik Sabry's definition, one he associates with a 'deterritorialization' and 'reterritorialization', and an engagement from 'a point of *différance*'. It is a way to analyse Arab culture through a 'relational/ conjunctional structure'.[86] Sayad's discussion of 'naturalization' must be looked at in its relation to the historicity and geography with which it is connected. His conversation stems from a colonialized and subsequently post-colonial, identity of Algerian migration to France, one of 'a double domination', from the historical – 'the colonizing country's dominance over the country that is its colony' – and a more 'contemporary' sense – 'the dominance of the country of immigration over the country of emigration'.[87] Attempting to nullify or diffuse the power structures embedded within this relationship of colonized/colonizer is thus to dispense with an integral point of analysis in this 'beginning' of migration and its attitudes towards 'naturalization'. It is as Sayad writes, 'to immigrate together with one's history' and 'all the other social, political and mental structures of one's society'.[88] Participants from London and Doha in this study differ from Sayad's samples, coming from a plethora of backgrounds and migrating under diverse circumstances from various trajectories of politics, economics, violence and sociocultural motivations. Trying to homogenize migratory, as well as 'naturalization' experiences, thus erases the necessary discourse through which to conduct such analysis. To draw on Hannah Arendt's analogy, 'To live together in the world means essentially that a world of things is between those who have it in common, as a table is located between those who sit around it; the world, like every in-between, relates and separates men at the same time'.[89] Ignoring sociopolitical and historical narratives in such a discussion would be to host these 'men' without a table – or chairs for that matter. It is to dismiss and disregard the needs and purposes of individuals in their migration, as well as to assume a hermeneutic of sameness. So while Sayad argues, 'Almost all those who have been naturalized have a fairly strong feeling of having excommunicated themselves',[90] he is essentially referring to specific forms of 'naturalization', which sees individuals of a previously colonized state conforming, or submitting, to the colonizing nation. It is both an internalized and externalized struggle for power in a case of 'double domination'.[91]

However, in order to continue this dialogue on 'naturalization' it is necessary to 'dislocate' and 'reterritorialize', to 'begin the process of connective creating; a kind of creativity that is conscious and assured of its own time and place'.[92] It can be argued that even with the host of power dynamics found within notions of 'naturalization' among Sayad's participants, incorporating their post-colonial identity, their internalized resistance to 'naturalization' bears relevance to the 'authenticity' and 'commitment' present within *iltizam*, but also it brings to the surface ideas of *hybridity* and *intercontextuality* found among members of the Arab diaspora in this study. This 'dislocation' thus allows *iltizam* to become 'intercontextual', as it accommodates 'new political expressions and new spaces of resistance'.[93] Drawing on Kraidy's concept of '*intercontextual hybridity*', which he describes as the 'mutually constitutive interplay and overlap of cultural, economic and political forces'[94] among diasporic communities, and merging this with the *meta-* and *micro-habitual* situations of respondents, offers a lens through which we can see how attitudes towards naturalization and citizenship are shaped and are able to influence the intercontextuality of *iltizam*. It is through both the 'deterritorialization' and 'reterritorialization' of *iltizam*, the 'dislocation' as well as the 'creative connectivity' that produces new forms of *iltizam* and drives its 'intercontextuality' that Mariam feels '*a massive cultural gap*' between members of her family in Qatar but still craves '*the humour of the Arabs, like the laughing through your eyes' nostrils*', when she is in London. However, it is her British passport that allows her to satisfy her '*friendships . . . with Arabs*', but also her '*extremely westernized*' sense of self, since she is able to move freely across geographical space. Her acquisition of a British passport ensures she is not stuck with 'the nationality of private and domestic life',[95] as it is not one with which she feels comfortable. The examples of Mariam and Leila give insight into the differences in social behaviours towards the mobility of women, which feed into their individual *meta-* and *micro-habitual* situations. Even within genders, among the members of the Arab diaspora, there are thus disparities in movement, which are evidenced through discussions on naturalization.

However, it is not only gender that is affected by naturalization. This ease of movement as a consequence of naturalization is also evident with Ahmad and Ayman, refugees from Iraq and Syria, who both live in London. The two men express movement across space that is possible, but that is hindered and cumbersome. Both examples show how *meta-habitual* situations, such as war and displacement, can upset the gender scheme of nationality, highlighting the emancipatory role of what Sayad calls, the 'female nationality', or 'the nationality of origin',[96] since it is one which confines and limits movement. Attaining 'male nationality'[97] thus becomes a necessity rather than an option, since it is the only means to reach freedom of movement. It is this flexibility of motion that affects the intercontextuality of *iltizam* and shapes perspectives on naturalization.

With this foundation, it is important to discuss Helene, Kathem and Marwan, who bring up Fairouz in discussions on mobility and naturalization in various ways. With her British passport, Helene is able to travel to Palestine to visit her friend and experience Fairouz in an atmosphere of '*sorrow and misfortune*'. A place that is forbidden due to her 'nationality of origin',[98] Palestine provides Helene with another backdrop against which to appreciate Fairouz's music, which takes on a deeper and more affective significance, '*I started crying so much, because I never heard her songs in that way and manner. Her songs meant more to me when I was in Palestine. They felt more powerful.*' The significance of travelling to Palestine in the realm of naturalization needs to be looked at affectively, in 'the organization of social and bodily space',[99] but also through the lens of intercontextual *iltizam* and the acquisition of naturalization. A cause that has been discussed at some length in this study, the plight of Palestinians under Israeli occupation is something virtually all participants talked about during their interviews. Almost as a rite of passage towards 'Arabness', the Palestinian cause is intertwined with notions of *iltizam*. However, and as mentioned previously, the ways in which respondents react and take position in relation to the cause are intercontextual. Listening to Fairouz in Palestine thus not only brings with it themes of naturalization but also shows affective defiance on a political and personal level. Helene's ability to occupy this 'social space' in Palestine is due to her naturalization. It is, in effect, a 'reforming' of 'bodily space' through the process of citizenship.[100] This links to Sayad, who writes, 'we present ourselves and are present through our bodies, and the body is the bearer of social identity: it is that identity', since this new body, this 'reformed body' (due to naturalization), acts as 'bearer of social identity' and 'presents' itself in a forbidden space.[101] So it is about not only the movement of the 'body' across 'social' space that is relevant but also the implications and connotations that exist within that 'body' and its relation to 'social space'.

With no passport for over two years, Kathem, a refugee from Iraq, is unable to travel. For him, Fairouz provides an escape, and '*I won't care about the rest of my problems. I'll want only, to live my life*'. Offering a different perspective from Ayman and Ahmed, Kathem is stuck due to his lack of naturalization. As someone who has lived in the UK for over six years, his 'body' remains stagnated as a refugee, it lodges a 'social identity' associated with a lack of power and belonging. A victim of circumstance – and *meta-* and *micro-habitual* situations – this 'body' remains motionless across space. Through her music, Fairouz is able to affectively '*change my mood*' and allow for '*positive emotions*' in a 'social space' that marginalizes, and is nonchalant about, the 'bodily space' Kathem inhabits.

While all the aforementioned examples are about naturalization in the UK, Marwan provides another opportunity through which to view naturalization in view of residing in Doha. Living in Qatar for over forty years, Marwan '*left only for four years to Canada to acquire the Canadian citizenship*'. Due to the country's strict citizenship laws, Marwan will never be able to apply for a Qatari passport. In addition, during the time of the interviews, non-Qataris working in the peninsula required an exit permit from their Qatari sponsor to leave the country.[102] Marwan's example sheds light on non-naturalization and controlled movements, the way 'bodily space' continues to remain 'foreign', incongruous and never fully absorbed into 'social space'. In his quest for naturalization in Canada, it is Fairouz who '*accompanied me on all these trips*'. Able to freely mobilize through her songs,

Fairouz remains part of the process of naturalization, accompanying participants on their journeys and giving them '*hope*' during times of '*sorrow and misfortune*'.

Power geometries and the domestic sphere

Notions of gender arise both publicly and privately in the diverse geographies and scattered abodes of Doha and London. While the previous sections have dealt with discussions on gender, movement and the public sphere, what Arendt[103] calls 'the common world', one of 'appearances', and 'politics', which 'relies on the simultaneous presence of innumerable perspectives and aspects', a space where 'being seen and being heard by others derive their significance from the fact that everybody sees and hears from a different position',[104] this section will focus on gendered diasporic experiences within domestic spaces, or 'the sphere of household and family.[105]

In the introduction to their book *The Domestic Space Reader*, Chiara Briganti and Kathy Mezei argue, 'Just as the home is affected by and replicates national and capitalist ideologies and agendas in microcosm . . . the social geography of the house itself charts the course of relations between sexes and classes'.[106] Similarly, Gaston Bachelard contends, 'For our house is our corner of the world', it is 'our vital space' which we 'inhabit' with 'all the dialectics of life'.[107] Trying to separate the private and public spheres is thus ineffective, since the private ultimately incorporates 'dialectics' from the public. This is especially significant in the discussion about those in the Arab diaspora. This section will examine the ways in which the *meta-* and *micro-habitual* situations of participants shape and affect relationships within the domestic environment. Namely, it will examine responses by married participants who describe their experience of Fairouz in the context of their homes, and in light of their spouses, since 'the house is a device for articulating differences and defining a hierarchy in the meanings one lives by'.[108] Beginning with Dina and Maha, two female respondents, both living in London and married to a Frenchman and an Englishman, respectively. The women offer an interesting perspective on gendered space, which incorporates temporal elements and intersectional qualities pertaining to the *meta-* and *micro-habitus*:

> *Julien would look at me and say: 'Man,' You know? And then I'll be putting music. I'll be coming to the kitchen and I start playing music and I start cooking. And he's like: 'Oh my God, she's going to do her thing again.' You know? It's maybe because I wanna retreat to a place where I can feel at home, and they can't make me feel at home. I have a home with them, but it's not the home that I left. I can't say that I'm mad about going to live [in Lebanon] now, but I'm a very passionate person who does all her work about Lebanon and the diaspora. (Dina, 42, Lebanese, London)*

> *On Sunday mornings, because my husband sleeps in, I will always, when I have a Sunday off, I will make my 'Rakwet Kahwe',[109] put my Fairouz on and sit down and sip my coffee and catch up on the news. It's like my little two-hour window of being me, you know? Nobody can touch that. That's a beautiful feeling. There*

was a period when this was being disrupted by my lovely stepdaughter, who's now twelve; she's not technically a teenager but in action, believe me, she's a teenager. She wants to wake up and the first thing she wants to do is just watch TV, so the living room, which was my area for doing my 'Rakwet Kahwe' and listening to my Fairouz, was suddenly taken over (laughs), you know? By, like, crappy teenage dance shows. I just felt like my space was being infringed upon, so we had to, like, have a negotiation of space, yeah! Because we'd literally race to who got there first to the living room. (Maha, 35, Syrian/Lebanese, London)

Providing an acoustic *'retreat to a place where I can feel at home'*, Fairouz creates a space within a space for the two respondents. For Dina, this space is a contrast to the *'home with them'*, *'them'* being her husband and two sons, who *'can't make me feel at home'*. It is an erratic, yet comforting, space, a place of pleasure and familiarity, a space opposite to her husband and children, where *'she's going to do her thing again'*. For Maha, this is a space, which provides a *'little two-hour window of being me'*. A space, which *'nobody can touch'*, it is a space which allows Maha to disconnect from immediate space and connect to another space that is more in line with *'being me'*. For both participants, Fairouz plays a part in the setup towards what is best described, literally and conceptually, as a 'dwelling place'. From his ontological discussion in, 'Building, Dwelling, Thinking', Martin Heidegger, writes, 'the basic characteristic of dwelling is to spare, to preserve'.[110] It is 'to remain at peace within the free, the preserve, the free sphere'.[111] This ability to 'preserve' and 'dwell' incorporates elements linked to past preferences and cultural familiarity. In their chapter, 'Children, Media as "Equipment" and Worldliness', Sabry and Mansour draw on Heidegger's concepts of 'Worldliness', as a 'totality in which media is constituent' and an 'ontological experience of being-in-the-world' and *'equipment'*, in order to examine 'the total system of *equipment* and practices which gives sense to the child's Worldliness'.[112] The authors explore how through 'equipment', such as media technologies and programming, children are able to 'extend' the 'spatial, the temporal and the imagination'.[113] Using these notions of 'Worldliness' and equipment, it can be argued that, with Dina and Maha, Fairouz offers such extension. As equipment, Fairouz is the soundscape of the 'preservation' of 'being-in-the-world', but also she is able to transport the women from their London flats to create a recognizable 'dwelling space', both away from and within it, spatially as well as temporally, she is a reversion back to 'Worldliness' through an acknowledgement of its existence in its current form. 'Worldliness' here is thus associated with lived and imagined experience, via the mnemonic imagination. Linking this to Sara Ahmed, who quotes the term 'dwelling place' with an affective conceptualization that brings in notions of 'attachments' and 'connections', we are able to understand 'dwelling place' in accordance with its spatial and temporal meaning.[114] It is 'what moves us, what makes us feel' which 'holds us in place or gives us a dwelling place'.[115] Fairouz as 'equipment' is that affective 'dwelling place', positioning participants in their diasporic environment while simultaneously guiding them across space and time. Through Dina's conversation, the ability to combine temporality with spatiality unfolds. Describing the '*home*' she is in as '*not the home that I left*', Dina compares past and present so as to situate herself spatially. Fairouz thus allows a recreation of the '*home that I left*' for Dina and provides Maha with a 'dwelling place' in order to preserve '*being me*'. The women define a specific role that Fairouz plays in crafting and maintaining a sense of space and time, which is recognizable and reassuring for them amidst another space and time, which does not provide the same sense of 'dwelling'.

These examples also show the ways Fairouz is able to feminize space, an excursion back to 'female nationality' within the masculine context of migration and subsequent 'masculine nationality'. Migration is best defined as a masculine process, one associated with political and economic factors. It is, as Sayad describes, a 'weaning from the mother-society'.[116] These responses within the private sphere can thus be seen as 'microcosms' of the public sphere, based on 'opposition' and power relations.[117] However, what these instances also show is a cultural, linguistic, behavioural and spatial disconnection between the women and their spouses, which is evidenced in further discussions with participants:

The other connection, and probably the reason I have that poster [of Fairouz] at home as well is, there's a language, a kind of cultural language I speak, that no one in my family here in London speaks. My family in London consists of my husband, who's English-Italian, and his parents, who are English and Italian, and my stepdaughter, who's English-French. So, there you go. And so, for me, this is my connection in terms of the Diaspora; it's Fairouz and the songs of Fairouz and the image of Fairouz, which they don't understand, they don't understand it. I wouldn't put it past my husband. I'm sure he's said it at one point. Waking up on a Sunday morning, listening to me listening to Fairouz and saying, 'what is this racket?' I wouldn't put it past him, and I wouldn't be surprised, if he had said it already, because he wouldn't understand her, he wouldn't understand her. (Maha, 35, Syrian/Lebanese, London)

Yeah, I do tear up easily [when I hear Fairouz's songs]. Maybe because I miss my mum a lot, and my brother I do miss home a lot, and I do live with foreigners. I mean my family doesn't have my background. They do understand me a lot, and my husband loves it, where I come from and everything. He knows me now very well, but still, sometimes he tells me 'I don't know what I can tell you, I really don't know what to say.' (Dina, 42, Lebanese, London)

There was one specific song that resonates, and it was 'Dakhilik ya Emme Medre Shu Bene, Trekini Bi Hamme Ziha'ni El Deni',[118] or something, and it was just, it wasn't . . . I don't remember that there was a narrative around the song, but I think my mum started singing it, and I started imagining her talking to her mother, and, so that song kind of always, I mean, my mum has a number of favourite songs that I now know, so whenever I hear them, I think of her, but from that period that song really, really, resonates . . . and, again, I think it was, uh, God, I'm actually tearing up now because I think it was for me, it was kind of, getting to see my mum, like recognizing that my mum was actually uprooted from her family and from her country, and sharing that moment with her, of connecting to it. (Maya, 46, Lebanese, Doha)

In his article 'Belongings: Place, Space and Identity in a Mediated World', David Morley describes a scene from within the household of a British/Barbadian journalist in London, with a 'Barbadian flag behind the front door of the house – signifying that whatever happened in the wider world, the territory within . . . was to be inhabited by Barbadian rules'.[119] Within her 'territory', Maha has hung up '*a big poster of Fairouz*' on the wall of her home, so '*when you first walk in, the first thing you see is a big poster of Fairouz*'. The reasoning behind this decision is both similar and different to Morley's example. While Morley explains his example to be associated with power relations between the public and private sphere, Maha's example shows power relations within the private sphere itself, one which is not only based on 'cultural autonomy' but on gender autonomy as well. The poster of Fairouz acts as an assertion of identity, a signifier of presence. It is a '*kind of cultural language I speak, that no one in my family here in London speaks*'. Through the poster, Maha is able to mark a place for herself in line with the '*cultural language*' she possesses. The poster acts as 'equipment' of presence and an extension of self. The '*cultural language*' Maha mentions describes a need for autonomy, a small break from the everyday social language she is expected to speak, but also it indicates inherent power relations operating within that language. Language thus becomes entwined with space, the two absorbing and exuding power mixtures to form different sets of relations based on language. It is necessary, here, to bring in Doreen Massey's concept of the 'power geometry of time-space compression', which she argues places 'different social groups, and different individuals' according to 'flows and interconnections' laced with power.[120]

It is this 'power geometry', which gives insight into the domestic relationships of these women with their spouses (Dina and Maha), as well as with their parents (Maya). For Maha, the poster of Fairouz is part of the '*Rakwet Kahwe, put my Fairouz on and sit down and sip my coffee*' ritual. It is Maha's way of re-connecting in domestic space and her '*little two-hour window of being me*'. It highlights the difference between her and her husband, who '*wouldn't understand [Fairouz]*'. This cultural gap is also felt with Dina and her '*foreign*' family. For both women, Fairouz is familiar territory in an absence of '*understand[ing]*' and a shared '*background*'. It is an affective connection to the '*diaspora*', to '*my mum*' and '*brother*' and to '*home*'. It is also a disconnection from an '*English-Italian*' husband, an '*English-French*' stepdaughter, and a family of '*foreigners*'. Through the music of Fairouz, respondents highlight their own position within the private sphere, which is reflective of their situation of being in diaspora, and also of marrying spouses who do not share their '*cultural language*'.

While Maha and Dina outline the 'power geometries' present among their spouses and children in their domestic households, Maya brings in a daughter's perspective. Reflecting on her mother's position in being '*uprooted from her family and from her country*', by way of the lyrics of Fairouz, Maya is able to affectively imagine a conversation between her mother and grandmother. What

Maya alludes to is that her mother was '*uprooted from her family and from her country*' because of her father's job. As discussed previously, most of the women interviewed for this study had migrated because of their husbands or their parents (namely, their fathers). Interestingly, Maha and Dina came to London to pursue their university degrees and met their husbands in London. So, although a male counterpart did not determine their movements across geographical space, their subsequent movements within domestic space are gendered. Understanding these dynamics within and across spaces is best seen through the *meta-* and *micro-habitus*. These two forms of *habitus* allow for a holistic overview in the analysis of diasporic behaviour, which traces past, present and future, as well as encompassing spatial and geopolitical factors and allows for a gender-based overview of diasporic experience. The examples given by the three women highlight how space and gender operate politically and affectively, but also how their relationship is determined by 'power geometries' put in place by *meta-* and *micro-habitual* situations. To further highlight how men dominate the domestic space, it is necessary to compare the excerpts from male respondents in reference to listening to Fairouz in the private sphere:

> *My wife is foreign, but she's started listening to Fairouz because I always listen to her. She started speaking Arabic, so she started listening to Fairouz and she's seen Bint il Haress,*[121] *Safar Barlik.*[122] (Michael, 36, Lebanese, London)

> *Yes, and I re-married a Russian. She listens too . . . not as much as my first wife, but she does listen to [Fairouz], she has . . . well she listens to it everyday because it is in the car, and it's in the house.* (Tarek, 36, Lebanese, London)

> *I listen to [Fairouz] with my wife, who is not Lebanese, she is from Georgia. but she loves her, she really loves her voice.* (Wassim, 42, Lebanese, London)

> *My son does [listen to Fairouz] when he leaves for school, he tells me to play [Fairouz's] songs. My wife doesn't like listening to her music, because it makes her feel depressed. Maybe because she feels that the music takes her back to Lebanon, that's why it depresses her, just maybe, I'm assuming. (Rodger, 38, Lebanese, Doha)*

> *I think speaking English for a while, and getting the English logic and not forgetting things, but starting to see things differently . . . maybe from the English perspective. You start to read words differently. I think, with Fairouz, you'll say this is incredible. This is at the same time distorting. That's why someone like me would struggle . . . Like Mira maybe . . . Would struggle in being in a relationship with a Western partner.* (Ayman, 34, Syrian, London)

The quotations from male participants, earlier, show the differences in listening behaviours between the sexes, especially in relation to the domestic sphere. Michael, Tarek and Wassim live in London, are married to '*foreign*' women, and take pride in the fact that their wives '*started listening to Fairouz because I always listen to her*'. It can be said that the male participants dominate the space here. While with the female respondents, Fairouz was heard in the kitchen or the living room as a private moment aimed at personal consumption, with the males, Fairouz is the audio-scape in all shared spaces. It is the males who take ownership of the sound waves, playing Fairouz '*everyday because it is in the car, and it's in the house*'. While the female participants express how language proves a barrier between them and their husbands in the context of Fairouz, '*he wouldn't understand her*', this was not the case for the males. For Michael, his wife '*just started speaking Arabic*', and Wassim explains his wife '*is from Georgia but she loves [Fairouz], she really loves her voice*'. The discrepancies between the male and female interviewees highlight the 'power geometries' at work in the domestic sphere, but also they highlight gendered attitudes towards the home. Rodger's excerpt bridges both private and public spheres. Even though he is married to a Lebanese woman, the initiative to move to Doha to pursue job opportunities was his idea. So while his son '*tells me to play [Fairouz's] songs*', his '*wife doesn't like listening to her music because it makes her feel depressed*'. Rodger assumes his wife finds Fairouz depressing because '*the music takes her back to Lebanon*', back to the familiarity to which she is accustomed and away from the migration she has had to undertake because of her husband.

Ayman's quotation shows how space also provides a 'power geometry' of its own. Expressing tension in trying to understand Fairouz as someone who has recently acquired a more '*English perspective*', Ayman finds listening to Fairouz in his new position within British space '*incredible*' and, at the same time, '*distorting*'. It is thus not only about individuals' dominance over space, but also the way space exerts dominance over individuals. To ignore power embedded within space, in the context of the Arab diaspora, is to ignore the social, political and economic trajectories which shape the dominant currents found within that space. Individuals inhabiting new space need to affectively 'reform bodily space' according to 'social space'.[123] Consumption of Fairouz and her music thus alters with this reformation of 'bodily space', which Ayman finds challenging, especially within the framework of relationships and gendered interactions. Consequently, Ayman asserts he '*would struggle in being in a relationship with a Western partner*', one who does not know the music of Fairouz, but, more importantly, one who would not have to 'reform' in a similar manner to him in 'social space'. Ayman provides interesting insight in trying to navigate this new 'social space' in light of Fairouz. Outlining how it has affected his outlook on relationships, it is necessary here to further draw on parts of Ayman's interview to observe the ways in which he tries to re-contextualize Fairouz in a different 'social space', embedded with separate rules and interactions:

> *So, anyway, I started to experience how horrible it is, and how scary it is to be vulnerable and to be passionate with people. I started to look back and try to study why am I like this? Why have I thought for a long time that they are wrong, and I am right? Why do I have this high level of love, and this high level of doubt? Why do I have the demand of being with a person and talking to them? Why do I have Fairouz's images in my head? Why do I have these poetic images? Why, when I'm having a f**king espresso in Soho, I'm thinking of 'Bteshrab men Fenjanak Beshrab men 3aynayk*[124]' *Why? I came from a culture where if you respect and*

love a girl, you'll tell her that you'll marry her. You'll tell her that you see in her eyes the mother of your children. Here, it's f**king scary. I was thinking that this is because they are superficial.... They are not. They are only different, and they don't have f**king time for you to talk about this shit. They are busy doing their work.... They have different ways of dealing with people. Some people have sex on the same night they meet, and then they take two months to be courageous to say 'I like you', and they say, oh, it's too early, but they keep having sex. (Ayman, 34, Syrian, London)

So, Fairouz, to me here, in a way was horrible. That's the way I see it. She's all about the love of touch and the eyes and, you know. This can last two or three days, but you can't live it as a way of life. Our culture is funny.... It doesn't happen here. In our culture, we are very poetic, we are into platonic love, as in Qays and Leila or Antar and Abla. When we are in bed, we turn into animals. We want to hear words and say words. We hold this contradiction. Here it's similar in a way. In life, women fight for feminism and equality. To me, the culture of Fairouz... Fairouz and Gibran Khalil Gibran, were for a certain group of people. Their effect here is damaging. (Ayman, 34, Syrian, London)

I think bringing Fairouz's attitude to the Western world is scary to people. It is scary. Imagine you have.... As a man, if I have a wife who will talk to me... let's say she doesn't know Fairouz. She'll talk to me about lyrics similar to Fairouz. It's going to be overwhelming. I fear that I might get bored in a while. No one refuses Fairouz; we think she's perfect. Well, she is, because this is how we received Fairouz. (Ayman, 34, Syrian, London)

These excerpts present the challenges Ayman faces in trying to adapt Fairouz and her lyrics to his life in London, especially in attempting to steer through variant notions of masculinity and femininity. Reflecting on his own position within this new 'social space', Ayman complains, '*Fairouz to me, here in a way was horrible*'. Incongruous to the London dating scene, Fairouz '*is damaging*' as '*she's all about the love of touch and the eyes*', which is both unsustainable and '*doesn't happen here*'. Through Fairouz, Ayman provides comparative insight into the cultural logistics of relationships and gender constructions between the Arab world and London, but also reveals how, through space, meanings can shift and so '*bringing Fairouz's attitude to the Western world is scary to people*'. This love Fairouz sings about, while once '*perfect*', becomes '*overwhelming*' in London. However, the conflict lies in the way Fairouz has been engrained into notions of love and romance, which is difficult for Ayman to be disassociated from in his new environment, '*I started to experience how horrible it is, and how scary it is to be vulnerable and to be passionate with people*'. It is an attempt at acceptance, 'a spatial reconfiguration of an embodied self',[125] in which space becomes a dominating factor in relations between the sexes, but also Fairouz expresses 'Worldliness' that is at odds with the current space Ayman inhabits. Translating Fairouz into the setting of London requires Ayman to take on a different masculine role than the one he is used to, and simultaneously to try to understand a new 'language' of 'social relations'.[126] However, while Fairouz can be confusing for Ayman in London, and a point of difference in relationships, she remains for him, a connector of space and language:

> *Now I'm seeing an English girl, whose mother is Norwegian, her father is from Essex. When I sit with her, I find myself forced to play Fairouz's songs to her. She's just like Fairouz for me . . . this is amazing.* (Ayman, 34, Syrian, London)

To bridge the space between him and his English girlfriend, Ayman feels '*forced to play Fairouz's songs to her*'. Fairouz therefore immediately becomes a translator, even though, ironically, she will essentially have to be translated. It is important to note that it is not just the words Fairouz is conveying, rather, it is a spatio-temporal context through which Ayman wants to be seen. She is the prologue, the subtext and the footnote to his identity. Fairouz is the 'equipment' by which Ayman expresses his 'Worldliness' to his girlfriend, in the quest towards connection. It is an affective collision of music, time and space, within that 'Worldliness'. Even though Fairouz is thus '*horrible*' in London, Ayman continues to be part of the '*culture of Fairouz*' and so, in this way, by playing Fairouz's songs, Ayman is able to reassert his individual dominance over space, conducting himself on his own terms. The '*culture of Fairouz*' also unfolds in other households, where language is not necessarily a factor. Some participants, who were married to correspondingly Arab-speaking spouses, spoke about their pride in 'educating' them in Fairouz and her music, a means by which couples have grown through her music. In addition, other married couples credited their spouses with bringing Fairouz into their lives. Power, in this context, becomes more evenly spread, as Fairouz is no longer a point of dispute or a tool for domination, but, instead, she is a contribution to the marriage and the household. She becomes entwined in daily activities and is thus embedded in both space and time, and remains there. These spaces and moments therefore become associated with her and her music.

Intercontextuality, naturalization, Al-Watan and gendered space

It is within the songs of Fairouz that participants conjure up notions of an idealized *Watan*, drawing on both private and social understandings. A pre-modern structure, *Al-Watan* is a combination of imagery associated with Mediterranean landscapes and geographies, but also individualized ideas of 'home' and consequently the 'self'. Temporally, Fairouz stands with participants in recognizing the advancement of *Al-Watan* into the post-modern, reflecting on its past and recognizing its violent transformation from a pre-modern state.

Through conversations with the Arab diaspora, it is clear Fairouz is able to situate participants according to imagined and lived spatial elements, and these spatial elements provide deep insight into the mechanisms of diasporic behaviour and attitudes in both Doha and London. As space, both sampling pools could not be more different and thus Fairouz is able to unravel the emotional and functional realities faced in both contexts. The *meta-* and *micro-habitus* cannot be discounted from this narrative, since they, along with the mnemonic imagination, play key roles in the shaping and reflecting of space and the positioning of the 'self', the 'body' and the 'collective' within it. It is also difficult to disassociate the concept of intercontextual *iltizam* in this narrative, as it is this intercontextuality, which summons this *Watan* and either defines or blurs its borders. In addition, the 'intercontextuality' of *iltizam* assists in exploring the complexity of conceptualizations towards naturalization and the ways it pans out across junctions of gender and citizenship.

Whether it was a comment on Fairouz as a female artist, or through the interpretation of her lyrics detailing women's experiences, or, even more importantly, her role in navigating gendered spaces, gender came up in a myriad of ways. A crucial element in examining Arab diasporic encounters, gender gave this study a vital layer for analysis. As an artist, a 'figure', and a voice, Fairouz provides a narrative to examine the ways in which women in the Arab diaspora position themselves, individually and collectively. Through her persona, Fairouz embodies an ideal Arab woman, strong, yet conservative; maternal, yet political. It is through these dichotomies that female listeners are able to position themselves individually and socially. However, it is also through Fairouz, who has more '*freedom*' than others, that participants are able to explore personal and collective notions of naturalization and mobility. Fairouz offers a gendered benchmark by which respondents can assess the space they are connected to and their situation within that space. Fairouz is also able to chart a gendered historical context, from being a voice of acceptance to one associated with being '*haram*' or from one in which women are perceived as '*insignificant*' to one where they are given more '*value*'. In essence, through gender, we are able to see the ways the *micro-habitus* and *meta-habitus* of participants engage. Often, it is the *micro-habitus*, which gives insight into the *meta-habitus* of participants, since it is the individual in the space of the collective, but also the *meta-habitus* is a driver to a *micro-habitus*, and so the collective positions the individual.

By comparing male and female listening behaviours and attitudes to Fairouz's music, we become aware of the 'power geometries' operating within space. While most of the women interviewed in this study were married to Arab men, the ones who were not provided great insight into life within domestic spaces and the gendered power relations contained within them. There is evidence of male dominance and ownership of space, in both the public and private spheres, but also space brings in power of its own, shaping, distorting and constructing notions of masculine and feminine behaviours. The ways in which Fairouz filtered through by way of spouses who brought them into the domestic space were also apparent. As 'equipment', Fairouz becomes an embedded element within the home, a ritual and a shared guest, who lingers long after she has left. She is, moreover, a connector of individuals in space, an introduction and a pretext, a signifier of place, background, socio-historical circumstance and 'Worldliness'. She is a vocal activist for justice and *iltizam*, and through the 'intercontextuality' of *iltizam* the Arab diaspora is able to negotiate gendered phenomena, situating themselves within it.

Fairouz does not hold empty space, her songs are perforated with meanings, and while this chapter has thus far examined the ways Fairouz has raised themes with regard to her 'figure', as a female artist and a 'body of discourse',[127] her role in the private and public spheres, and the 'functionality' and 'purpose' she provides as 'equipment' in extending and explaining 'Worldliness'.[128] The next chapter takes on a more temporal discussion, looking at how Fairouz moves through time stratospheres and how, essentially, she will remain timeless.

Chapter 7

FAIROUZ, TIME, GENERATIONAL LINEAGE
AND THE MNEMONIC IMAGINATION

In countries like Syria, Iraq and Qatar, it is Fairouz's voice that is heard across the morning airwaves on national radios or television channels. The singer is usually associated with the morning, and although this attribute was mentioned among participants in the Arab diaspora in Doha and London, especially as a ritualistic element to starting their days, it will not form the focal point of this chapter. Instead, this chapter will outline the ways in which time formulates different relationships with Fairouz's music. Whether respondents talked about how Fairouz offered comfort during times of war, or in comparisons of how individual and collective evolutions transform understandings of Fairouz, or the ways in which memory manages to occupy various positions within the minds of participants or, finally, how Fairouz is an inherited artist, spanning generations and continuing her legacy. This chapter travels through the eventual timelessness of Fairouz and her ability to be both keeper and disseminator of time.

It was evident through conversations with participants that Fairouz is able to define and describe time. However, she is also able to adapt to time, taking on significance at various chronological points. Her relevance as an aural backdrop to war, violence and the plight of refugees transcends ages to accommodate new situations. From providing a historical narrative to being temporally appropriated, Fairouz travels through shared experiences and nestles in the private minds and hearts of the Arab diaspora in both London and Doha. She is representative of both the collective and the individualized, chronicling them both and giving them each transformative meaning.

Memory: Mnemonic, associated, reconstructed and adapted

In their book *The Mnemonic Imagination: Remembering as Creative Practice*, Keightley and Pickering argue for the conjoining of memory and imagination to comprehend 'the relationship between past, present and future'.[1] The authors also make the case that media and imagination work in harmony, 'both at the time we are immersed in music or fictional narrative and subsequently, as what is given to us through our imaginative engagements with them become interwoven with our own social and historical experience'.[2] In the same vein, Astrid Erll also raises the importance of media in cultural memory, since 'media and symbol systems are two of the coordinates which play a significant role in determining in which "mnemonic mode" the past is being remembered'.[3] So, it is through this intersection of memory, imagination and the *meta-* and *micro-habitus* among the Arab diaspora, which is key here. How do Fairouz and her music transform over time? What roles do they play in the past, present and future of participants in this study? From the interviews conducted, forms of memory fell into a spectrum of three main (at times overlapping) categories: associated, reconstructed and adapted. Associated memory combines the mnemonic imagination with affect theory, in the sense that Fairouz, as an artist or through her music, has played a part in recreating a memory, leading to affect. This is not to say that the mnemonic imagination is not affective in itself, but that, with its position of association, affect was prominent. Examples of how associated memory was affective were when participants shared memories of Fairouz during wartime, or in conversations about loved ones, both present and lost or linked Fairouz to space and to past moments when she was heard and shared. Reconstructed memory refers to a revised form of remembering, it is visualized, with a conscious or subconscious sense of awareness that it may have never been lived personally, but which has instead been lived through the experience of others. Finally, the third form of memory, adapted memory, involves the application of memory from past to present events. While the first two forms of memory mostly involve the *meta-habitus* and its effects on the *micro-habitus*, adapted memory stems from the point of the *micro-habitus* and its presence within the *meta-habitus*, in the sense that memory is centrifugal and emanates from the individual to the communal. Adapted memory highlights the ways in which Fairouz and her 'aura' amalgamates, forming new experiences reliant on previous events, giving her listeners the autonomy to interpret and appropriate her music in their own ways. Using Keightley and Pickering's description of the 'remembering subject' as someone 'who is operative within the social relations sustained in the practices of everyday life', but who is also 'capable of thinking about herself and her situation', forms the criteria through which the three categories of remembering are placed.[4] As both a social and personal activity, remembering is 'operational'. In the case of Fairouz and her listeners, remembering is a linking mechanism between *micro-* and *meta-habitual* experiences. From here, it is important to give examples of the three forms of memory so as to best understand their relationship to Fairouz, time and the Arab diaspora, beginning with associated memory.

Associated memory: People, places, war and violence

A discussion of previous memory studies is important in laying the foundation to try to describe what associated memory implies. Using Erll's definition of 'episodic memory', which 'encompasses memories of life experience' and is 'tied to a specific time and context',[5] associated memory draws on 'life experience' to provide links with Fairouz's music. Associated memory finds commonality with 'episodic memory'. However, through the medium of Fairouz's songs, this memory becomes associated with time and space, often becoming inseparable. 'Episodic memory' connotes a severing of time, of compartmentalization and linearity. Whereas associated memory is instigated cyclically through the *meta-* and *micro-habitus*, it is a constant continuation of 'life experience', which absorbs and releases in its temporal and spatial journey. Arguably, 'episodic memory' can trigger 'associated memories' but, in the case of Fairouz and her listeners, it cannot be seen as an end result. Associated memory brings in memories related to the people and places participants remember while listening to Fairouz. These are affective memories, ones that evoke emotion. Associated memories are not necessarily happy memories, at times they are reminders of violence and war, examples of which will be given as this section unfolds:

'Nassam 3alayna al Hawa',[6] *I try not to play it anymore, because it just makes me get Goosebumps, but every time it's my dad's birthday, I put it on YouTube and tell the guys, this is, uh, happy birthday dad, because I knew he loved it. Yeah, I try to avoid listening to some songs now, because it – emotionally, it gets me emotional.* (Shams, 40, Iranian/Palestinian/Lebanese/English, Doha)

Ok, very often I cry, because . . . not all the time, but there's, there are a few songs that will just hit so close to home, because I just remember being in the car with my Jiddo,[7] *and having him explain it to me. . . . No one ever sat down with me. . . . My grandfather was at least sixty years older than me, not sixty, haram no, maybe 54, 56 years older than me at the time, and so, when I was nine and ten and he was an extremely busy chemical engineer, working on a crazy project, he'd take the time out of his day to come sit with me, and drop me off to school in the morning, and explain to me all of these things, it's just so, there's been so much invested in me, and Fairouz helped build that relationship, the same way my grandfather helped build my relationship with Fairouz.* (Tania, 20, Palestinian, Doha)

My children listen to her, my relatives, I remember, my niece in Beirut, my brother's daughter – when she was very young, I used to visit Beirut and see her and she would sing Fairouz songs, 'Ya Karm El 3alali',[8] *she would sing that song for me. I reminded her, she is grown up and she has children now, and her children, one of them is in Australia now, they're in New Zealand, I reminded her when I talked to her, I said, I still remember that song, she was crying you know, I still remember you singing me that song.* (Ziyad, 82, Iraqi, Doha)

[She reminds me of] My mother . . . I'm going to start crying in a bit . . . she is my second mum. The mother that you live with in the house raises you, and she also raises you. (Mona, 45, Lebanese, Doha)

There have been songs which my ex-wife actually used to adore a lot . . . she is Russian, she didn't know, she didn't understand her words, but she used to love that song, 'Boukra Inta w Jayi'[9] *and she would put it on every morning. So whenever I listen to that, I remember my ex. We had a wonderful marriage for ten years, and it had to end. So whenever I listen to that song now, I remember my wife now, and*

. . . at first it brought hurt, but now it brings joy, so, you know, like I said, time sometimes it's funny the way it works, time is a healer. . . . But it's good now that I listen to that song and it brings me wonderful memories of my ex-wife. (Tarek, 36, Lebanese, London)

As is evident, the intertwining of affect with the mnemonic imagination is the foundation of associated memory. For Shams, the song '*Nassam 3aleyna al Hawa*' is rooted in memories of times with his father, and so listening to the song after his death is '*emotional*'. Similarly, Tania '*cries*' when hearing '*a few songs*', as they '*hit too close to home*'. A reminder of her maternal grandfather, who took '*the time out of his day to come sit with me, and drop me off to school in the morning, and explain to me all of these things*', Fairouz '*helped build that relationship*' with Tania's grandfather, '*the same way my grandfather helped build my relationship with Fairouz*'. Fairouz affectively fills the empty space and time occupied by participants' lost ones through her songs and music. She is associated with a time in which her listeners shared moments with loved ones and so, in their absence, she transforms through the 'movement between the horizons of experience'.[10] This temporal shift of presence and absence, past and present, merges Fairouz and her music to take on new meaning. It must be noted that while absence in the examples of Shams and Tania means death, for Ziyad, Mona and Tarek, absence means a lack of presence created by some sort of distance. For example, Ziyad relates Fairouz to his niece, who lives in Beirut and who used to always sing one of Fairouz's songs for him. Mona is reminded of her mother, whom she is separated from geographically.

Associating Fairouz with being a mother figure was common among participants in this study and was previously discussed, to some extent, in the last chapter. However, Mona's claim that Fairouz is her '*second mum*', since '*she also raises you*', is suggestive of her constant presence through the ages. So even though Mona associates Fairouz with her mother, Fairouz is a separate entity who incorporates the same attributes found in her real mother. Being in diaspora, and so far away from her mother, is affective for Mona. However, it is the association with Fairouz that drives an emotional response. In this way, Fairouz is able to straddle two personas at once. First, one in which she is a singer, an artist, and also a mother in her own right, and second, as a replacement for the real mother. In diaspora, Fairouz becomes an interchangeable signifier of motherhood for Mona, catalysing the consequent affect, which arises from that associated personal memory. With Tarek, Fairouz triggers memories of his ex-wife and '*at first it brought hurt, but now it brings joy*'. Time, in this instance, '*is a healer*' for Tarek, illustrating the ways in which affect can change through the intersection of the mnemonic imagination and time, in their consequent relationships with the *micro-habitus*. In a sense, this can be related to nostalgia, since it 'is dependent on a sense of temporal dislocation' which 'is felt primarily as drastic loss'.[11] This combination of association through the mnemonic imagination along spatio-temporal tangents in *micro-habitual* situations thus leads to forms of affective nostalgia, expressed towards the home, loved ones and old relationships. It is, as Amar in Doha contends:

Nostalgia, you know, it invades you more when you're away, you listen to Fairouz and it's as if you've taken medicine, she sedates you, it sedates you, it takes away this pain of missing, it makes you feel like you're home again, it compensates for being away, it's enough, it's like she's medicine for migration that makes you feel like you're back in Lebanon, this is how I connect it. (Amar, 39, Lebanese, Doha)

Fairouz, as both a suppressor and instigator of '*this pain of missing*', or what has been defined as nostalgia, is dependent on spatio-temporal contexts, since '*it invades you more when you're away*'. Like the examples given earlier, this nostalgia is acknowledged, and as Keightley and Pickering argue 'nostalgia is by no means necessarily stultifying'.[12] Instead, it is, as these authors demonstrate, 'a more active effort at reclaiming what seems lost'.[13] Jo Tacchi in her chapter 'Nostalgia and Radio Sound' also attests to the 'activeness' of nostalgia. Tacchi's research on radio sound in households in Bristol, for which she draws on various notions of nostalgia, argues for a more 'productive' idea of nostalgia, one which is seen as 'both a mode of consumption and a mode of production – it is consumed through radio and music and at the same time it is practiced, it is a mode of production'.[14] So, in this way, by means of association, Fairouz as memory does not remain motionless but is instead a 'productive', 'active' and dynamic way for participants to express, calm and generate nostalgia. Amar describes Fairouz as '*medicine for migration*', a way to soothe the nostalgia arising '*when you're away*'. This path, for Amar, leads back to Lebanon, and while Lebanese participants were not the only ones sought for this study, it is important to turn to their discussion on war and the music of Fairouz, as another form of associative remembering:

You listen to it in the shelters during the bombing. So, yes, in a way, it reminds you of a lot of things, Fairouz. It's not just nice songs, or just a song that fits in a place. Like, I have almost every song of Fairouz and I know why it relates to me and for what reason, but, in total, it's something that reminds you of home. (Dina, 42, Lebanese, London)

Then I told them that I wanted to sing them a song that I really love, so I sang 'Al Qamar Bidawi 3al Nas'.[15] *Some of them cried when I sang it. . . . It touches everyone. Every person that lived in the war, or experienced love, will be touched. Her songs are full of meanings of our daily lives.* (Sara, 46, Lebanese, London)

The song 'Bhebak Ya Libnan'[16] *was released during the time of the war; we were migrating from one area to another, trying to escape the destructive war. When we used to listen to the song it gave us courage, and supplied us with the energy needed to continue in this country. . . . I still feel the mixed feelings of courage and anger that I used to feel during the times of the war. It is difficult to prefer one song of Fairouz over the other. However, of course, there are some songs that touch me more. Each song has a special and unique taste.* (Abouna Yousef, 60, Lebanese, London)

Ever since we were kids. . . . When we were children and the war was going on there wasn't anyone but her, even on the radio. Between the radio and TV, there was mostly Fairouz. . . . My parents and the environment around us. . . . We used to gather and wait for breaking news about the bombings, or if any village was being hit during the war. . . . In between, all the stations were playing Fairouz. Until today, by coincidence, we heard from some Jordanian friends that when they used to listen to Fairouz they felt that the war had started, since Jordanian TV would put Fairouz, and this would signal that there's a conflict going on. . . . She used to make us feel safe. All the news was very bad except for her voice. (Ghassan, 45, Lebanese, Doha)

I vividly remember the days during wartime when I was young. My mother used to prepare us breakfast to take with us to school, and my father would turn on the TV to listen to the news. . . . In between news segments, they used to play Fairouz's songs. Can you see the contradiction? We were living a war and listening to Fairouz at the same time . . . I think that they were trying to calm people down. We were living a time of killing and kidnapping. . . . Some people left their houses in the morning, and never returned at night. The policy of most radios and channels was to play Fairouz, hoping that she might calm people down . . . Fairouz's music calmed people down. It probably prevented a bigger explosion in the situation at that time. At war, with all the bombings, shootings and people talking, tension will rise among people. Fairouz is a stress reliever. She'll decrease the doses of tension. She's a kind of painkiller. That's why I believe they used to play her songs. Fairouz is not related to time. She's important at any time. This is the truth. Fairouz was important in the past. She's important now, and she'll be important in the future. (Elie, 50, Lebanese, London)

I was one of the people where Fairouz's war songs really allowed me to overcome the war. [She sings] 'Li Beirut, men Albe Salamon li Beirut'.[17] She never swore, she never destroyed the image of Lebanon. Even in the midst of war, she kept on engraving the beautiful images. 'Kubalon lil Ba7ri',[18] she keeps this sincerity always. Sure, there are bad memories, but her songs really saved the war that could have been much worse on our wellbeing. She was the hope. The TV stations, I remember, how old were we? The TV stations when they would put songs of Fairouz, they were still hopeful. No one said that they would throw down their weapons, or resign from their country. Fairouz kept bringing them together, all the stations, all the political factions, all of them, used to play Fairouz during the war. This is the biggest indicator that when someone separates us we separate, but when someone brings us together, we really are brought together. (Mona, 45, Lebanese, Doha)

'Yalla Tnam Rima'[19] reminds me of my childhood. The songs from Petra, remind me of [the] Lebanese war, whenever we were getting bombed, on Voice of Lebanon or Free Lebanon they would put Fairouz's songs and tell us that we were being bombed. I get a memory, whenever I hear nationalistic songs, of the days we were in the bomb shelter, when we were bombed, the destruction that happened. Fairouz summarizes all the phases during which Lebanon has passed. I'm 42, if I go back 20 years as well. She summarizes sixty years of the life of a Lebanese person. (Wassim, 42, Lebanese, London)

Fairouz taught me a lot of things. She used to take me back every time. We are Jeel El Hareb, the war generation, we didn't live in a loving environment for our country, so we surrendered quickly, and the first opportunity we had to leave the country, we did. So, she's that one thing that stays with you, she follows you and she teaches us to take Lebanon with us everywhere we go. She takes you back to your roots, and she teaches you without even knowing it. . . . Also she helps you raise your family and nourish it without you knowing it. So, yeah, Fairouz taught me a lot, and she's also teaching my family. But our country is not learning from her, unfortunately. (Nora, 37, Lebanese, Doha)

Even though these excerpts highlight the collective experience of living through the Lebanese civil war, it is important to look at the ways the war translated into individual experiences through the music of Fairouz. All participants mentioned the songs of Fairouz as a juxtaposition to the war which was unfolding outside. Offering 'courage', 'calmness' and 'hope', Fairouz's voice, broadcast on TV and radio, was heard in bomb shelters and homes during the Lebanese civil war, providing a contrast to the violent soundscapes. Tacchi states:

The textured soundscapes that are created with the help of radio sound, in the homes of listeners, is, similarly, personal, and it extends beyond the sound that their radio sets emit, it is a 'productive engagement' with wider society, yet it can be contained in the domestic sphere. (2003, p. 292)

Using Tacchi's thesis, it can thus be argued that Fairouz offers this link between the 'personal' and the 'wider society'. She is a form of 'productive engagement', a spatio-temporal connection to the war. While, in the nineteenth and twentieth centuries, war drums often heralded the call to war, a warning, an announcement, Fairouz, through her music, is also seen as such a signifier. '*In between news segments*' Fairouz would be played, '*they would put Fairouz's songs and tell us that we were being bombed*'. As a signifier '*that there's a conflict going on*', but also '*she used to make us feel safe*', an indicator and a comforter during war is the contradiction that lies in this merged soundscape. As experience for '*every person that lived in the war*' (Sara, London), Fairouz's music becomes associated with a shared and collective associated memory. She is at once a '*painkiller*', a voice of '*hope*' and a definer of the Lebanese '*war generation*' or '*jeel el hareb*'. However, it is also important to note the individual experiences of Fairouz during the Lebanese war. For Dina, Sara and Abouna Youssef in London, Fairouz offers an affective spectrum of music to draw from, '*I have almost every song of Fairouz, and I know why it relates to me and for what reason*' (Dina, London), but also her music is reminiscent of violence and destruction. For Abouna Youssef, Fairouz's voice offered '*courage*' during the Lebanese conflict, but he '*still feel[s] the mixed feelings of courage and anger that I used to feel during the times of war*'. It is the association of Fairouz with times of war, which shapes this relationship affectively, but also, through Fairouz, this affect moves across time and space. Ghassan, Elie, Wassim and Mona compose a vivid memory of the aural landscape during the war, with Elie and Mona focusing on Fairouz's ability to calm the situation down. For Elie, a musician in London, and Mona in Doha, Fairouz's role during the bloodshed was not one which should be disregarded. Both participants credit the singer for '*sav[ing] the war*'. For Mona, it was Fairouz's songs, which '*really allowed me to overcome the war*' on a personal level, and also '*Fairouz kept bringing them together, all the stations, all the political factions, all of them, used to play Fairouz during the war*'. Echoing this sentiment, Elie links the singer to a '*painkiller*', but also posits that her music '*probably prevented a bigger explosion in the situation at that time*'. Fairouz thus holds a neutral place, in that, politically, she was claimed by all sides, a way for the Lebanese warring factions to be, as Mona puts it, '*brought together*'. A point of convergence during a time of division, Fairouz is associated not only with the soundscape of the war but also with being an 'active' player at both an individual and collective level. However, for Elie, Wassim and Nora, Fairouz's role does not end with the Lebanese civil war but, instead, travels through space and time connecting and charting other events on the way. In Wassim's opinion, '*Fairouz summarizes all the phases during which Lebanon has passed. I'm 42, if I go back 20 years as well, she summarizes sixty years of the life of a Lebanese person*'. Although relieving Fairouz of being tied down to the specific time of the Lebanese civil war, Wassim anchors the singer to the '*life of a Lebanese person*' in the past. However, the gist of his statement is of importance, especially in this idea of Fairouz and time. As an accompaniment for the last '*sixty years*', Fairouz is a source of Lebanese history. She is able to transmit key milestones of the eras, but also she cannot stay there, she is, as Nora says:

> that one thing that stays with you, she follows you, and she teaches us to take Lebanon with us everywhere we go. She takes you back to your roots, and she teaches you without even knowing it. . . . Also, she helps you raise your family and nourish it without you knowing it.

Nora keeps Fairouz locked in Lebanese importance, but, here, she frees her from the confinement of '*sixty years*' to travel and to '*teach us*' about the past, which is how '*she helps you raise your family and nourish it*'. Although conversation about Fairouz being passed on through generations will be discussed later in this chapter, Nora's statement hints at this idea of passing on this history associated with Fairouz to her family, which, in a sense, is a way to prolong a sense of time. Interestingly, Elie states, '*Fairouz is not related to time. She's important at any time. This is the truth. Fairouz was important in the past. She's important now, and she'll be important in the future.*' Fairouz is thus both evocative of time and transcends it. She is associated with a certain historical and geographical context, but she does not remain there. In this way, Fairouz is temporally and spatially omnipresent, a timeless timekeeper, an anchoring nomad and a body of contradictions. While the earlier examples show the ways in which participants associate Fairouz and her music to a certain time, place or person, there was often an overlap between the different paths the mnemonic imagination took. An instance of such an overlap is

found in the following extract, taken from interviews with Noor and Nicholas, a
married couple living in London:

> **Noor:** *I was thinking now, in the car, you asked me what Fairouz is to you . . . it*
> *reminds me for the time of the war, during the time of the war, and whatever*
> *the lyrics are, it just, it just makes you feel that you belong to this country, it*
> *makes you feel Lebanese, somehow . . . but there is no particular song that*
> *I listen to . . . anything I listen to from Fairouz would speak to me. It gives*
> *me a sense of identity, if that makes any sense. No other artist in Lebanon*
> *embodies this, which is amazing, I have to say . . . There is a particular song,*
> *always when I listen to it I see Ba'albeck and the moon, even though I've*
> *never, never attended a festival in Ba'albeck.*
> **Nicholas:** *Probably because I told you the story.*
> **Noor:** *Yes, but it always – when I listen to it, I see a full moon in the sky, it's just*
> *beautiful, I can't remember the name of the . . .*
> **Nicholas:** *Nihna wil Qamar Jiran*[20]
> **Noor:** *Nihna wil Qamar Jiran, it's just beautiful*
>
> (Nicholas and Noor, 47 and 45, Lebanese, London)

This example highlights the interlaying of associated and reconstructed memory.
While Noor recounts listening to Fairouz during the war and the sense of *'identity'*
it evokes in her, she also visualizes a scene of Fairouz performing *'Nihna wil Qamar
Jiran'*, even though she has never *'attended a festival in Ba'albeck'*. This image she
recounts is not one she has experienced herself but, instead, is one reconstructed
by her from conversations with her husband, who *'told [her] the story'* of being
there. So, even though Noor associates the song with the image of the *'full moon in
the sky'* in *'Ba'albeck'*, it is not a memory she has experienced first-hand. From here,
it is important to move to a discussion of reconstructed memory and the ways in
which the mnemonic imagination, combined with elements of storytelling, takes
participants on a sonic and visual journey through the lived experiences of others.

Reconstructed memory: Remembering through the lives of others

Reconstructed memory refers to a form of remembering, which mixes 'lived
experience' with 'second-hand experience'. As both a social and personal process,
reconstructed memory finds roots in 'semantic memory', in that it can be a
'memory of historical events not personally experienced'.[21] However, 'semantic'
memory implies distance between events and memories, which comes with a sense
of detachment. With reconstructed memories, there is an affective awareness that
these memories have been passed down and taken on, forming components of
individual, as well as social, identities and creating a sense of affective belonging.
Explicitly hosting social aspects, since memories are relayed through people,
communities and various other media, and can be related to a lost homeland
or an imagined sense of nationhood, but also depending on the *micro-habitus*,

reconstructed memories can implicitly harbour deeply personal and subjective dimensions, with memories being reconstructed according to private circumstances and desires. Placing associated and reconstructed memories in the context of the mnemonic imagination elucidates the distinctions of how, in certain cases, memory and imagination fluctuate in terms of their relationship with the 'remembering subject'. Associated memories will be biased towards the mnemonic component, while with reconstructed memories imagination is key:

> *Um, and so Fairouz kind of wove to me, kind of my mum's youth, in a big way, but also, growing up in the Emirates, it was also drawing for me a picture of Lebanon through my mum's eyes, or through, again, my grandma's eyes. I mean, not that my grandmother was around then, but just imagining my grandmother listening to it, or appreciating it, or forming a sense of my grandmother's sensibility towards it at the time.* (Maya, 46, Lebanese, Doha)

> *I'm Palestinian, and I would consider it my home, but, unfortunately, I've never visited. I've, uh, read about it, I've heard about it, I've listened to songs about it, but I've never had the privilege of visiting.* (Tania, 20, Palestinian, Doha)

> *I mean my parents are, like, my family is extremely Palestinian, and I interact with all sorts of people from the Levant but, um, I think you sort of lack it, if you're not living in a specific place, you're unable to relate to the way the nature comes about. Like, she always talks about the seasons, ya3ni, there's a song, 'Aam bit Dawi al Shams',[22] she talks about the seasons and, basically, you know, planting and so on, and if you've never lived in a farm-like place, or if you've never lived in a place where there's greenery, then you don't really appreciate that much. Ya3ni, here, yes, my grandfather has jasmine hedges, he has fil[23] hedges, but it's not the same.* (Tania, 20, Palestinian, Doha)

Maya and Tania's discussion of Fairouz in light of their parents or grandparents is significant. For Maya, who grew up in the United Arab Emirates around the time of the Lebanese civil war – and was unable to travel there – Fairouz '*wove*' *to* her, her '*mother's youth*', as well as drew her '*a picture of Lebanon through my mum's eyes, or through, again, my grandma's eyes*'. Reliant on the memories of her mother and grandmother, Maya was able to reconstruct memories of Lebanon through the depictions found in the music of Fairouz. Reconstructed memory is thus imagined with an underlying awareness that it was lived through the experience of others. Maya is able to visually assemble the spatial concept of Lebanon, through her '*mum's eyes, or through . . . my grandma's eyes*'. It is an innate vision of Lebanon, which moves from the past to Maya's present. This Lebanon of Maya's mother and grandmother is a simulated stand-in for the real thing for Maya, even with the acknowledgement that it was not a version she has experienced herself.

Similarly, Tania, who is Palestinian and who has '*read about [Palestine]*', '*heard about [Palestine]*' and has '*listened to songs about [Palestine]*' yet has never been there, identifies with being part of that space. Her description of growing up in Doha, away from '*seasons*' and '*farm-like*' green spaces Fairouz sings about, is something she associates with an envisaged space away from the one she presently occupies. For the two participants, Fairouz plays a role in relaying memories of their elders in imagining a place, which is central to the construction and understanding of their sense of self. To better explain this argument, it is important to put reconstructed memory in conversation with the concept of postmemory. Marianne Hirsch defines postmemory 'as a *structure* of inter- and trans-generational transmission of traumatic knowledge and experience. It is a *consequence* of traumatic recall but . . . at a generational remove'.[24] It is 'to grow up with such overwhelming inherited memories, to be dominated by narratives that preceded one's birth or one's consciousness'.[25] Hirsch explains postmemory in the context of the Holocaust, as 'inherited memories', its central theme being trauma. Reconstructed memory is not necessarily traumatic, but it can be. Time and space play key parts in its reconstruction. For Maya and Tania, their inability to travel to Lebanon and Palestine because of violence and occupation, indicates an imbued trauma in both the spatial and the temporal. It is also about a lost homeland, in both the symbolic (Maya) and literal (Tania) senses. So, for Maya and Tania and their older relatives, it is not only about the reconstruction of memories, or of time, but subsequently the reconstruction of land and space. However, reconstructed memories are not only about land and war, and are not only about generational narratives. Jihad, in Doha, for example, reconstructs a different setting through the songs of Fairouz:

> It touches you. Ya3ni, the use of the lyrics and the music, it takes you to places you've never been before and you'll never be in the future. It's that moment, where you are in a certain mood and a certain song is being played, like, for example, ya3ni, one of her songs that always touched me is the song of, Ya Reit Inta w Ana Fil Bayt, Shi Bayt, Ab3ad Bayt Meghfi Wara Hdood il Hatab,[26] I don't know what, and it's snowing outside, while we are alone inside an old house, and there is that candle, uh, lighting upon us and it's a quiet and content space. Ya3ni, if I had like three shots of wine, and I listen . . . I might cry [laughs]. Because I've always wanted to be in such a room, with such a person you love so much to feel that you are so separated from the whole universe, not only the planet Earth. (Jihad, 51, Palestinian/Jordanian, Doha)

This instance of reconstructed memory differs from those passed on through generations. It is more of an individualized form of reconstruction, drawing on the *micro-habitus*, but it also has elements of storytelling, provoking its reconstruction. Jihad laments that the lyrics and music of Fairouz '*takes you to places you've never been before and you'll never be in the future*'. It is the acknowledgement of not living through such experiences but imagining that one has. Jihad describes a form of reconstructed individual memory he has acquired through Fairouz's songs, but also it shows an example of another overlap in memory, interlacing the reconstructed with the adapted. Adapted memory brings past memories and relates them to present events. Jihad's reconstructed memory thus transforms into one he would like to recreate for himself, since '*I've always wanted to be in such a room, with such a person*'. It is an active synthesis of reconstructed and adapted memories through the *micro-habitus*, which allows for them to engage and build with/on each other.

While associated and reconstructed memory mostly involves the *meta-habitus*, and its effects on the *micro-habitus*, adapted memory stems from the point of the *micro-habitus*, and its presence within the *meta-habitus*, in the sense that memory is centrifugal and emanates from the individual to the communal. Using the lyrics of Fairouz, participants are able to disassociate the contexts of the song from their historical and geographical settings to apply them to current situations. It is thus a case of the 'deterritorialization' and 'reterritorialization' of memory, or what Tarik Sabry would call 'dislocation' and 'creative connectivity',[27] to acclimatize to the ebbs and flows of the *meta-habitus*.

Adapted memory: Prospective, retrospective, pre-mediated and re-mediated

Describing memory as a 'switchboard', Astrid Erll introduces two terms – 'prospectively' and 'retrospectively' – that she argues 'organize experience'.[28] Erll defines 'prospectively' as 'cultural memory' or 'the source of schemata which already pre-form experience . . . decid[ing] what will even enter the individual's consciousness and how this information will be further processed', and 'retrospectively' as 'cultural remembering' which relies on 'creat[ing] experience as an interpretation of events that guides future action'.[29] In this model, Erll essentially contends pre-existing circumstances drive and assist in future forms of 'cultural remembering'. However, while Erll implies the passing of time through this process of 'remembering', spatial transformations are neglected. It is therefore important to bring in both the *meta-* and *micro-habitus* of participants to this discussion to show how space and time trajectories contribute to both 'cultural memory' and 'cultural remembering'. In addition, there is a missing component to remembering, which is an active form of 'retrospection' among members of the Arab diaspora in this study. Memories are consciously adapted by way that the *micro-habitus* reflects on the *meta-habitus*, but with assistance from the media, in this case, the music of Fairouz. In her chapter 'Media and Memory', Erll reflects on the terms 'remediation' and 'pre-mediation'. The author contends 'remediation' allows us to 'fathom the evolution of media technology as a mnemonic process', which 'tends to solidify cultural memory, creating and stabilizing certain narratives and icons of the past'.[30] 'Pre-mediation' brings 'attention to the processes of mediated memory that are at work even *before* the choice for representing a matter in a certain fashion is made', meaning that 'existent media circulating in a given context provide schemata for future experience'.[31] Combining 'prospective' and 'retrospective' with 'pre-mediated' and 're-mediated' gives insight into how adapted memory can surface. With the 'stabilizing' power of 'certain narratives' and the 'schemata of future experience', the 'remembering subject' is not only able to recollect and interpret but also to 're-mediate' memories and apply them to different experiences in the fluctuating environment of the '*meta-habitus*'. So, while associated and reconstructed memory rely on social instigators in their materialization, adapted memory is a way in which the 'remembering subject' situates himself/herself within his/her environment and navigates the relationships of 'prospective', 'retrospective', 'pre-mediation' and 're-mediation' accordingly so as to form new meanings and 're-mediate' new memories:

There is a song for Fairouz that really suits the refugees it's called 'Ihtarafto L Hozna Wal Intezar'.[32] *It says 'Kaborto fil Kharej, Banayto Ahlein Akhareen, kal Shajar Astanbethon fa Wakafo Amami, Wa Ha Ana Astawtino il Faragh, Shoredto 3an Ahli Maratayen'.*[33] *This song was for the Palestinian refugees and it's also applicable for the Syrian refugees. A cliché follower of Fairouz might summarize our current situation by making a lame choice as 'Al Ardo Lakom fal Ardo Tabtahijo, Al Ardo Lana wa Anta Akhi Limaza Izan Tokatiloni*[34] *'I don't like the cliché Fairouz anymore. I prefer the critical and sarcastic part of Fairouz.* (Mounir, 37, Lebanese, London)

I love London to bits, that's why I can't leave, because I don't know where to go, but my other choice would be Berlin, Germany, and for one reason, to follow the immigrants, the migrants, and try to help them accommodate to Europe. So I try to give them an island in my life. And these guys listen to Fairouz all the time . . . I went to Macedonia. It's true they just left Syria, but they're not listening to Syrian people, they're listening to Fairouz. All the camp was Fairouz, Fairouz . . . So, it was beautiful. . . . We were laughing about it. I was telling them. 'Yeah, because you're at war now, you listen to Fairouz, and it was a joke. Because they said 'We never really listened to Fairouz that much.' (Dina, 42, Lebanese, London)

Yeah, she was there, part of that era she's part of the revolution you know, or the Arabness that was supposed to be. (Nafie, 35, Sudanese, Doha)

In 2006, during the Israeli invasion in 2006, I rediscovered Fairouz. I was here . . . I was very sad about what was happening to Lebanon. I wanted to be there, I wanted to feel connected. So, I've always had a rejection of being Lebanese. I've always rejected it; I've always associated being Lebanese with being shallow and materialistic; which doesn't really make sense, because a lot of my friends in Lebanon, and a lot of people I knew and hung out with, were very cool, intellectual, interesting people. So the idea was that, umm . . . I don't know why I had that image of Lebanon and where it came from. But once I got here, after the first two years of kind of gaining some distance and finding some air, if you like, I got to know Lebanon on my own terms, and Fairouz was one of those terms. I was listening a lot to 'Li Beirut',[35] *and I would literally weep while listening to it. So Fairouz just found her way into me on my own terms, not as something that you're supposed to love as a Lebanese person, but someone that I discovered on my own journey and learnt to love. . . . Giving what's happening in Syria and in Lebanon and in Yemen, not too long ago also in Egypt, and is continuing to happen in Egypt and in Bahrain, so what's known as the Arab Spring, although I have a big problem with that terminology. That label, Um . . . a lot of Fairouz's songs became very poignant,*

so, 'Shadi', the song about the young boy who gets lost in the minefield, these kind
of songs started to have a particular resonance, because it was no longer just about
Lebanon and the Lebanese civil war; it became about so much more than that.
(Maha, 35, Syrian/Lebanese, London)

Even though her songs are decades old, Dina and Mounir are able to appropriate them for the Syrian refugees who have been fleeing their country since 2011. This is the essence of adapted memory. It is the ability to make sense of, and describe, the *meta-habitus* through Fairouz's songs and their place within the *micro-habitus* of her fans. In this way, Fairouz is an infinite storyteller. She is able to capture the plights of generations of refugees, who all come from different places and times but who converge in the lyrics of her songs.

The song Mounir highlights was meant *'for the Palestinian refugees, and it's also applicable to the Syrian refugees'*. Similarly, Dina who often travels to assist volunteers in their camps around Europe points out that in Macedonia, *'all the camp was Fairouz, Fairouz'*. According to Dina, the refugees themselves thus seek out Fairouz's songs as a source of comfort during times of war, since they *'never really listened to Fairouz that much'* before the war started. Nafie and Maha's excerpts further expand on the notion of adapted memory at both the collective and individual level. For Nafie, Fairouz was *'part of that era, she's part of the revolution'*. In this way, Nafie connects Fairouz temporally, through her past and *'that era'*, but also her relevance in the controversially termed 'Arab Spring' and its aftermath. Nafie links the singer to *'the Arabness that was supposed to be'* in the context of the *'revolution'*. This authenticity of the revolution is what Nafie alludes to, the *iltizam* of its people and their *iltizam* towards 'Arabness'. Nafie's example shows the ways in which time conducts new forms of *iltizam* or what has been described in this study as the 'intercontextuality' of *iltizam*. Time factors into this 'intercontextuality', defining its presence and being defined by its presence. So, although the 'intercontextuality' of *iltizam* is affected *by* and *through* time, Fairouz remains its key proponent, a standard of Arab 'authenticity' and a proxy by which memory can be adapted and appropriated by her diverse listeners.

Maha, in London, retreats to her own personalized experience of the 2006 Lebanese war with Israel. During that time, Maha *'rediscovered'* Fairouz. It was a way for her to remain *'connected'* to a place she felt estranged from, since she has *'always associated being Lebanese with being shallow and materialistic'*, but *'after the first two years of kind of gaining some distance and finding some air',* Maha was able to get *'to know Lebanon on my own terms, and Fairouz was one of those terms'*. Maha interlinks getting to know Lebanon with getting to know Fairouz, and so her movement through time and space, two years after relocating to London, changes her understanding of both Lebanon and the singer. Maha is able to reconstruct memories of Lebanon and Fairouz through her new appreciation of both in a different spatio-temporal framework. Maha is also able to contextualize Fairouz with regard to *'what's happening in Syria, and in Lebanon and in Yemen, not too long ago also in Egypt, and is continuing to happen in Egypt and in Bahrain'*. Maha's affiliation with Fairouz is no longer only related to Lebanon or cemented to a specific space and time but, instead, it becomes '*so much more than that*'. It is through the adapted memory of Maha, at both the individual and collective level, that she is able to transform the significance of Fairouz and her music to occupy new spaces in new temporal settings. It is not only about the changes occurring within the *micro-habitus* but also about the ways in which the *meta-habitus* is in constant flux. So, here, Fairouz negotiates meanings between the *micro-habitus* and the *meta-habitus*, in their relationship with adapted memory.

Fairouz's infinite ability to transform and represent key cruxes in time and space, and her flexibility at the levels of both the *micro-* and *meta-habitus*, were also important in discussions that extended beyond memory. In conversations with the Arab diaspora in London and Doha, many raised this notion of Fairouz and timelessness. This idea that no matter what the circumstances, Fairouz and her music would live on forever, not just in acoustic space but also within participants and the generations to follow. While a discussion of Fairouz and her continuity among generations follows this section, it is important here to look at how participants expressed Fairouz affectively in terms of their own bodies and the way in which she has become engrained within their very beings through bodily memory:

> *Fairouz, Fairouz, in every song of her songs, it has a story, for sure, that has passed in every person's life. So, some of Fairouz's songs, it reminds us of our childhood and our past, present and future. Fairouz means a lot, a lot, for every Arab person.* (Amin, 27, Palestinian, London)

> *Because she talks about reality, more than any other singers in the world, Fairouz in one song is able to bring you all your life's flashbacks, from the moment you [had your first] milk bottle until after death, you know? Its starts with us from here, the army time, she's there in every memory. Sometimes, I can't listen to her because I am sad.* (Akram, 37, Syrian/Lebanese, London)

> *'Wa aneen l nay yabka ba3da an yafna l wojoud',[36] Fairouz is just like this; she'll remain until the end of time. She doesn't need anyone to remind us of her existence. Fairouz is not waiting for anyone to write articles about her, because she'll never be forgotten.* (Elie, 50, Lebanese, London)

> *I feel that I'm living with [Fairouz]. I don't have to remember her because she is always with me.* (Sara, 46, Lebanese, London)

> *The fact that [Fairouz] is in your cells' memory; in your body cells' memory, so, for me, I can hear someone singing about Beirut, Lebanon, Syria, and not get too emotional. I mean, I do listen to other Arab musicians, especially musicians that are up and coming. For example, Souad Massi, Yasmine Hamdan. I'm into that kind of music, but they don't reach me the way Fairouz does. I think it's because she's in my body memory, you know? Like, my body remembers her. So, when I hear her, my body responds to her, you know? It doesn't even reach the reasoning level; there's no reasoning for listening to her, because I was listening to her ever since I was a child, probably when I was in my mother's womb, my mom was listening*

to her, so she's very much a part of my physicality and who I am, and I think that's why she evokes a response from me, more than others. (Maha, 35, Lebanese/ Syrian, London)

By interlacing Fairouz's songs with '*every Arab person*', Amin conjoins the singer temporally and spatially with her listeners. She is a reminder of the past, still very much present and will remain for the future. For Amin, Fairouz is not just a backdrop but also a guide through the ages, since her songs contain '*a story, for sure, that has passed in every person's life*'. Similarly, Akram traces his own personal journey through time with Fairouz '*from the moment you [had your first] milk bottle, until after death*'. Fairouz's presence is felt in '*every memory*' accompanying both respondents throughout their life journeys. For Elie, Fairouz transcends memory, since she exists even without it and is timeless, since '*she'll remain until the end of time*'. This sentiment is echoed by Sara, who, like Elie, does not need to be reminded of Fairouz, because the singer '*is always with*' her. Fairouz's existence thus extends beyond time and space. She is thus both 'postmemory', in that she is a shift away from memory, 'it approximates memory in its affective force',[37] but she is also not postmemory, in the Hirsch sense, since Fairouz is not just limited to 'trans-generational transmission of traumatic knowledge'.[38] For Maha, Fairouz is '*in your cells' memory; in your body cells' memory*'. She is part of the affective self, which goes beyond any '*reasoning*'. It is a self, which has been constructed '*probably when I was in my mother's womb*'. It is a self at the intersections of the *micro-* and *meta-habitus*, of *iltizam* and its intercontextuality, and of affect and '*reasoning*'. Fairouz thus remains timeless and untouchable, she exists, defines and transforms both time and space, but she remains protected and settled within the bodies and minds of her listeners.

Musical continuity and generational lineage: Fairouz as inheritance

Tania meets me at a coffee shop on the lavish grounds of the Qatar Foundation in Doha. A pre-med student and, at twenty years old, the youngest participant in this study, eloquent beyond her years, Tania's interview spans two and a half hours, in which she gives a comprehensive overview of Fairouz and her discography, as well as the ways in which Fairouz has given her '*a sense of belonging on so many occasions*'. Introduced to Fairouz and her music through her maternal grandfather '*when I was eight*', because '*I was studying at a school that only had English, and that really upset [him]*'. During morning drop-offs to school '*he would always play Fairouz, and explain the lyrics to us*'. While at first resistant, '*I'd sort of roll my eyes at it*', Tania then '*would constantly listen to Fairouz*', finding solace in her songs, and '*felt that Fairouz, at some point, became an escape*'. Raised in a '*very Arab, very traditional*' household, Tania felt at odds in her international high school, where '*maybe [out of] 120 students, three were Arab*'. Incongruous in her surroundings, Tania often found herself '*as the only one who would be doing the right thing, between my friends*', and although '*I don't want to say I was bullied*' but '*[the other students and I] never really clicked*, and so Fairouz *'really helped me pull through a lot of, a lot of times'*. Typecast as the *'nerd'*, or the *'whatever'*, by her peers, Fairouz offered Tania a comforting and non-judgemental space, one where she was able to tune out negativity, *'sometimes people annoy me at university, or whatever, I'll just plug my headphones in and be, like, 'bye guys. I'm done. Discuss your own thing, I'm in my own world.'* After her grandfather passed away in 2012, Fairouz occupied an affective space for the pre-med student, one associated with absence and presence, with memory and experience, loss and inheritance. Tania's example shows the different ways time came up in relationships with Fairouz across the families in the Arab diaspora, but also how her role changes among generations.

Keightley and Pickering argue, 'The mnemonic imagination allows experience to fund new temporal meaning in the present and for those meanings to be shared, as for instance across generations or between different social groups'.[39] So, while Fairouz played an important role in the relationship between Tania and her grandfather, over time it took on 'new temporal meaning[s]', associated with both reminders of the times spent with him and forms of comfort in the absence of belonging. While previous sections of this chapter focused on past and present, Tania's example foreshadows the future of Fairouz and her migratory listeners, but also it outlines how respondents were adamant that they would pass on Fairouz to their children, especially in cases when parents had themselves inherited Fairouz from their own parents.

In his book *Musical Elaborations*, Edward Said begins by thanking his mother, who had passed away before being able to read it. Said writes that he owes his love for music to his mother, 'It is to my mother's own wonderful musicality and love of the art that I owe my earliest interest in music.'[40] The significance of this acknowledgement enhances the findings of this study. While many authors, intellectuals and theorists often pay gratitude to their family members, it is this idea of musical continuity that is worthy of attention, this notion of music as inheritance. In a 1982 interview with American singer, songwriter and producer, Luther Vandross for *The New Black Magazine*, Kalamu ya Salaam asks the singer about his musical upbringing:

VANDROSS: Because my musical awareness was broad. It extended to the left and right of the people whom I like, and whom my mother likes. It was funny, because there is a marked difference between black families and white families. To me the difference is this: in white families, the mother and the father like Frank Sinatra and Liza Minnelli, and the sons like Pink Floyd and the Rolling Stones, whereas in Black families, the mother loves Aretha Franklin and the sons and daughters love Aretha Franklin. The mother loves Gladys Knight and the Pips, and the sons and daughters love Gladys Knight and the Pips.

SALAAM: You're talking about musical continuity?

VANDROSS: I'm also talking music as an integral part of a culture, as opposed to a trendy contribution to the culture.

SALAAM: So, you're saying that Aretha is more than entertainment for us?

VANDROSS: This woman ain't entertainment. She's done opened the books to my life and told everybody. Like Roberta Flack used to say in 'Killing Me Softly,' 'I thought he found my letters and read them all out loud.' We can relate that to everybody. She was the spokesperson for a lot of people and how they feel. (Salaam, 1982, n.p.)

In this excerpt, Vandross alludes to this idea of 'musical continuity', where in 'black families', the children or younger generations often harbour the same listening behaviours in regard to music as their parents or elders. Musical continuity is an important concept to discuss in relation to Fairouz and the Arab diaspora, especially in terms of affect, 'Arabness' and *iltizam*. While I have argued that 'Arabness' does not possess specific traits in terms of definition among the Arab diaspora, it is important to briefly revisit the term by bringing in Ramy Aly's work in *Becoming Arab in London*. For Aly, 'Arabness' is 'best understood not as a form of authentic "being" but as repertoires of "doing"'.[41] It is, as Aly argues, a form of performance, an act of 'doing Arab'. What roles do Fairouz and her music play in the relationship of 'doing Arab' and musical continuity? This is a key question when, later in the section, I analyse responses from those parents who stated that they 'forced' their children to listen to Fairouz.

Many participants were introduced to Fairouz by their parents, thus listening to her music brings back memories of times spent with them, or of them, specifically, which is both pleasurable and nostalgic, but also many respondents were eager to pass on Fairouz and her music to their children. Musical continuity is the link between diaspora, Fairouz, aura, affect, space, time and the mnemonic imagination. It is an inherited continuation, an extension of time and space, and a means towards the infinite:

We listened to it as kids every day. So, whenever I hear songs . . . that have poetry in them, which most Fairouz songs are . . . it brings me a lot of joy. So that's my connection with her. (Tarek, 36, Lebanese, London)

One of the things related to Fairouz is that my mother raised us on the songs of Fairouz, so Fairouz means my mother, now I'm talking about the emotional stuff. (Amar, 39, Lebanese, Doha)

For example, when I miss my parents, the songs that talk about Lebanon will touch me the most, such as 'Hkili Hkili An Baladi'.[42] I love this song with all my heart, it reminds me of my parents. (Sara, 46, Lebanese, London)

Yeah, and I came to live with my dad later on. So, yeah, I lived with him for five years before he passed away, in which I caught up with him. But, yeah, my dad taught me the expat Fairouz education. As in, these are things you need to have. When he died, he had a lot of Fairouz CDs. So I was happy to acquire them. (Dina, 42, Lebanese, London)

Respondents often mentioned ritualistic aspects that were associated with Fairouz from living at their parents' house. While this has previously been discussed in other chapters in the context of space, the focus here is on time and the ways Fairouz and her music become associated with family and family life. Tarek, Amar and Sara credit their parents for listening to Fairouz during their childhood. It is an affective associated memory, especially for Amar, who lost her mother in the 2006 war in Lebanon, and Sara, whose parents live in Lebanon. Fairouz triggers *'the emotional stuff'* with Amar, for a time, when her mother was still alive. For Sara, it is the songs *'about Lebanon'* which *'will touch me the most'*, since her memories are linked to being home with her parents. It is an affective nostalgia for both the spatial and the temporal, since they are bound together in her memories. Dina, in London, attributes her knowledge of Fairouz to her father, who taught her the *'expat Fairouz education'*. This relationship with Fairouz is one nurtured in being in diaspora *'as in these are things you need to have'*. Fairouz is seen as a *'need'* to be able to handle expatriation, a survival kit, or what Sabry and Mansour would define as 'equipment'. By drawing on Heidegger's concepts of 'Worldliness' and 'equipment', the authors seek to unravel the ways in which 'equipment', such as media or, more specifically, television, contribute to 'shaping' the 'Worldliness' of children in Beirut, Casablanca and London. By taking Sabry and Mansour's use of the term 'equipment', we can better understand how, for Dina's father, Fairouz is 'equipment' for living in diaspora. It is a way of preparing Dina to live in that state and to ensure her 'survival'. However, this type of 'Worldliness' differs from that, which is discussed by Sabry and Mansour, in that rather than being used 'as outwardness',[43] Fairouz, as 'equipment', here is used as a means for reflection, a reflection of presence within diasporic space. It is an internal 'extension', a going back in order to move forward.[44] Respondents were quite vocal in wanting to preserve a sense of 'Arab' identity with their families in diaspora, often referring to Fairouz as a school, an educator of values in line with their own. However, the reasons behind this musical continuity were not homogenous and thus need to be explored in some detail:

> *When my kids were younger, I made them listen to old songs of Fairouz on cassettes, until they were sick of it, when I would drop them off and pick them up from school. They were very bored, because I would play the same songs, so I changed the songs a little bit in the end. . . . They love her a lot, they know that Fairouz is my life . . . my kids were born and raised here, [so] they're more [like] foreigners, but I taught them [how] to speak Arabic and they are used to our values and traditions, and they know that I don't tolerate them to be wild.* (Viviane, 56, Lebanese, London)

> *I forced [my children] to listen to Fairouz in the morning. I didn't let them change her songs. Whenever they wanted to change the song, I told them that the morning is for Fairouz. The boy listens to Fairouz now, but the girl listens more. I made them love her.* (Sara, 46, Lebanese, London)

Viviane *'made'* her children *'listen to old songs of Fairouz'* almost everyday *'until they were sick of it'*. Similarly, Sara *'forced'* her children *'to listen to Fairouz in the morning'* and *'made them love her'*. Born and raised in London, Viviane and Sara's children are '*more [like] foreigners*' and thus the women resort to Fairouz as a means to extend their 'Worldliness'. For Viviane, Fairouz is used as 'equipment' for speaking '*Arabic*' and '*to our values and traditions*'. Unwrapping this form of musical continuity is thus to explore the ways in which the *micro-* and *meta-habitus* interact to create new trajectories of identity. While both respondents are, in fact, singers themselves and view Fairouz with the highest regard, their persistence in educating their children on the music of Fairouz goes beyond the aesthetic qualities of the singer. Fairouz is a means to reconnect, a spatio-temporal bridge for the mothers and their children. She is a way of 'performing Arab', since she is deeply associated with the '*values and traditions*' of Arabness and *iltizam*, something the mothers were keen to pass on to their families. For some respondents, Fairouz was an essential constituent of ritual:

> *So sometimes if we're drinking coffee in the morning, we listen to Fairouz, you know, when you don't feel like talking to anyone, she's the only one that can clear the air, but for me it is a daily ritual: Fairouz, coffee, and a cigarette, and I feel that I should teach this to my children, even if they don't understand, they need to get used to it. When my kids say they want to listen to Fairouz, you have no idea what I feel, I feel like I've accomplished something! It's an achievement!* (Amar, 39, Lebanese, Doha)

Amar's notion of musical continuity is also linked to space and time and her own experience of appreciating Fairouz. As mentioned earlier in this section, Amar links Fairouz to her deceased mother, who would play Fairouz constantly for her and her siblings. Successfully passing on this ritual to her children is seen as Amar's '*achievement*'. For all three women mentioned thus far, it is not only about wanting Fairouz to be part of their children's lives, but also it is about the children '*lov[ing]*' and '*want[ing]*' to listen to Fairouz independently, without their mothers' encouragement. Similarly to the example of Dina's father, Fairouz is a type of survival kit, 'equipment' for living in diaspora and a rooting of 'Worldliness'. However, while Sabry and Mansour explain the idea of media as 'equipment' for the extension of 'Worldliness', in the cases discussed in this section, Fairouz is an 'equipment' to the past, a temporal extension to heritage and to memories associated with older family members, and this is evident in the extract from the interview with Elie, a musician in London:

> *I have memories of my childhood that I'd like my children to live and know about. There were games that we used to play, when I was young, and they ceased to exist today. I would have liked my son to experience them. Once, in Lebanon, I took my son to an area I used to like. We used to play there and carve on the trees . . . I didn't find any trees. . . . Everything was cut down. Also, the playground that we used to play in was demolished, and there were buildings in its place. Therefore, they [had] erased my memories. This upsets me. These are the things that I constantly tell my son about, because I can't show them to him. Fairouz is the only thing left from my memories. Therefore, she's the only thing that I can pass down to my children. My*

children can only inherit the love of Fairouz from me. When my children grow up,
Fairouz will help them remember their memories. Fairouz and the music. I believe
that there are two great senses that the human needs. These senses are hearing and
smelling. They are senses that can change a human, and they can transport you
from one place to another in seconds. Sometimes, you smell something and it will
take you years back. Music has the same effect. Sometimes, you hear something
and you feel that you've heard it before, or it will take you to some place you
know. . . . It's what people call déjà vu. The quality of music today is degrading
and descending. Fairouz is a heritage that we should all pass down to our children.
This way she'll keep on spreading, and her continuity and reach to people will be
ensured. Fairouz should be in every home. I can't imagine a time with no Fairouz.
Therefore, Fairouz should always be present. She should always exist among us. I
want people to still talk about Fairouz after a hundred years. I don't want people
to talk about her as if she's something from the past. (Elie, 50, Lebanese, London)

For Elie, 'Fairouz *is the only thing left from my memories'*. Disappointed that his
children are growing up in a different environment than he is used to, but also that
the environment he was accustomed to '*was cut down', 'demolished'* and '*erased',*
Elie is unable to share his history and the elements linked to it with his children. The
only thing left to '*pass down'* is Fairouz's music. For Elie, Fairouz encompasses the
spatio-temporal attributes of his past, which he can no longer locate in the present.
It is further evidence of the affective autonomy of Fairouz's 'aura', which is able to
resurrect and adapt *with* and *through* the mnemonic imagination and the habitual
situations of participants. Fairouz is a reminder of collective and individual history
and is able to stand in for both. This is why Elie's plea that '*[Fairouz] should always*
exist among us' is about not only the singer but also the time and space which she
represents for him. Fairouz is the unique bearer of this past, carrying it through
her music for future generations. Fairouz '*will help them remember their memories',*
this overlapping of associated, reconstructed and adapted memory is the essence
of the musical continuity Elie wants for his family, one which has roots in a certain
geo-historical context but one which can also morph and take shape in its own
journey. Similarly to Viviane, Sara and Amar, Elie wants his children to '*inherit*
the love of Fairouz from me'. This interesting need for participants to have their
children '*want*' or '*love*' Fairouz is affective, but also it is a way to bond the past to
the future, where older and younger generations are able to connect through the
music of Fairouz and the signifiers correlated with her and her music:

Sometimes, I like my kids to listen to it, just to get familiarized with it; they don't
like it, at all. That doesn't help, so it makes me down a bit. Ya Allah,[45] *my kids don't*
like Fairouz, it's like a big deal. (Dina, 42, Lebanese, London)

In his chapter 'Differential Intensities of Social Reality: Migration, Participation
and Guilt', Ghassan Hage presents the ways in which the Lebanese community in
Sydney respond to news about Lebanon. The author explores how 'the reading of a
news item in the Lebanese paper is a totally Lebanese experience where belonging

to the Australian physical space becomes immaterial and suspended'.[46] Central to his study are the ways readers relate to content, what Hage calls 'strategies of intensification', an affective method of negotiating with certain news events.[47] Hage explains 'strategies of intensification' as being 'guilt-ridden moves within a general moral economy of social belonging'.[48] Drawing on Marx and Nietzsche, Hage contends the need for individuals to 'repay the gift' of 'social and communal life' through 'a life-time of participating in it'.[49] It is the feeling of being in constant debt to the 'communal group' that has given individuals the 'gift of community'.[50] In cases of migration, the process itself is 'guilt-inducing', since 'to leave the communal group to which one is indebted is precisely to refrain from paying the debt'.[51] For Dina, in London, listening to or '*lik[ing]*' Fairouz can be seen as a form of 'participating' in the 'communal group'. By playing Fairouz's music to her children, Dina is contributing to the singer's continuity over time, which can be seen as a way to 'repay' the 'debt'. However, her children not liking Fairouz '*is a big deal*', since it contributes to the 'guilt' induced by the lack of 'participation'. Dina's dismay at her children not liking the singer is thus twofold. It is an individual defeat in that Dina, a fan of Fairouz and someone who is deeply involved with the Arab community in London, cannot transmit this sense of identity to her children, but also it is a collective failure to repay the debt of participation to the 'communal group' to which she belongs. The need for musical continuity among participants is thus very much related to their positions within social environments and the ways they negotiate and navigate those realms. Contextualizing musical continuity alongside a geo-historical and political narrative is the essence of understanding how Fairouz is passed on and inherited by generations of Arab diaspora in London and Doha.

Timeless memories

Interweaving collective and individual experience, Fairouz provides a sonically contrived archive of space and time. Communally, respondents turn to Fairouz to express pivotal events in the Middle East, but also Fairouz is there at the personal level, charting individual phases and providing a soundtrack to individual narratives. Through the agency of her 'aura', Fairouz is able to straddle past, present and future, provoking nostalgia, yet simultaneously surfacing as an indicator of hope. This is a more 'productive' type of nostalgia, one which 'may foster a form of longing that is quite compatible with hope'.[52] Although, at times, participants did not offer any remedies to the nostalgic past they linked with Fairouz, some of them did, seeing her songs not only as historical reminders but also as optimistic visions of the future.

The agency of participants to temporally and spatially travel through their mnemonic imaginations was evident. This is formulated in three, frequently overlapping ways. First, in associated memory, which is the most affective form of remembering. This involved memories of loved ones and of times of war, especially among the Lebanese respondents in this study. These memories often led to affect resulting in emotional responses in their recollections. Second, through reconstructed memory, participants showcased a modified way of remembering, with awareness that experiences were not lived personally but instead lived through the memories of others. Reconstructed memories are very much linked to space and time, in that it is not only the music of Fairouz that is disseminated but also images of 'home', landscapes and concepts of belonging. Reconstructed memory serves as a reminder that notions of home are not stagnant in space but float and take shape across time. For associated and reconstructed ways of remembering, the *meta-habitus* leads the *micro-habitus*, in the sense that circumstances and environmental factors often drive the mnemonic imagination towards a form of remembering. However, with adapted remembering, it is the *micro-habitus*, which assesses and reflects on the *meta-habitus* in the construction of memory. Adapted memory takes on memories from the past to apply them to the present. Through Fairouz's lyrics, participants were active in this application, furthering the notion of Fairouz as timeless and accommodating limitless geopolitical, sociocultural and historical situations.

Moving through generations, Fairouz occupies various roles, and so the need for musical continuity among participants, their children and their parents is very much related to their positions within social environments and the ways they interact with and understand those surroundings. Placing musical continuity within a relative framework thus helps to deconstruct the ways Fairouz and her music find significance among both older and younger generations in Doha and London, and also highlights her presence in the past, present and future. In some cases, she is not found externally to the individual but resides within the body's memory. It is, as Ali in London attests, that '*she remained in a different place. She stayed in our imagination*', and it is through the conjoining of the imagination and Fairouz that allows for a timeless trajectory in understanding, appreciating and appropriating Fairouz and her music.

UNDERSTANDING DIASPORIC EXISTENCE
THROUGH THE SONGS OF FAIROUZ

This book began as an attempt to explore the role Fairouz played in the lives of the Arab diaspora in London and Doha, focusing on how participants positioned themselves according to Fairouz and her music, and to elucidate forms of identity construction and belonging in that process. However, narratives moved beyond mere identity. Essentially, discussing Fairouz meant discussing diasporic life, ushering in a host of converging and diverging trajectories that gave insight into both individual and collective experiences, as well as exploring them in accordance with spatial and temporal aspects. Arab diasporic occurrences are diverse in their history and actuality, whether members are migrants or refugees, leaders or followers in migration, or whether they are socially integrated or isolated.

It is exactly this lack of homogeneity that was found in conversations on Fairouz. In addition to acting as a soundtrack to the daily routines of participants, Fairouz brought to the surface the various quotidian experiences and encounters to which members of the Arab diaspora were subjected. The diverse geographical locations between Doha and London, and the timeframe in which the research was conducted, all played a part in this discourse. It is here that the concepts of the *meta-habitus* and *micro-habitus* emerge to illuminate and accommodate these disparities. It is through the interrelation between the two types of *habitus*: the overarching consequence of the political, social, cultural and environmental dynamics in which participants reside, and the more specific situations, such as domestic arrangements, familial ties and gender roles, that guide the consumption and reception of Fairouz and her music. The double layers of *habitus* highlight the fluctuating global and private environments surrounding the samples in this study, setting the stage for discussions on Fairouz and unravelling stories of living in migration.

Affectively, migration found itself encircled by childhood, war, love and loss, by past and future. With the *micro-* and *meta-habitus*, migration was not the beginning, nor was it the end, and it was through the music of Fairouz that these historical and geographical elements were emphasized. Fairouz also opened up opportunities for looking at diasporic gender relations, of naturalization and citizenship and of exploring memory. Tangents of 'Arabness' were explored, showing how the singer cannot be confined to one monolithic homeland, expanding on Christopher Stone's argument that Fairouz was a 'post-colonial, nation-building project'.[1] Instead, Fairouz is able to simultaneously represent all Arab nations, a particular

Watan,[2] or none at all, depending on the 'subject positions' and 'intersectional' qualities of her listeners, and their relationship to the *meta-* and *micro-habitus*. Fairouz is a driver of patriotism and resistance, of *iltizam*, commitment and its intercontextuality. Through her songs, such themes are navigated across webs of sociocultural and geo-historical attributes and circumstances. By way of her 'aura', Fairouz is able to travel, mould and encapsulate, defying Walter Benjamin's assertion that art is best appreciated in its spatio-temporal setting. The 'aura' of Fairouz takes on deeper significance and affective strength the further it moves away from the context with which it is associated. Fairouz simultaneously emits and embodies 'aura', transporting her listeners to moments and places, but also she is able to construct, share and maintain space and time with her songs. It is through the *micro-* and *meta-habitus* that individual experience with Fairouz and her 'aura' are understood, reflected on and interpreted, giving way to comprehending the individual and the social complexities that arise in audience reception, especially when it is seen through an affective framework. The interplay of Fairouz, as a 'figure', the strength of her 'aura' and the affective positioning of her listeners, generates a multiplicity of meanings and maintains her significance across spatial and temporal lines.

Moreover, affect provides a platform from which to analyse the ways participants situate themselves in accordance with their environment and through the music of Fairouz. Concepts such as 'Arabness', or what it means to be Arab, differed among participants, but also found points of commonality. As a method by which to 'do' Arab, but also as a symbol of 'Arabness', Fairouz offers private and collective correlations for her listeners to respond to. At the same time, 'Arabness' was seen as a flexible framework, which was affective, discursive, negotiated, performed and imagined. Performing 'Arab' did not always share similarities but also drew on personal affective descriptions. However, a key constituent of 'Arabness' is *iltizam*, or commitment. The evolution of *iltizam* takes shape through the *meta-* and *micro-habitus*, establishing it as a multi-layered concept, reliant on numerous factors for its production and preservation. It is no longer seen, as originally intended, as a unifying force among Arab communities. Rather, *iltizam* is subjectively 'intercontextual', allowing for fluctuations in the *meta-* and *micro-habitus* to position identity.

The intercontextuality of *iltizam* shows the inconsistencies in 'commitment' among participants, in an era punctuated with polarized politics and an increase in religious fundamentalism. These dynamics manifest as affect, as affect works across these non-linear gradients, policing self-identity and positioning the self in relation to others. So, arguably, while *iltizam* was a purpose through which to unite, 'intercontextual' *iltizam* indicates division and fragmentation. Intercontextual *iltizam* also highlights the autonomy of what to remain committed to. It is a contested space, where commitment is contingent on dynamic processes and affective agendas that are put in place by the *meta-* and *micro-habitus*. Offering her fans a wide periphery to find and form those key elements that contribute to their sense of self, Fairouz is seen as a hybrid identity space. Hybrid in the sense that she encapsulates multiple segments of identities, which diasporic communities are able to actively sift through, to claim or reject cross-cultural attributes in their own self-representation. Fairouz thus acts as an intermediary between 'authenticity' and 'hybridity' on the pathway to 'becoming Arab' and 'doing Arab'.

The relationship between the *meta-* and *micro-habitus*, the intercontextuality of *iltizam* and affect, is also manifested in contrasting perceptions of 'home' and nationhood. Through the mnemonic imaginations of respondents, a merging of memory and imagination, alongside the temporal and spatial, affective and private notions of 'home' and 'belonging' resulted. Symbolically housing her listeners in the rich landscapes and familiar alleyways found in her lyrics, Fairouz creates an 'affective state'. This 'state' can be understood literally and conceptually as nationhood and homeland, but also as condition and circumstance. Home was not always a physical place but, at times, affectively intangible. Tapping into the individual and collective mnemonic imaginations of her listeners, Fairouz offers affective concepts of belonging, adhering to intersectional subject positions and *meta-* and *micro-habitual* contours. She is a reminder of home, but that home cannot always be defined, it is the feeling of home, of belonging, one which is both affective and imagined. It is important to note that affect is not contained within Fairouz or her music, nor is it contained within her listeners but, instead, affect is generated through 'the movement between signs',[3] this further stresses the importance of the *meta-* and *micro-habitus* in discussion of Fairouz and her fans, since together they capture the contextual and discursive structures working towards affect.

The 'aura' of Fairouz in space and place

A factor in this contextual structure is space. Space is a means through which participants are linked *with*, and linked *to*, Fairouz and her songs. Place is personal and affective, whereas space is fluid and nodal, with the potential for affect. Space is dynamic and active in containing, shaping and interacting with Fairouz and her music. The spaces and places where Fairouz is heard, and their relationship to the *meta-* and *micro-habitus*, are foundational to examining the behaviour, understanding and appreciation of her songs, since as the body moves through space and place, so does Fairouz's 'aura'. Travelling with respondents, Fairouz not only creates an affective space with her music, but her 'aura' is one that also grounds her listeners in 'place'. By way of her songs, Fairouz is able to mobilize through 'space' to create a parallel 'space', which participants tap into through their mnemonic imagination. Such space is one of familiarity and comfort, regardless of its existence in actuality, but precisely because it exists in Fairouz's songs. For Abdelmalek Sayad, the process of migration leads to 'frustration' of being away from the 'mother-society' and 'nurturing land'.[4] Being in the non-nurturing land, participants are removed from this Fairouzian space, which is linked to her music. Being embedded within this 'nurturing' space, Fairouz, through her 'aura', thus becomes its representation the further removed her listeners are from it. Adding to this is an affective element since, as the body moves through space, it needs to 're-habit', 'reform' and 'reconfigure' according to its surroundings and new environment.[5] Through Fairouz's music and the affective spaces of 'home' and 'not home', 'nurturing' and 'non-nurturing', the individual 'reconfigures' his/her position in relation to the collective. It is the interplay of bodies, space and affect that constructs a sense of 'home', and subsequent belonging, in the context of Fairouz. However, this movement is not only spatial but also temporal between 'the horizons of experience, expectation and possibility', which gives room for the 'synthesis' of Fairouz and her music to 'achieve new meaning in the present'.[6] Through the temporal and spatial dislocation of participants and the 'aura' of Fairouz, there is room for a reflection of presence and absence. The occupying of space that leads to that, which becomes memory, not only alters the relationship with Fairouz and her 'aura' but also instigates different forms of affect, since the body 'infolds *contexts*'.[7] Amalgamating through 'space', 'contexts' are acknowledged affectively through mnemonic imaginings of presence and absence.

Presence and absence determine the positions of respondents in space, as well as show how affect and the mnemonic imagination work in tandem with participants' intersectional qualities and their *micro-* and *meta-habitus* to produce different forms of consumption and interpretation. Fairouz represents both presence and absence, since she is able to reflect both. Travelling with participants, Fairouz provides a 'presence' of 'place' in its 'absence', a reminder of the past, but also a substitute for the present and the future. She is strategic in 'reforming' 'space' to occupy the feeling of 'place', transgressing space to occupy an affective state in the realm of absence and presence, but also, through the *meta-* and *micro-habitus* of participants, the singer takes on different connotations and functions. In this way, place moves beyond rigid and private structures. Place is dynamic and in constant engagement. It is a point of reflection, drawing on 'a distinct *mixture* of wider and more local social relations'.[8] Fairouz and her music act as spatial locators allowing for a contemplative journey across the relationships of place to space, absence to presence, and '*Al-ghurba*' to '*haneen*'. *Al-ghurba*, or expatriation, is the absence from one's country – a shift in space, but it also occupies a range of significances depending on the context with which it is associated and the geo-historical point from which it is expressed. Understanding *Al-ghurba* requires knowledge of cultural and social discourses surrounding the 'pre-thinking' that is required to be able to express and translate the term.[9] The *meta-habitus* and *micro-habitus* assist in this 'pre-thinking' to better explain the term in relation to respondents. Importantly, *Al-ghurba* is a state of affect, especially when coupled with the affective state of *haneen* – nostalgia, craving, longing and yearning. Space is a major contributor to *haneen*, since it is *within* space that *haneen* occurs and also *through* space that it travels. Similarly, *Al-ghurba*, as a spatial shift, inherently carries space and recognizes the self as a 'foreign body' within that space. *Al-ghurba* and *haneen* are mutually exclusive but are affectively powerful when together. The two states are continuously evolving. They are spectra across which vectors of individual and collective *micro-* and *meta-habitus* subject positions and mnemonic imaginations intersect.

Al-ghurba and *haneen* are intricately linked to a sense of belonging found within *Al-Watan*. *Al-ghurba* gives rise to the comparative state of *Al-Watan*, since it is its polar opposite. *Haneen* is a longing for belonging in *Al-Watan*. Whatever the differences in their perceptions of *Al-Watan*, participants make a distinction between it and the space they occupy in diaspora, or in *Al-ghurba*. Peter Blickle positions the German notion of Heimat as a response to modernization, a 'longing' for the 'pre-modern state'.[10] The pre-modern, Arabized imagery of *Al-Watan* is broadcast through Fairouz's lyrics but is acknowledged through the mnemonic imagination. Individualized, and at the same time shared, *Al-Watan* is constructed centrifugally, through the familiar images Fairouz projects in the lyrics of her songs, as well as centripetally, through the mnemonic imagination which selects, links, filters and merges experience with landscape, loved ones and cherished moments. Fairouz provides a flexible space for both 'personal' and 'popular' memory to unite and reconstruct so as to form *Al-Watan*. A combination of imagery associated with Mediterranean landscapes and geographies, of village life and the accompanying simplicity found there, but also individualized ideas of 'home', and consequently of the 'self', *Al-Watan* comprises the romanticism of *iltizam*, but also the realism of its intercontextuality. It is difficult to disassociate the sociopolitical climate of *Al-Watan*, since Fairouz's appeal is not just limited to one specific nation, and thus it absorbs the tensions, violence and destruction found in Arab world history.

Naturalization, 'power geometries' and worldliness

The intercontextuality of *iltizam* was also found in conversations about naturalization and citizenship. Flexibility of motion across spaces shapes perceptions of naturalization and its relationship with *iltizam*. Migration, or mobility across space, is dependent on *micro-* and *meta-habitual* factors. Women and refugees are more prone to experiencing limited movement in the absence of naturalization since a British passport contributed to the ease of motion through borders. Due to strict citizenship laws, the Qatari nationality is rarely an option, highlighting some of the key differences between diasporic samples in Doha and London in respect of ideas of 'home' and belonging. Naturalization facilitated movement among members of the Arab diaspora, especially women and refugees. Interestingly, gender played a big role in the acceptance of naturalization, since it was equated with freedom of movement. Mobility across space was found to be a gendered phenomenon, in that, in Doha, women were mostly there because of fathers or spouses. In London this was true of half the women interviewed, showing the disparity in movement that was raised by discussions on naturalization. Migration thus needs to be framed as both a subjective and collective experience, dependent on amalgamating factors arising from the *meta-* and *micro-habitus*. Through her music, Fairouz gives a peek into the gendered public and private lives of the Arab diaspora living in London and Doha. Via her gender, the singer provides insight into differences among the women recruited in this study, thus highlighting the various positions they occupy within space. However, issues around gender were not only limited to public spaces, they also manifested in domestic spaces. Space and gender operate politically and affectively, but also their relationship is determined by power dynamics put in place by *meta-* and *micro-habitual* situations. These dynamics arise in domestic relationships, where males took ownership of the sound waves, especially in cases where Arab men were married to 'non-Arab' women. For Arab women married to 'non-Arab' men, Fairouz plays a part in the setup of a place of contemplation, one where the women could reflect on and recharge their sense of self. In addition, the singer acted as 'equipment' to express 'Worldliness'.[11] As 'equipment', Fairouz is the soundscape for preservation, offering a gendered benchmark by which respondents can assess the space to which they are connected, and their situation within that space, effectively and affectively positioning and guiding them across space and time.

Fairouz, as 'equipment', for the extension of 'Worldliness' can also be used in a temporal sense, especially in the context of musical continuity and the Arab diaspora. Unlike Sabry and Mansour's argument for an 'outwardness' with regard to 'equipment' and 'Worldliness',[12] one that looks at ways for participants to extend their knowledge further outside their surroundings, in this case, Fairouz is used among the Arab diaspora as 'equipment' for a reflection of presence within diasporic space, an internal 'extension', a going inwards to move forwards in the effort to preserve the identity and meaning found within Fairouz's songs and in her symbolic representation among her listeners. Fairouz is thus 'equipment' for preservation, of musical continuity among the generations of the Arab diaspora who associate her music with 'Arabness' and *iltizam*. Preservation, here, is thus seen as a connection with authenticity and to 'Arabness'. In addition, Fairouz, through her songs, is able to trace the evolution of modern Arab society over time, giving room for participants to reflect on their own growth in that evolution. She provides a spatio-temporal narrative of both individual and collective experience. This falls in line with arguments for the implementation of 'cultural memory', since 'sociocultural contexts' allow for a deeper analysis of memory that takes into consideration the environment in which memories are 'recalled'.[13] The relationship of respondents to time and memory is reliant on 'culture-specific schemata', which 'preform every single experience we have' in a 'cultural context' that influences what is remembered and the ways it is expressed.[14] The *meta-* and *micro-habitus* play a key role here in conceptualizing and generating modes of remembering, since they are responsible for 'every single experience' individuals confront, as well as the 'cultural context' in which those are encountered. Modes of remembering among the sample in this study are categorized into three groups: associated, reconstructed and adapted memory.

Remembering as mediated engagement

Associated memory fuses the mnemonic imagination with affect theory, in the sense that Fairouz's songs play a part in recreating a memory and, as a result, lead to affect. That is not to say that other forms of memory are not affective, but affect in associated memory is prevalent, since associated memory resurrects moments of wartime or of times spent with loved ones. Associated memory brings together people, places and shared experiences, which materialize individually through the music of Fairouz and are instigated cyclically through the *meta-* and *micro-habitus*. This mnemonic process is a constant continuation of 'life experience', which is absorbed and released through its temporal and spatial journey. Reconstructed memory is a revised form of remembering, with a cognizant or intuitive sense of awareness that experience may not have been lived through personally, but rather has been lived through the experience of others. Combining 'lived experience' with 'second hand experience',[15] reconstructed memory harbours personal and subjective dimensions, since memories have essentially been passed down and taken on. While associated memory is biased towards the mnemonic component of the mnemonic imagination, reconstructed memory skews towards the imagination segment. Memory and imagination thus sway according to the relationship between the mnemonic imagination and the 'remembering subject'. On the other hand, adapted memory is an active way of 'retrospection'. It is the application of past memory to present events. While associated and reconstructed memory arise from the *meta-habitus* and its interaction with the *micro-habitus*, adapted memory takes shape from the point of view of the *micro-habitus* and its presence within the *meta-habitus*. It is an individual perspective on the communal, and it is assisted by the presence of media texts, such as Fairouz's music. By way of adapted memory, the 'remembering subject' is not only able to summon and decipher memories but is also able to 'remediate' and apply them to different situations in the shifting conditions of the *meta-habitus*. In this way, Fairouz remains an infinite storyteller, since no matter what the circumstances among the Arab diaspora Fairouz finds significance. Even though Fairouz is reminiscent of a certain historical and geographical context, she does not remain there, instead, she occupies different positions within time to acquire a timelessness that is at once an extension of the past, a present relevance and a sense of hope for the future.

Representative of 'Arabness' and *iltizam*, Fairouz, as a 'figure', embodies a spectrum of meanings. By distancing her private life from her audience, she remains ascribed and integrated with the messages in her songs. This distance provides her listeners with the opportunity to appropriate her and her music in ways that best suit them and their needs. Fairouz is thus able to incorporate the 'social space' of her listeners within the 'dwelling space' of her songs, encouraging her fans to navigate, contest and interact through these spaces according to their *meta-* and *micro-habitus*. She is omnipresent, existing in transitions of 'social space' and timeframes, in memories and moments, in the present and the future, bringing different meanings to the Arab diaspora in London and Doha. Borderless, Fairouz takes 'flight', yet she remains rooted and grounded through the mnemonic imagination of her listeners, effectively becoming 'reterritorialized'.[16] She is simultaneously reminiscent of time and place, but also shifts to inhabit different 'planes' of self-reflection and creativity so as to live on, not just in acoustic space but also within the bodily memory of her listeners and their offspring.

Fairouz and the fields of research: An overview

While there have been many calls by researchers for the non-fixity of diaspora and a need to understand them as a heterogeneous and dynamic evolving body, they should also be seen within contexts and structures undergoing constant change. These fluctuations are both spatial and temporal, and they are integral in studying diasporic communities as part of a shifting environment that goes beyond individual experience. The *meta-* and *micro-habitus* not only allow for such a framework among members of the diaspora but also help in looking at audiences in general, especially when they are interacting with media texts. While previous studies have considered the sociocultural context in their work on audiences and media, these need to be seen through a double-layered lens, one that encompasses the individual amidst the domestic, the local and the global.

Positioning audience members in this way is not only indicative of how private media interpretation can change according to environmental and personal intersections but also shows how media texts can find relevance amidst these alterations and circumstances. Popular culture is essential in providing insight into the everyday experience of audiences and members of the diaspora. This is especially important among Arab diasporic groups, who harbour a plethora of individual and collective characteristics that are further diversified due to the actualities of where and how they live. By way of the *meta-* and *micro-habitus*, the Arab diaspora is thrust into the expanding arena of Arab cultural studies, where they are armed with new 'beginnings' to detach them from the historical and geographical phenomena by which they are usually framed and, instead, to move forwards to encompass the new realities in which they are embedded. In this way, the diaspora is given 'concretised foregrounding' allowing for a conjunctional examination 'between the social, political, economic, existential and the anthropological'.[17] Arab cultural concepts thus take on new meaning, blossoming geographically and historically from their original narratives, they are essentially 'displaced' and 'reterritorialized', paving the way for 'creative connectivity' to incorporate the present.[18] In addition, the everyday, or banal, modes of popular media – such as Fairouz's songs – in Arab culture make way for new models of identity and belonging to materialize in discussions with those in the Arab diaspora about how they situate, and are situated by, such media. While hybridity and intercontextual hybridity have formed key arguments in the negotiation of 'transnational cultural dynamics',[19] to examine how identities and other social constructions are able to merge and diversify, of letting go and taking in, intercontextual *iltizam* acts as an accompaniment to that morphing, in that it illustrates agential forms of commitment, of holding on and of keeping. Moreover, intercontextual *iltizam* moves away from the political and homogenizing pan-Arab milieu with which it was associated to demonstrate the divisiveness among Arab communities that runs along vectors of commitment and authenticity. Fairouz allows for that gauge between hybridity and authenticity, giving her listeners the opportunity to traverse both.

Fairouz can thus no longer be seen as a singer associated with a specific time and place as argued by Stone, who used the 1998 Ba'albeck International Festival to analyse the singer and the Rahbani coalition, stating:

> Fairouz had come to represent nothing less than the nation itself, a position which required that she be an incarnation of romantic ideals about the female Lebanese mountain peasant while at the same time being virtually a bodiless, sexless, motionless, mute and haloed angel. (Stone, 2008, p. 172)

Cementing Fairouz to a certain time and place limits her appeal and erases the power of her 'aura' to reach fans outside the Lebanese nation. Fairouz's 'aura' is not only strengthened across space and time but is able to also incorporate and emit spatio-temporal elements. Instead, Fairouz must be seen as timeless, omnipresent and as an affective force in constructing her own spatio-temporal 'aura'. She must be 'deterritorialized' to become 'reterritorialized'. So far, studies on Fairouz have been biographical and disco-graphical, focusing on her role as a singer, her evolution over time, her development in the era of radio technology, her songs and her strong connection to folklore, using ethno-musicality as a foundation for research. This book differs in that audiences, and specifically diasporic audiences, are at the forefront of analysis. Using an ethnographic approach helps to decipher the ways in which Fairouz is heard among her listeners and the various functions she performs in the lives of Arab diaspora. Symbiotically, Fairouz, as a proxy, gives way to understanding the behaviours of diaspora through interviews and discussions, adding audience perspectives to existing work on the singer, as well as in the field of music studies. The affective interlacing of music and audience brings to light new ways of understanding both. Literally, then, Fairouz gives participants a voice, not in the clichéd sense but one which they are active agents in constructing. Sorting and filtering through her songs, the Arab diaspora in London and Doha is able to find ways to express their experiences and identities, both as individuals and as groups.

Paving the way to discerning relationships between space and time under the auspices of the Arab diaspora, Fairouz is able to situate participants accordingly. Spatio-temporalities, such as *Al-ghurba* and *haneen*, offer other ways to understand 'foreignness' and 'nostalgia', away from the ethno-centric language limitations placed on the terms. Both terms provide a spectrum of meanings that is dependent on the *micro-* and *meta-habitual* situations of individuals and communities, and in which members of the diaspora are able to locate themselves. *Al-ghurba* and *haneen* are not only positions in space and time but are also markers of identity and belonging – or non-belonging. Through them, respondents are able to articulate constructions of self, as well as to examine that self in its social state.

However, one cannot ignore the role of the mnemonic imagination in forming these relationships between Fairouz and her audience. Taking on concepts from cultural memory, and expanding on them, illustrates the ways the mnemonic imagination morphs through the interaction with media texts in three different, yet at times overlapping, ways to incorporate past, present and future. By way of

Fairouz and her music, audiences are able to activate their memories and apply them, or 'remediate' them, to present-day situations. Adaptation of memory is thus a process by which the *micro-habitus* works to emit memory towards the *meta-habitus*. Using lyrics in Fairouz's songs, participants transfer them to current events to better explain and contextualize them. Fairouz thus remains timeless and relevant, expanding through the mnemonic imagination to encompass generations of her listeners. While adapted memory stems from the *micro-habitus*, associated and reconstructed memory are formed through the *meta-habitus* and find place within the *micro-habitus*, as both lived experience and 'second hand' experiences, respectively. These three forms of remembering highlight the dynamism found within memory that is not compartmentalized but, rather, grows and blooms over time and space. However, although this study does not contain enough samples or data to elaborate on collective memory processes, it does allow for insights into individual memory systems, especially in light of Fairouz and her music.

Secrets of existence

While participants mostly spoke about Fairouz positively, sometimes she was criticized for giving a false sense of reality through her songs, or she was accused of disseminating submissive messages to women. In some cases, assumptive comments were made about her role as a mother, and others complained her music was overbearingly depressing and melancholy. It is important to note, this research does not claim to be symptomatic of Fairouz's listeners around the world, nor is it suggestive of the behaviours and experiences of all Arab diasporic communities. The purpose of this study was never to romanticize Fairouz's role among the Arab diaspora but, rather, to explore the mediatory role she played in their lives. Through her music, Fairouz opens up dialogue and gives insight into processes that shape relationships with her listeners, situating them according to their spatio-temporal surroundings and allowing them to construct versions of their identity in the context in which they are presented.

Thus, to ignore Fairouz is to ignore an important 'Arab' icon. Through her songs, Fairouz has touched the lives of many Arab diasporic communities around the world and while this book focused solely on two geographical locations, she is heard globally.[20] For Lebanese listeners, Fairouz remains a constant. Her significance at a national level is unprecedented and she remains untouchable and immaculate. She is reminiscent of a better Lebanon, of the 'golden age' whether or not that has ever existed is irrelevant. Her position as a Lebanese 'national treasure' is never disputed, neither is her power to connote 'Lebaneseness' and promote patriotism. However, her role cannot and does not end at the borders of Lebanon. Between Arabs who are fans of her music she bridges differences and highlights common trajectories while transporting them to a world that only exists in her songs. It is through these songs that the secrets of existence among the Arab diaspora in London and Doha can be found and heard.

NOTES

Chapter 1

1 Habib, 2005, p. 1.
2 Although, in his dissertation, *The Superstar Singer Fairouz and the Ingenious Rahbani Brothers*, Kenneth Habib (2005) conducted a number of interviews with fans of Fairouz's music, his purpose was to further highlight the cultural significance of Fairouz and the Rahbani brothers, rather than to try to understand forms of identity construction that move beyond Lebanese nationals.
3 Stone, 2008, p. 1.
4 Stone, 2008, p. 1.
5 Stone, 2008, p. 10.
6 Taylor, 1989, p. 47.
7 Taylor, 1989, p. 47.
8 Taylor, 1989, p. 50.
9 Stewart, 2010, p. 344.
10 Bourdieu, 1990, p. 54.
11 Bourdieu, 1990, p. 60.
12 Fiske, 1994, pp. 70–3.
13 Benjamin, 1936, n.p.
14 Sabry, 2012, pp. 17–19.
15 Massumi, 1995, p. 88.
16 Keightley and Pickering, 2012, p. 84.
17 Keightley and Pickering, 2012, p. 84.
18 Seigworth and Gregg, 2010, p. 1.
19 Ahmed, 2004a, p. 119.
20 Ahmed, 2004b, p. 127.
21 Ahmed, 2004a, p. 120.
22 Ahmed, 2004b, p. 28.
23 Ahmed, 1999, p. 342.
24 Ahmed, 2004a, p. 120.
25 Taylor, 1989, p. 36.
26 Taylor, 1989, p. 36.
27 Taylor, 1989, pp. 46–7.
28 Sabry, 2012, p. 13.
29 Sabry, 2012, p. 14.
30 Kadi, 1994, xix.
31 Jamal and Nader, 2008, p. 2.
32 Karlyn, 2009, p. 180.
33 Sabry, 2012, p. 14.
34 Karlyn, 2009, p. 180.
35 Levin, 1993, p. 2.

36 Smith, 1994, p. 238.
37 Smith, 1994, p. 233.
38 Smith, 1994, p. 234.
39 Smith, 1994, p. 236.
40 Street, 2012, p. 1.
41 DeNora, 2003, p. 17.
42 Street, 2012, p. 8.
43 Street, 2012, p. 6.
44 Brah, 1996, p. 181.
45 Slobin, 1994, p. 243.
46 Slobin, 1994, p. 244.
47 Slobin, 1994, p. 244.
48 Schaefer, 2015, p. 496.
49 Schaefer, 2015, p. 497.
50 Schaefer, 2015, p. 503.
51 Schaefer, 2015, p. 505.
52 Frishkopf, 2010, pp. 17–18.
53 Abdel-Nabi et al., 2004, p. 231.
54 Abdel-Nabi et al., 2004, p. 232.
55 Gilman, 2014, p. 15.
56 Gilman, 2014, p. 13.
57 Gilman, 2014, p. 209.
58 See Racy, 1986.
59 See Racy, 2003.
60 See Racy, 1996.
61 Mansour and Sabry, 2019, p. 3.
62 Mansour and Sabry, 2019, p. 3.
63 Al-Taee, 2002, p. 59.
64 Al-Taee, 2002, p. 42.
65 Al-Taee, 2002, pp. 44–5.
66 Schade-Poulsen, 1999, pp. 26–7.
67 Schade-Poulsen, 1999, p. 37.
68 Schade-Poulsen, 1999, p. 101.
69 Schade-Poulsen, 1999, p. 103.
70 Schade-Poulsen, 1999, p. 109.
71 Schade-Poulsen, 1999, p. 166.
72 Harb and Bessaiso, 2006, p. 1063.
73 Harb and Bessaiso, 2006, p. 1074.
74 Harb and Bessaiso, 2006, p. 1063.
75 Harb and Bessaiso, 2006, p. 1064.
76 Harb and Bessaiso, 2006, p. 1064.
77 Harb and Bessaiso, 2006, pp. 1072–3.
78 Harb and Bessaiso, 2006, pp. 1070–3.
79 Matar, 2006, p. 1027.
80 Matar, 2006, p. 1029.
81 Matar, 2006, p. 1036.
82 Matar, 2006, p. 1037.
83 Matar, 2006, p. 1031.
84 Matar, 2006, pp. 1032–4.
85 Miladi, 2006, p. 948.

86 Miladi, 2006, p. 959.
87 Miladi, 2006, p. 953.
88 Miladi, 2006, p. 959.
89 Tsagarousianou, 2016, p. 67.
90 Tsagarousianou, 2016, p. 73.
91 Tsagarousianou, 2016, p. 75.
92 Tsagarousianou, 2016, p. 78.
93 Tsagarousianou, 2016, p. 78.
94 Kadi, 1994, xix.
95 Sabry, 2012, p. 13.
96 Mansour and Sabry, 2017, p. 216.
97 Brah, 1996, p. 181.
98 Massey, 1994, p. 149.
99 Lawler, 2001, p. 326.
100 Aly, 2015, p. 9.
101 Stone, 2008, p. 55.
102 *Al-ghurba* can be translated to mean expatriation; absence from one's own country, but arguably it can also be a state of feeling alienated and foreign.
103 Anthias, 1998, p. 557.
104 Mansour and Sabry, 2017, p. 215.
105 Anthias, 1998, p. 557.
106 Bourdieu, 1990, p. 54.
107 Bourdieu, 1990, p. 55.
108 Bourdieu, 1990, p. 55.
109 Bourdieu, 1990, p. 55.
110 Bourdieu, 1990, p. 56.
111 Bourdieu, 1990, p. 51.
112 See Khalili, 2017; Bachmann and Sidaway, 2016; Virdee and McGeever, 2017.
113 Virdee and McGeever, 2017, p. 1803.
114 Virdee and McGeever, 2017, pp. 1803–4.
115 Names of all participants and interviewees in this book have been changed.
116 Loosely translated, *heiki* means like this. The decision to keep the word in its original Arab format was purposeful.
117 Translates as: My homeland.
118 Keightley and Pickering, 2012, p. 115.
119 Stone, 2008, p. 144.
120 Tsagarousianou, 2004, p. 52.
121 *Iltizam* can be translated into the word 'commitment'.
122 Fiske, 1994, p. 69.
123 Keightley and Pickering, 2012, p. 72.
124 Blickle, 2002.
125 Keightley and Pickering, 2012, p. 10.

Chapter 2

1 Pont, Lacroix, and Mitterrand, 1998.
2 Abu Murad, 1990, p. 39.
3 Roughly translated as: Amazing Sunset.

4   Translated as: We are returning.
5   Abu Murad, 1990, p. 43; Bishalani, 2009, p. 21; Habib, 2005, p. 54.
6   Habib, 2005, p. 54.
7   Bishalani, 2009, p. 21.
8   Habib, 2005, p. 34.
9   Habib, 2005, p. 336.
10 Habib, 2005, p. 91.
11 Aliksan, 1987, p. 98.
12 Bishalani, 2009.
13 Habib, 2005, p. 25.
14 Habib, 2005, p. 27.
15 Habib, 2005, p. 31.
16 Stone, 2008, p. 144.
17 Nasr, 2018, p. 3.
18 Nasr, 2018, p. 33.
19 Nasr, 2018, p. 175.
20 Nasr, 2018, p. 129.
21 Nasr, 2018, p. 176.
22 Habib, 2005, p. 34.
23 It is important to note that Umm Kulthum's music appeals to a very specific audience. Although she is a respected and revered artist in her own right, she was somewhat positioned politically, which alienated some listeners.
24 Danielson, 1997, p. 167.
25 Schade-Poulsen's book on Rai music in Algeria also focuses on how the relationship of production and consumption of music factors into audience reception. His work brings to surface the ways in which certain genres of music such as Rai tap into social dynamics in Algeria. For Schade-Poulsen, the emergence of Rai coincided with political tensions in Algeria, creating a specific temporal following. Rai created a form of subculture that brought to surface men's opinions on women and relationships as well as acting as a tool towards combating Islamic extremism. Schade-Poulsen looks at the commercial side of the genre, explaining that the social aspects and lived experiences of the music in cabarets, weddings and studios embedded the listener in both the production and consumption of the songs. In this way, Schade-Poulsen describes Rai as intertwined within activities of Algerian society, something understood culturally and socially.
26 Stone, 2008, p. 74.
27 Stone, 2008, p. 41; emphasis in original.
28 Stone, 2008, p. 55.
29 Nasr, 2018, p. 6.
30 Nasr, 2018, p. 121.
31 Habib, 2005, pp. 32–3.
32 Trad and Khalifa, 2001, p. 26.
33 Trad and Khalifa, 2001, p. 28.
34 Stone, 2008, p. 1.
35 It must be noted here that all references to Fairouz are done with the acknowledgement of the Rahbani family as an integral force in the intricate creation of her persona and 'musical works'. However, they will not form the central theme of this book. Instead, it is Fairouz who takes centre stage.
36 Williams, 1983, p. 269.

37 Williams, 1983, p. 269.
38 Benjamin, 1936, n.p.
39 Peirce, 1931–58, CP 2.299.
40 Peirce, 1931–58, CP 2.279.
41 Habib, 2005, p. 108.
42 Stone, 2008, p. 17.
43 Stone, 2008, p. 10.
44 Habib, 2005, p. 108.
45 Nasr, 2018, pp. 9–11.
46 Stone, 2008, p. 31.
47 Fiske, 1994, p. 68.
48 Fiske, 1994, p. 69.
49 Fiske, 1994, p. 73.
50 Fiske, 1994, p. 70.
51 Fiske, 1994, p. 73.
52 Fairouz's carefully crafted persona, which is discussed later in the book, allows for her 'figure' to be appropriated and used in various ways.
53 Tomkins, 2009, p. 163.
54 Gregg and Seigworth, 2010, p. 1.
55 Gregg and Seigworth (2010) define affect as 'vital forces insisting beyond emotion – that can serve to drive us toward movement, toward thought and extension. . . . Indeed, affect is persistent proof of a body's never less than ongoing immersion in and among the world's obstinacies and rhythms, its refusals as much as its invitations'. (p. 1).
56 Ahmed, 2010, p. 31.
57 Ahmed, 2010, p. 31.
58 Ahmed, 2004a, p. 120.
59 Ahmed, 2004a, p. 119.
60 It should be noted that Lebanese migration preceded these conflicts with numerous 'push' and 'pull' factors dating back to the nineteenth century. Prior to the Lebanese civil war, factors such as internal and external conflicts, lack of local job opportunities, concern of recruitment into the Ottoman army and the collapse of the Lebanese silk industry pushed many Lebanese people to migrate to countries in Europe, the Americas, Australia, West Africa and the Gulf States. The first known migrant from the nineteenth century was Anthonius Al-Bishalani, who migrated to the United States in the 1850s (Ferson, 2010). Middle East experts and historians have mainly highlighted five waves of Lebanese migration starting from the 1880s during Ottoman rule to the present day (see Ferson, 2010; Tabar, 2010). Paul Tabar (2010) also discusses the migration of Syro-Lebanese Christians to Rome in order to become members of the clergy. After some relative peace, in the second half of the nineteenth century, churchmen who returned from Rome began setting up missionary schools to educate the population. This created an 'internal exodus' from Mount Lebanon towards Beirut. The first wave of migration from the second half of the nineteenth century to about the First World War saw Mount Lebanon as a scene of internal religious conflicts mainly between Maronite Christians and the Druze, causing many to flee the area. The population of Beirut almost doubled, with a high number of educated people competing for work in a limited employment market. This motivated many skilled and unskilled Lebanese to migrate for economic opportunities. In addition, during

this time, a large number of men fled to avoid mandatory military service in the Ottoman army (Ferson, 2010; Tabar, 2010; Hitti, 1924). According to Tabar, Western influences introduced by the missionary schools were also factors in 'pulling' Lebanese youth to Europe and the Americas, as were the developing economies in Egypt and Brazil. The second wave of migration from 1915 to 1945 was characterized by a three-year lull as a result of the First World War sea blockades and consequent famine. The third wave of migration just before the Lebanese civil war was characterized by the abundance of educated men and women seeking employment opportunities. The Lebanese civil war, from 1975 to 1990, marks the fourth wave of migration with an estimated one million people leaving the country as a result of the violence, economic instability and structural destruction (Ferson, 2010; Taber, 2010). The fifth wave of migration, post-1990, was distinguished by Lebanese looking for economic, social and familial stability (Tabar, 2010). Arguably, there is a sixth wave of migration from October 2019 to the present, which saw a mass exodus of Lebanese as a result of a rapidly deteriorating economy and unstable political and financial environment (see Mendelek, 2022).

61 Barnard and Pendock, 2012, p. 47.
62 Brah, 1996, p. 186.
63 Brah, 1996, p. 182.
64 Brah, 1996, p. 183.
65 Anthias, 1998, p. 561.
66 Brah, 1996, p. 16.
67 Brah, 1996, p. 192.
68 Robins and Aksoy, 2006, p. 86.
69 Robins and Aksoy, 2006, p. 87.
70 Hall, 1990, p. 231.
71 Tsagarousianou, 2004, p. 52.
72 Tsagarousianou, 2004, p. 52.
73 Tsagarousianou, 2004, p. 52.
74 Cohen, 1994, p. 65.
75 See Birks and Sinclair, 1979; Feiler, 1991.
76 Thiollet (2011) also reveals, 'Naturalization which the oil-rich states had opened to "ethnic" Arab migrants in the 1960s – 1970s had become virtually impossible by the mid-1970s' (p. 107).
77 Both Feiler (1991) and Thiollet (2011) discuss the 'social exclusion' some migrants face, especially those who constitute unskilled labour. They are usually swept to the peripheries, even living in areas outside the main cities in labour camps. Many of them are single men, who are unable to afford bringing their families and they are often not allowed to mix with other communities in the receiving countries. As Thiollet (2011) writes, 'Categories under which foreign nationals are labelled indicate the limits and extent of their rights, duties and freedom of movement' (p. 115).
78 Thiollet, 2011, p. 104.
79 Feiler, 1991, p. 144.
80 Thiollet, 2011, p. 108.
81 Thiollet, 2011, p. 108.
82 Norman, 2021, p. 248.
83 Birks and Sinclair, 1979, p. 90.

84 Thiollet, 2011, p. 107.

85 Russell and Teitelbaum (1995). International migration and international trade. *World Bank*.

86 Thiollet (2011) argues, the 'World's highest ratio of migrants to national population is in the Middle East' (p. 103).

87 Aly, 2015, p. 63.

88 Up until the early 2000s, high school graduates in Qatar would have to travel abroad to continue their education, as there was a lack of universities. Thus unlike the UK, which saw a greater influx of students, Qatar's Arab diaspora consists mostly of families or individuals (mostly men) who have travelled for economic opportunities or to also escape violence in their own countries.

89 Aly, 2015, p. 35.

90 Aly, 2015, p. 32.

91 Aly, 2015, p. 32.

92 Aly, 2015, p. 68.

93 Aly, 2015, p. 170.

94 Aly, 2015, p. 69.

95 Aly, 2015, p. 125.

96 While there is no empirical study on the attitudes of Arabian Gulf youth towards other Arabs, Thiollet (2011) discusses notions of 'Arabness', inclusivity and unity in her article. Her study provides a historical overview of policies of migration in the Gulf States, rather than an ethnographic discussion. However, she makes some interesting points regarding the inclusivity of 'Arabness' through means of integration and non-integration. According to Thiollet, the absence of participation by Gulf States in attempts at institutionalized Arab agreements such as the League of Arab States and so on showcases the selective ways in which Gulf countries exhibit forms of 'Arabness'. In addition, their refusal at signing 'any binding convention concerning the access to their labor markets for foreign nationals' bestows on them control and autonomy over all migrants that cross their borders (Thiollet, 2011, p. 112). Although this does not explicitly highlight their stance regarding other Arabs, it does position them on an uneven standing of power. For Thiollet (2011), migration in the Middle East is a 'political phenomenon' with 'migrants and refugees' playing the roles of the 'political actors' (p. 117).

97 Mansour and Sabry, 2017, p. 216.

98 Mansour and Sabry, 2017, p. 218.

99 Mansour and Sabry, 2017, p. 218.

100 Jamal and Naber, 2008, p. 2.

101 See Tsagarousianou, 2016; Miladi, 2006; Harb and Bessaiso, 2006; Matar, 2006.

102 Appadurai, 1996, p. 4.

103 Appadurai, 1996, p. 190.

104 Stone, 2008, p. 78.

105 MacFarquar, 1999.

106 Ang, 2008, p. 242.

107 Crenshaw, 1991, p. 1244.

108 Appadurai, 1996, p. 31.

109 Athique, 2008, p. 34.

110 Keightley and Pickering, 2012, p. 2.

111 Keightley and Pickering, 2012, p. 7.

112 Keightley and Pickering, 2012, p. 5.

113 Keightley and Pickering, 2012, p. 63.
114 Taylor, 1989, pp. 46–7.
115 Taylor, 1989, p. 36.
116 Taylor, 1989.
117 Keightley and Pickering, 2012, p. 12.
118 Anderson, 1983, p. 15.
119 Keightley and Pickering, 2012, p. 76.
120 Keightley and Pickering, 2012, p. 94.
121 Keightley and Pickering, 2012, p. 17.
122 Slobin, 1994, p. 244.
123 Keightley and Pickering, 2012, p. 17.
124 Gibbs, 2001, p. 1.
125 Ahmed, 2010, p. 37.
126 Ahmed, 2010, p. 31.
127 Ahmed, 2010, p. 31.
128 Keightley and Pickering, 2012, p. 51.
129 Barrett et al., 2010, p. 390.
130 Barrett et al., 2010, p. 390.
131 Barrett et al., 2010, p. 391.
132 Keightley and Pickering, 2012, p. 11.
133 Cited in Keightley and Pickering, 2012, p. 11.
134 Boym, 2001, pp. xv–xvi.
135 Boym, 2001, p. xv.
136 Boym, 2001, p. 44.
137 Boym, 2001, p. 54.
138 Boym, 2001, p. xvi.
139 Boym, 2001, p. 346.
140 Tacchi, 2003, p. 292.
141 Tacchi, 2003, p. 282.
142 Keightley and Pickering, 2012, p. 115.

Chapter 3

 1 Names of all participants and interviewees in this study have been changed.
 2 Seigworth and Gregg, 2010, p. 1.
 3 Shouse, 2005, n.p.
 4 The translation of 'Al-ghurba' is expatriation or absence from one's native country.
 5 It is common practice in the Middle East to hire a live-in domestic worker from countries in Asia and Africa to assist in household chores as well as childcare. Qatar, like other countries in the Gulf, outsources more non-Arab workers than Arab workers for many reasons, one of which is to bring down labour costs.
 6 Fiske, 1994, p. 69.
 7 Fiske, 1994, p. 69.
 8 Fiske, 1994, p. 72.
 9 Fiske, 1994, p. 71.
10 Fiske, 1994, p. 71.
11 Benjamin, 1936.
12 A type of oven-baked bread.

13   Firth, 1996, p. 121.
14   Firth, 1996, p. 109.
15   Goffman, 1956, p. 17.
16   Goffman, 1956, p. 13.
17   Goffman, 1956, p. 13.
18   Goffman, 1956, p. 17.
19   Goffman, 1956, p. 69.
20   Goffman, 1956, p. 17.
21   Goffman, 1956, p. 17.
22   Williams, 1977, p. 130.
23   Aly, 2015, p. 1.
24   Aly, 2015, p. 15.
25   For example, a singer like Umm Kulthum was often affiliated with 1950s Egyptian president Jamal Abdel Nasser and his politics, so her audiences were divided accordingly. Fairouz on the other hand remained more neutral as both a private figure and a public one.
26   El-Ariss, 2017, p. 45.
27   El-Ariss, 2017, p. 576.
28   El-Ariss, 2017, p. 579.
29   El-Ariss, 2017, p. 581.
30   El-Ariss, 2017, p. 581.
31   Alshaer, 2016, p. 115.
32   El-Ariss, 2017, p. 46.
33   Translated from the Arabic word *aseel*.
34   Mansour and Sabry, 2017, p. 215.
35   Ruddick, 2010, p. 28.
36   Ruddick, 2010, p. 27.
37   Goffman, 1956, p. 6.
38   Pickering, 2001, p. 49.
39   Ahmed, 2004a, p. 123; italics in original.
40   Ahmed, 2004a, p. 123; italics in original.
41   A type of drum also called Darbuka or Katim.
42   Aly, 2015, p. 8.
43   Mikhail, 1979, p. 596.
44   Mikhail, 1979, p. 596.
45   Ahmed, 2004b, p. 26.
46   Keightley and Pickering, 2012, p. 83.
47   Keightley and Pickering, 2012, p. 18.
48   Seigworth and Gregg, 2010, p. 2; emphasis in original.
49   See Ashcroft, Griffiths and Tiffin, 1998; Spivak, 1999.
50   Kraidy, 2002, p. 320.
51   Joseph, 1999, p. 2.
52   Joseph, 1999, p. 2.
53   Bhabha, 1994, p. 1.
54   Seigworth and Gregg, 2010, p. 1.
55   Bhabha, 1994, p. 1.
56   Bhabha, 1994, p. 1.
57   Aly, 2015, p. 2.
58   Ruddick, 2010, p. 30; emphasis in original.

59 Kraidy, 2002, p. 333.
60 Kraidy, 2002, p. 333.
61 Hall, 1990, p. 223.
62 Hall, 1990, p. 223.
63 Aly, 2015, p. 15.
64 Hall, 1990, p. 225; emphasis in original.
65 Hall, 1990, p. 225; emphasis in original.
66 Hall, 1990, p. 226.
67 There are numerous residential compounds in Qatar. These are gated housing communities, usually encompassing villas and communal clubhouses with recreational areas and sometimes a swimming pool.
68 Keightley and Pickering, 2012, p. 8.
69 Keightley and Pickering, 2012, p. 19.
70 Barrett et al., 2010, p. 390.
71 Barrett et al., 2010, p. 390.
72 Barrett et al., 2010, p. 390.
73 Barrett et al., 2010, p. 391.
74 Barrett et al., 2010, p. 390.
75 Barrett et al., 2010, p. 390.
76 Keightley and Pickering, 2012, p. 112.
77 Firth, 1996, p. 110.
78 Ahmed, 1999, p. 343.
79 According to Higham, Ellaby and Thomas, changes in the Qatari immigration laws means that as of 9 October 2020, residents no longer require exit permits (Law no. 19 of 2020). However, at the time of the interviews for this book, exit permits were still required for non-Qataris leaving the country.
80 Williams, 1977, p. 134.
81 Williams, 1977, p. 134.
82 See Chapter 6.
83 Silva, 2004, p. 21; emphasis in original.
84 Stone, 2008, p. 145.
85 As previously mentioned, although there may be truth to Stone's argument with regard to Fairouz and the Rahbani brothers being part of a Lebanese nation-building campaign, the issue here is that this ignores the sphere of influence Fairouz has on her listeners and dictates that only those from Lebanon identify with her songs.
86 Stone, 2008, p. 144.
87 Stone, 2008, p. 38.
88 It is important to mention here that almost all of Fairouz's songs, except for a rendition of 'We Wish You a Merry Christmas' on her Christmas album, are sung in Arabic. This shows how linguistically, Fairouz is able to create an Arab identity through her commitment to the Arabic language.
89 Stone, 2008, p. 11.
90 Stone, 2008, p. 10.
91 Translates as: The Flower of all cities.
92 Translates as: 'God forbid'.
93 Secretary General of the Lebanese political and parliamentary party, Hezbollah.
94 Ahmed, 2004a, p. 120.
95 Ahmed, 2004a, p. 127.
96 Ahmed, 2004a, p. 121.

97   Jean-Klein, 2001, p. 84.
98   Jean-Klein, 2001, p. 84; emphasis in original.
99   Abu-Lughod, 1990, p. 42.
100   Mansour and Sabry, 2017, p. 215.
101   Iyengar, Sood, and Lelkes, 2012, p. 407.
102   Iyengar, Sood, and Lelkes, 2012, p. 406.
103   Massumi, 1995, p. 104.
104   Translates as: 'the resistance', but they are contextually known as Hezbollah.
105   Kraidy, 2002, p. 333.
106   *Haram,* in this context, can be translated as taboo. In this instance, it has religious connotations.
107   Naber, 2005, p. 480.
108   Naber, 2005, p. 479.
109   Ahmed, 2004a, p. 127.
110   Translates roughly as: Shameful.
111   Translates as: Jesus.
112   Keightley and Pickering, 2012, p. 19.
113   Keightley and Pickering, 2012, p. 7.

Chapter 4

1   Foucault, 1986, p. 23.
2   Keightley and Pickering, 2012, p.10.
3   Blickle, 2002, p. 2.
4   Blickle, 2002, p. 28.
5   Sabry, 2012, p. 13.
6   Sabry, 2012, p. 13.
7   Fiske, 1994, pp. 68–9.
8   Goffman, 1956, p. 69.
9   Translated as: Cedar tree, the symbol of the Lebanese flag.
10   Ahmed, 2004b, p. 27.
11   Ahmed, 2004b, p. 33.
12   Ahmed, 1999, p. 342.
13   Ahmed, 1999, p. 339; emphasis in original.
14   While her songs are often political and a call for action, they are ambiguous in their positioning, thus allowing for multiple interpretations of her music, and the ability for different political parties/opinions to claim Fairouz as their own. Her silent persona reinforces this, as she is not vocal about supporting any particular side. Although some participants brought up their own views regarding Fairouz's politics, based on rumours in the media, unless indicated otherwise in this book, participants often discarded or dismissed them. Aly's argument that 'collective "Arabness" was intimately informed and organized around political figures, causes and allegiances' is important here, since it shows how Fairouz did not align herself 'around political figures' or 'allegiances' and thus was seen as someone who embodied all and no politics at once (2015, p. 43).
15   Translates as: Shadi is lost.
16   de Certeau, 1984, p. 117.

17   Sabry, 2012, p. 19.
18   Baudrillard, 2004, p. 369.
19   Keightley and Pickering, 2012, p. 72.
20   Keightley and Pickering, 2012, p. 72.
21   Ahmed, 2004b, p. 33.
22   Keightley and Pickering, 2012, p. 72.
23   Ahmed, 2004a, p. 120.
24   Ahmed, 1999, p. 333.
25   Sayad, 2004, p. 28.
26   Ahmed, 1999, p. 342.
27   Ahmed, 2004b, p. 27.
28   The word *akeed* in Arabic is the equivalent of 'for sure' in English.
29   Translates as: The Lebanese way. Here it is the name of a community-based and community-driven initiative in Doha to introduce Lebanese youth on the customs and traditions of Lebanon.
30   Sayad, 2004, p. 225.
31   Sayad, 2004, p. 225.
32   Ahmed, 1999, p. 342.
33   Ahmed, 2004a, p. 128; emphasis in original.
34   Ahmed, 1999, p. 342.
35   Keightley and Pickering, 2012, p. 71.
36   Keightley and Pickering, 2012, p. 71.
37   Ahmed, 1999, p. 342.
38   Keightley and Pickering, 2012, p. 81.
39   Keightley and Pickering, 2012, p. 63.
40   Ahmed, 2004b, p. 27.
41   Ahmed, 1999, p. 342.
42   de Certeau, 1984, p. 108.
43   de Certeau, 1984, p. 117.
44   de Certeau, 1984, p. 108.
45   Gregg and Seigworth, 2010, p. 1; see also Massumi, 1995.
46   Translates as: We and the moon are neighbours.
47   Translates as: The wind breezed upon us.
48   Massumi, 1995, p. 90.
49   Soja, 1989, p. 11.
50   Soja, 1989, p. 11.
51   Ahmed, 2004b, p. 33.
52   Ahmed, 2004b, p. 26.

Chapter 5

1   Foucault, 1986, p. 22.
2   Foucault, 1986, pp. 23–4.
3   Foucault, 1986, p. 24.
4   Foucault, 1986, p. 24.
5   Foucault, 1986, p. 25.
6   Darwish, 2011, p. 5.
7   Darwish, 2011, p. 50.

8   Darwish, 2011, p. 44.
9   Darwish, 2011, pp. 19–20.
10 Translates as: Oh God!
11 Translates as: Hookah.
12 An Arabic dish made from Jew's Mallow.
13 Foucault, 1986, p. 25.
14 Massey, 1994, p. 152.
15 Massey, 1994, p. 155.
16 See Morley, 2001; Massey, 1994; Soja, 1989.
17 de Certeau, 1984, p. 108.
18 Massey, 1994, p. 156.
19 Keightley and Pickering, 2012, p. 63.
20 Ahmed, 1999, p. 342.
21 Sayad, 2004, p. 213.
22 At the time of the interviews, trying to find work in Qatar if you become unemployed comes with a host of regulations, which may or may not allow you take up a new position. As a migrant in Qatar, you have to be 'sponsored' by a Qatari who owns the company you work for. If the 'sponsor' Qatari does not allow you to be released from your job, you will not be allowed to move freely to find any other job.
23 Aly, 2015, p. 1.
24 Blickle, 2002, p. 17.
25 Blickle, 2002, p. 61.
26 Sayad, 2004, p. 26; emphasis in original.
27 Darwish, 2011, p. 42.
28 Foucault, 1986, p. 23.
29 Sabry and Ftouni, 2017, p.8.
30 Sabry and Ftouni, 2017, p. 7.
31 Translates as: Bird, oh bird, flying at the edge of the world.
32 Translates as: Living in *Al-ghurba*.
33 Translates as: Those who live in *Al-ghurba*.
34 Can mean a deeper affiliation for, or a craving.
35 Translates as: The place of *Al-ghurba*.
36 Stewart, 2010, p. 344.
37 Sayad, 2004, p. 26.
38 Darwish, 2011, p. 19.
39 Stewart, 2010, p. 344.
40 Darwish, 2011, p. 44.

Chapter 6

1   Blickle, 2002, p. 1.
2   Baalbaki, 2001.
3   Bensaid, 2013, p. 150.
4   As cited in Bensaid, 2013, p. 151.
5   Bensaid, 2013, p. 151.
6   Bensaid, 2013, p. 149.
7   Bensaid, 2013, p. 149.
8   As cited in Bensaid, 2013, p. 155.

 9 Bensaid, 2013, p. 157.
10 Bensaid, 2013, p. 158.
11 Also known as: *Al-Umma Al-Arabiya*, the Arab state.
12 Bensaid, 2013, p. 164.
13 Bensaid, 2013, p. 164.
14 Bensaid, 2013, p. 166.
15 Bensaid, 2013, p. 165.
16 Bensaid, 2013, p. 166.
17 Bensaid, 2013, p. 169.
18 See Darwish, 2011; Alshaer, 2016.
19 Blickle, 2002, p. 4; emphasis in original.
20 Ahmed, 2004a, p. 343.
21 Blickle, 2002, p. 4.
22 Blickle, 2002, p. 7.
23 Blickle, 2002, p. 8.
24 Blickle, 2002, p. 20.
25 Blickle, 2002, p. 17.
26 Blickle, 2002, p. 27.
27 Blickle, 2002, p. 28.
28 Translates as: The Station.
29 Translates as: Go back to your home, go back.
30 Translates as: Why should I go back? My home is with me, my home is with me.
31 Translates as: Year after year.
32 Translates as: Take me and plant me in the soil of Lebanon.
33 Translates as: The moon of Mashghara (an area in Lebanon).
34 Translates as: Give me the nay (oriental flute) and sing.
35 Translates as: For Beirut or To Beirut.
36 Translates as: Ashen.
37 Contextually translated as: I can't believe how beautiful your eyes are, Alia.
38 Translates as: To Beirut, from my heart, a greeting to Beirut.
39 Translates as: Kisses to the sea.
40 Translates as: I come with the unfortunate/poor people.
41 Translates as: Like.
42 Translates as: We shall return one day.
43 Translates as: We are returning.
44 This is a difficult word to translate, as the intensity gets lost. But it means a kind of zeal or activism.
45 Translates as: country, nation or homeland.
46 Translates as: One day we will return to our neighbourhood.
47 Translates as: What's wrong with me? I'm growing and you're growing in my heart.
48 Translates as: The Nation.
49 Translates as: The Flower of all cities.
50 Translates as: My father closed the gate and I jumped out the window.
51 This is difficult to translate, but it means of the highest standard, or the highest peak.
52 This is a line from the song 'Hanna the Drunkard'. Translates to: Those were the days, those were, there was a small shop in the shade.
53 Blickle, 2002, p. ix.
54 Blickle, 2002, p, 6.

55 Blickle, 2002, p. 20.
56 Ahmed, 1999, p. 343.
57 Ahmed, 1999, p. 343.
58 Blickle, 2002, p. 78.
59 Translated into English, *iltizam* means commitment. It is a politicized form of commitment with a host of socio-historical origins, linked to the 1950s pan-Arab vision of the former Egyptian president, Jamal Abdel Nasser. The term has since evolved to incorporate different meanings. Drawing on Marwan Kraidy's term 'intercontextual hybridity', which he defines as the 'mutually constitutive interplay and overlap of cultural, economic and political forces' among diasporic communities, which allow for 'us to comprehend how under certain conditions, in certain contexts, ideological elements coalesce in a certain discourse of hybridity' (Kraidy, 2002, p. 3), I argue the same concept can be applied to *iltizam*, which can also be considered 'intercontextual'.
60 Blickle, 2002, p. 6.
61 Translated as: I come with the unfortunate/poor people.
62 Blickle, 2002, p. 7.
63 Keightley and Pickering, 2012, p. 10.
64 A Lebanese singer often criticized for her lack of vocal talent and who is often hyper-sexualized.
65 Stone, 2008, p. 142.
66 Stone, 2008, p. 142.
67 Fiske, 1994, p. 71.
68 Sabry, 2012, p. 16.
69 Pickering, 2001, p. 48.
70 Massey, 1994, p. 178.
71 Massey, 1994, p. 186.
72 Massey, 1994, p. 178.
73 Translates as: Forbidden by Islamic law.
74 Translated as: Custodian.
75 This does not mean that women do not travel to Doha to work on their own accord, but rather it was telling of the female participants in this study.
76 Massey, 1994, p. 186.
77 Morley, 2001, p. 431.
78 Sayad, 2004, p. 237.
79 Mikhail, 1979, p. 596.
80 Sayad, 2004, p. 236.
81 Sayad, 2004, p. 29.
82 Sayad, 2004, p. 238.
83 Sayad, 2004, p. 238.
84 Sayad, 2004, p. 238.
85 Sayad, 2004, p. 238.
86 Sabry, 2012, p. 14.
87 Sayad, 2004, p. 234.
88 Sayad, 2004, p. 3.
89 Arendt, 1956, p. 52.
90 Sayad, 2004, p. 237.
91 Sayad, 2004, p. 234.
92 Sabry, 2012, p. 19.
93 Sabry, 2012, p. 13.

94   Kraidy, 2002, p. 333.
95   Sayad, 2004, p. 238.
96   Sayad, 2004, p. 238.
97   Sayad, 2004, p. 238.
98   Travelling to Palestine under Israeli occupation is illegal as a Lebanese citizen.
99   Ahmed, 2004b, p. 33.
100 Ahmed, 2004b, p. 33.
101 Sayad, 2004, p. 260.
102 The procedures for leaving Doha have since changed. For more information, see
     https://portal.moi.gov.qa/wps/portal/MOIInternet/services/inquiries/exitservices
103 While Arendt has been criticized by many feminist and political theorists for her
     notions of public/private spheres, and her concept of politics, as well as her dismissal
     of gender, these will not be tackled in this book (see Benhabib, S., 1993; Breen, K.,
     2007).
104 Arendt, 1998, p. 57.
105 Arendt, 1998, p. 28.
106 Briganti and Mezei, 2012, p. 7.
107 Bachelard, 2012, p. 20.
108 Verschaffel, 2012, p. 153.
109 Lebanese/Arabic/Turkish coffee, brewed and served in a traditional stovetop pot.
110 Heidegger, 2012, p. 25.
111 Heidegger, 2012, p. 24.
112 Sabry and Mansour, 2019, p. 101.
113 Sabry and Mansour, 2019, p. 102.
114 Ahmed, 2004b, p. 27.
115 Ahmed, 2004b, p. 27.
116 Sayad, 2004, p. 208.
117 See Briganti and Mezei, 2012; Bourdieu, 1970.
118 Roughly translates as: Please mother, I don't know what's wrong with me, leave me
     with my worries, I'm sick of this world.
119 Morley, 2001, p. 442.
120 Massey, 1994, p. 149.
121 The name of a film Fairouz performed in. Translates as: Daughter of the Guard.
122 The name of a film Fairouz performed in. The term is one commonly used during
     Ottoman Times, when there was a mass forced exodus and deportation of Lebanese,
     Syrian and Kurdish families during the Second Balkan War and the First World War.
     The term is Turkish and means mobilization.
123 Ahmed, 2004b, p. 33.
124 Translates as: You drink from your cup and I drink from your eyes.
125 Ahmed, 1999, p. 342.
126 Kaplan, 1982, p. 192.
127 Fiske, 1994, p. 73.
128 See Sabry and Mansour, 2019, p. 102.

Chapter 7

1   Keightley and Pickering, 2012, p. 7.
2   Keightley and Pickering, 2012, p. 2.

3   Erll, 2011, p.104.
4   Keightley and Pickering, 2012, p. 18.
5   Erll, 2011, p. 84.
6   Translates as: The wind breezed upon us.
7   Translates as: Grandfather.
8   Literally translates as: The highest of lands.
9   Translates as: Tomorrow when you come.
10 Keightley and Pickering, 2012, p. 72.
11 Keightley and Pickering, 2012, p. 113.
12 Keightley and Pickering, 2012, p. 114.
13 Keightley and Pickering, 2012, p. 115.
14 Tacchi, 2003, p. 289.
15 Translates as: The moon illuminates the people.
16 Translates as: I love you, oh Lebanon.
17 Translates as: For Beirut, I send a greeting from my heart, to Beirut.
18 Translates as: Kisses to the sea.
19 Translates as: Let Rima go to sleep.
20 Translates as: We and the moon are neighbours.
21 Erll, 2011, p. 93.
22 Translates as: The sun is shining.
23 Type of flower in the Jasminum Sambac family.
24 Hirsch, 2008, p. 106; emphasis in original.
25 Hirsch, 2008, p. 107.
26 Translates as: I wish you and I were in a house, some house, the furthest house hidden by the trunks of the trees.
27 Sabry, 2012, p. 19.
28 Erll, 2011, p. 112.
29 Erll, 2011, p. 112.
30 Erll, 2011, p. 141.
31 Erll, 2011, p. 142.
32 Literally translates as: I became an expert in sadness and waiting.
33 Literally translates as: I grew up away from home. I built another family, like trees they grew and stood before me. And here I am, I chose emptiness as a nation. I was separated from my family twice.
34 Literally translates as: The land is yours, so the land will rejoice. The land is ours and you are my brother, then why do you fight me?
35 Translates as: For Beirut.
36 Translates as: And the sighs of the nay (flute) remain till after the end of existence.
37 Hirsch, 2008, p. 109.
38 Hirsch, 2008, p. 106.
39 Keightley and Pickering, 2012, p. 201.
40 Said, 1991, viii.
41 Aly, 2015, p. 1.
42 Translates as: Tell me, tell me about my country.
43 Sabry and Mansour, 2019, p. 101.
44 See Sabry and Mansour, 2019.
45 Translates as: Oh God!
46 Hage, 2002, p. 196.
47 Hage, 2002, p. 197.

48   Hage, 2002, p. 203.
49   Hage, 2002, p. 203.
50   Hage, 2002, p. 203.
51   Hage, 2002, p. 203.
52   Keightley and Pickering, 2012, p. 119.

Understanding diasporic existence through the songs of Fairouz

1   Stone, 2008, p. 144.
2   Translates as: Nation.
3   Ahmed, 2004a, p. 127.
4   Sayad, 2004, p. 208.
5   Ahmed, 2004b; 1999.
6   Keightley and Pickering, 2012, p. 72.
7   Massumi, 1995, p. 90.
8   Massey, 1994, p. 155.
9   Sabry and Ftouni, 2017, p. 7.
10   Blickle, 2002, p. 27.
11   Sabry and Mansour, 2019.
12   Sabry and Mansour, 2019, p. 102.
13   Erll, 2011, pp. 8–9.
14   Erll, 2011, p. 91.
15   Erll, 2011, p. 93.
16   Sabry, 2012, p. 19.
17   Sabry, 2012, p. 14.
18   Sabry, 2012, p. 19.
19   Kraidy, 2002, p. 333.
20   The University of Pennsylvania teaches its students Fairouzian songs as part of its Arab Music Ensemble course.

BIBLIOGRAPHY

Abdel-Nabi, S., Agha, J., Choucair, J., and Mikdashi, M. (2004). 'Pop Goes the Arab World'. *Hawwa*, 2(2), 231–54.

Abu-Lughod, L. (1990). 'The Romance of Resistance: Tracing Transformations of Power through Bedouin Women'. *American Ethnologist*, 17(1), 41–55.

Abu-Lughod, L. (1991). 'Writing Against Culture'. In R. Fox (Ed.), *Recapturing Anthropology: Working in the Present* (pp. 137–62). Santa Fe, NM: School of American Research Press.

Abu Murad, N. (1990). *Al-Akhwan Rahbani: Hayat wa-Masrah*. Beirut: Dar Amjad li-al-nashr wa-al-tawzi.

Ahmed, S. (1999). 'Home and Away: Narratives of Migration and Estrangement'. *International Journal of Cultural Studies*, 2(3), 329–47.

Ahmed, S. (2004a). 'Affective Economies'. *Social Text*, 22(2), 117–39.

Ahmed, S. (2004b). 'Collective Feelings, or the Impressions Left by Others'. *Theory, Culture and Society*, 21(2), 25–42.

Ahmed, S. (2010). 'Happy Objects'. In M. Gregg and G. Seigworth (Eds.), *The Affect Theory Reader* (pp. 29–51). Durham: Duke University Press.

Arcury, T. A., and Quandt, S. A. (1999). 'Participant Recruitment for Qualitative Research: A Site-Based Approach to Community Research in Complex Societies'. *Human Organization*, 58, 128–33.

Arendt, H. (1998). *The Human Condition*. Chicago: The University of Chicago Press.

Al-Taee, N. (2002). 'Voices of Peace and the Legacy of Reconciliation: Popular Music, Nationalism, and the Quest for Peace in the Middle East'. *Popular Music*, 21(1), 41–61.

Aliksan, J. (1987). *The Rahbanians and Fairouz: 1000 Artistic Works, 50 Years of Giving*. Damascus: Talas Editions for Studies Translation and Publishing.

Alshaer, A. (2016). *Poetry and Politics in the Modern Arab World*. London: Hurst & Company.

Alsultany, E. (2011). 'Stealth Muslim'. In R. Abdulhadi, E. Alsultany, and N. C. Naber (Eds.), *Arab & Arab American Feminisms: Gender, Violence, & Belonging* (pp. 307–14). Syracuse: Syracuse University Press.

Aly, R. M. K. (2015). *Becoming Arab in London: Performativity and the Undoing of Identity*. London: Pluto Press.

Anderson, B. (1983). *Imagined Communities: Reflections of the Origin and Spread of Nationalism*. London: Verso.

Ang, I. (1985). *Watching Dallas: Soap Opera and the Melodramatic Imagination*. London: Methuen & Co Ltd.

Ang, I. (2008). 'Melodramatic Identifications: Television Fiction and Women's Fantasy'. In C. Brunsdon and L. Spigel (Eds.), *Feminist Television Criticism: A Reader* (2nd ed., pp. 235–46). Berkshire, England: Open University Press.

Ang, I. (2012). 'On the Politics of Empirical Audience Research'. In M. G. Durham and D. Kellner (Eds.), *Media and Cultural Studies: Key Works* (2nd ed., pp. 145–59). Hoboken, NJ: John Wiley & Sons LTD.

Anthias, F. (1998). 'Evaluating "Diaspora": Beyond Ethnicity'. *Sociology*, 32(3), 557–80.

Antoon, S. (2011). 'Translator's Preface'. In M. Darwish (Ed.), *In the Presence of Absence* (pp. 5–9). Brooklyn, NY: Archipelago Books.

Appadurai, A. (1996). *Modernity at Large: Cultural Dimensions of Globalisation.* Minneapolis: University of Minnesota Press.

Armbrust, W. (1998). 'When the Lights Go Down in Cairo: Cinema as Secular Ritual'. *Visual Anthropology*, 10, 413–42.

Ashcroft, B., Griffiths, G., and Tiffin, H. (1998). *Key Concepts in Post-Colonial Studies.* New York: Routledge.

Athique, A. (2008). 'Media Audiences, Ethnographic Practice and the Notion of a Cultural Field'. *European Journal of Cultural Studies*, 11, 25–41.

Baalbaki, R. (2001). *Al-Mawrid: A Modern Arabic-English Dictionary.* Beirut, Lebanon: Dar El-Ilm Lilmalayin.

Bachelard, G. (2012). 'The House from Cellar to Garret. The Significance of the Hut'. In C. Briganti and K. Mezei (Eds.), *The Domestic Space Reader* (pp. 19–21). Toronto: University of Toronto Press.

Bachman, V. and Sidaway, J. (2016). 'Brexit Geopolitics'. *Geoforum*, 77, 47–50.

Barnard, H. and Pendock, C. (2012). 'To Share or Not to Share: The Role of Affect in Knowledge Sharing by Individuals in a Diaspora'. *Journal of International Management*, 19(2013), 47–65.

Barrett, F. S., Grimm, K. J., Robins, R. W., Wildschut, T., Sedikides, C., and Janata, P. (2010). 'Music-Evoked Nostalgia: Affect, Memory, and Personality'. *Emotion*, 10(3), 390–403.

Baudrillard, J. (2004). 'Simulacra and Simulations'. In J. Rivkin and M. Ryan (Eds.), *Literary Theory: An Anthology* (pp. 365–77). Oxford: Blackwell Publishing.

Bauer, M. W., and Gaskell, G. (2000). *Qualitative Researching with Text, Image and Sound. A Practical Handbook.* London: Sage Publications.

Benhabib, S. (1993). 'Feminist Theory and Hannah Arendt's Concept of Public Space'. *History of the Human Sciences*, 6(2), 97–114.

Benjamin, W. (1936). *The Work of Art in the Age of Mechanical Reproduction.* Retrieved on 2 May 2011, from http://www.marxists.org/reference/subject/philosophy/works/ge/benjamin.htm.

Bensaid, S. (2013). 'Al-Watan and Al-Umma in Contemporary Arab Use'. In G. Salame (Ed.), *The Foundations of the Arab State* (pp. 149–74). Oxfordshire: Routledge.

Berlant, L. (2010). 'Cruel Optimism'. In M. Gregg and G. Seigworth (Eds.), *The Affect Theory Reader* (pp. 93–117). Durham: Duke University Press.

Bhabha, H. K. (1994). *The Location of Culture.* London: Routledge.

Birks, J. S., and Sinclair, C. A. (1979). 'International Labour Migration in the Arab Middle East'. *Third World Quarterly*, 1(2), 87–99.

Bishalani, B. (2009). *Fairouz.* Lebanon: USEK Publishing.

Blankenship, D. (2010). *Applied Research and Evaluation Methods in Recreation.* Sheriden, Wyoming: Sheridan Books.

Blickle, P. (2002). *Heimat: A Critical Theory of the German Idea of Homeland.* New York: Camden House.

Bourdieu, P. (1970). 'The Berber House or the World Reversed'. *Social Science Information*, 9(20), 151–70.

Bourdieu, P. (1990). *The Logic of Practice.* Cambridge: Polity Press.

Boym, S. (2001). *The Future of Nostalgia.* New York: Basic Books.

Brah, A. (1996). *Cartographies of Diaspora: Contesting Identities.* Abingdon: Routledge University Press.

Breen, K. (2007). 'Violence and Power: A Critique of Hannah Arendt on the "Political"'. *Philosophy and Social Criticism*, 33(3), 343–72.

Briganti, C. and Mezei, K. (Eds.). (2012). *The Domestic Space Reader*. Toronto: University of Toronto Press.

Cepeda, M. E. (2003). 'Shakira as the Idealized, Transnational Citizen: A Case Study of *Colombianidad* in Transition'. *Latino Studies*, 1, 211–32.

Chandler, D. (n.d.) *Semiotics for Beginners*. Retrieved on 4 December 2015, from http://visual-memory.co.uk/daniel/Documents/S4B/.

Clifford, J. (1983). 'On Ethnographic Authority'. *Representations*, 2, 118–46.

Clough, P., Goldberg, G., Schiff, R., Weeks, A., and Willse, C. (2007). 'Notes Towards a Theory of Affect-Itself'. *Ephemera*, 7(1), 60–77.

Cohen, A. P. (1994). *Self Consciousness: An Alternative Anthropology of Identity*. London: Routledge.

Crenshaw, K. (1991). 'Mapping the Margins: Intersectionality, Identity Politics, and Violence Against Women of Color'. *Stanford Law Review*, 43, 1241–99.

Cunningham, S. and Sinclair, J. (2001). 'Diasporas and the Media'. In S. Cunningham and J. Sinclair (Eds.), *Floating Lives, the Media and Asian Diasporas* (pp. 1–34). Lanham: Rowman & Littlefield Publishers.

Danielson, V. (1997). *The Voice of Egypt: Umm Kulthum, Arabic Song and Egyptian Society in the 20th Century*. Chicago and London: University of Chicago Press.

Darwish, M. (2011). *In the Presence of Absence*, trans. S. Antoon. Brooklyn: Archipelago Books.

De Certeau, M. (1984). *The Practice of Everyday Life*, trans. S. Rendall. Berkley: University of California Press (original work published 1980).

DeNora, T. (2003). *Music in Everyday Life*. Cambridge: Cambridge University Press.

El-Ariss, T. (2017). 'Hacking Rites: Recoding the Political in Contemporary Cultural Practices'. In T. Sabry and L. Ftouni (Eds.), *Arab Subcultures: Transformations in Theory and Practice* (pp. 44–61). London: IB Tauris.

Erll, A. (2011). *Memory in Culture*. London: Palgrave Macmillan.

Feiler, G. (1991). 'Migration and Recession: Arab Labor Mobility in the Middle East, 1982–89'. *Population and Development Review*, 17(1), 134–55.

Fersan, E. (2010). *Syro-Lebanese Migration (1880-present):"Push" and "Pull" Factors*. Middle East Institute. Retrieved on 6 September, from: Syro-Lebanese Migration (1880-Present): "Push" and "Pull" Factors | Middle East Institute (mei.edu).

Firth, S. (1996). 'Music and Identity'. In S. Hall and P. Du Gay (Eds.), *Questions of Cultural Identity* (pp. 108–27). London: Sage.

Fiske, J. (1994). *Media Matters: Everyday Culture and Political Change*. Minneapolis: University of Minnesota Press.

Foucault, M. (1986). 'Of Other Spaces'. *Diacritics*, 16(1), 22–7.

Frishkopf, M. (2010). *Music and Media in the Arab World*. Cairo: American University of Cairo Press.

Gibbs, A. (2001). 'Contagious Feelings: Pauline Hanson and the Epidemiology of Affect'. *Australian Humanities Review*, 24. Retrieved on 14 December 2015, from http://www.australianhumanitiesreview.org/archive/Issue-December-2001/gibbs.html.

Gillespie, M. (1989). 'Technology and Tradition: Audiovisual Culture among South Asian Families in South London'. *Cultural Studies*, 3 (2), 225–39.

Gilman, D. (2014). *Cairo Pop: Youth Music in Contemporary Egypt*. Minneapolis: University of Minnesota Press.

Goffman, E. (1956). *The Presentation of the Self in Everyday Life*. Edinburgh: University of Edinburgh Research Centre.

Gopinath, G. (1995). "Bombay, UK, Yuba City': Banghra Music and the Engendering of Diaspora'. *Diaspora: A Journal of Transnational Studies*, 4(3), 303–21.

Gregg, M. and Seigworth, G. (2010). 'An Inventory of Shimmers'. In M. Gregg and G. Seigworth (Eds.), *The Affect Theory Reader* (pp. 1–25). Durham: Duke University Press.

Grossberg, L. (1986). 'Is There Rock after Punk?' *Critical Studies in Mass Communication*, 3, 50–74.

Grossberg, L. (2010). 'Affect's Future: Rediscovering the Virtual in the Actual'. In M. Gregg and G. Seigworth (Eds.), *The Affect Theory Reader* (pp. 309–38). Durham: Duke University Press.

Habib, K. S. (2005). *The Superstar Singer Fairouz and the Ingenious Rahbani Composers: Lebanon Sounding*. Doctoral Dissertation, University of California, Santa Barbara.

Hage, G. (2002). 'The Differential Intensities of Social Reality: Migration, Participation and Guilt'. In G. Hage (Ed.), *Arab-Australians Today: Citizenship and Belonging* (pp. 192–205). Victoria: Melbourne University Press.

Hage, G. (2005). 'A Not So Multi-Sited Ethnography of a Not So Imagined Community'. *Anthropological Theory*, 5(4), 463–75.

Hall, S. (1990). 'Cultural Identity and Diaspora.' In J. Rutherford (Ed.), *Identity: Community, Culture, Difference* (pp. 222–37). London: Lawrence & Wishart.

Hall, S. (1993). 'What Is This "Black" in Black Popular Culture?' *Social Justice*, 20, 104–14.

Hannerz, U. (2003). 'Being There . . . And There . . . And There!' *Ethnography*, 4(2), 201–16.

Harb, Z. and Bessaiso, E. (2006). 'British Arab Muslim Audiences and Television after September 11'. *Journal of Ethnic and Migration Studies*, 32(6), 1063–76.

Haugbolle, S. and Kuzmanovic, D. (2015). 'Introduction: Towards a New Sociology of Icons in the Middle East'. *Middle East Journal of Culture and Communication*, 8, 5–11.

Heidegger, M. (2012). 'Building, Dwelling, Thinking'. In C. Briganti and K. Mezei (Eds.), *The Domestic Space Reader* (pp. 21–6). Toronto: University of Toronto Press.

Hennink, M., Hutter, I, and Bailey, A. (2011). *Qualitative Research Methods*. London: Sage Publications Ltd.

Higham, E., Ellaby, S., and Thomas, S. (2020). 'Qatar Employment and Immigration Laws Change'. *Global HR*, 9 October. Retrieved on 23 September 2021, from: https://www.shrm.org/resourcesandtools/hr-topics/global-hr/pages/qatar-employment-and-immigration-laws-change.aspx.

Hiller, H. H. and DiLuzio, L. (2004). 'The Interviewee and the Research Interview: Analysing a Neglected Dimension in Research*'. *Canadian Review of Sociology/Revue Canadienne de Sociologie*, 41(1), 1–26.

Hinds, J. and Sparks, P. (2008). 'Engaging with the Natural Environment: The Role of Affective Connection and Identity'. *Journal of Environmental Psychology*, 28, 109–20.

Hirsch, M. (2008). 'The Generation of Postmemory'. *Poetics Today*, 29(1), 104–28.

Hitti, P. (1924). *The Syrians in America*. New York: Doran & Company.

Issa, D. (2011). *Situating the Imagination: Turkish Soap Operas and the Lives of Women in Qatar*, Unpublished Master's Dissertation, London School of Economics, London, England. Retreived from http://bsps.org.uk/media@lse/research/mediaWorkingPapers/MScDissertationSeries/2010/Dissa.pdf.

Iyengar, S., Sood, G., and Lelkes, Y. (2012). 'Affect Not Ideology: A Social Identity Perspective on Polarization'. *The Public Opinion Quarterly*, 76(3), 405–31.

Jamal, A. and Naber, N. (Eds.) (2008). *Race and Arab Americans Before and After 9/11:From Invisible Citizens to Visible Subjects*. New York: Syracuse University Press.

Jayyusi, S. K. (1977). *Trends and Movements in Modern Arabic Poetry* (Vol. 2). Lieden: Brill.

Jean-Klein, I. (2001). 'Nationalism and Resistance: The Two Faces of Everyday Activism in Palestine during the Intifada'. *Cultural Anthropology*, 16(1), 83–126. Retrieved from http://www.jstor.org/stable/656603.

Jensen, K., and Jankowski, N. (Eds.) (1991). *A Handbook of Qualitative Methodologies for Mass Communication Research*. London: Routledge.

Joseph, M. (1999). 'Introduction: New Hybrid Identities and Performance'. In M. Joseph (Ed.), *Performing Hybridity* (pp. 1–25). Minneapolis: University of Minnesota Press.

Kadi, J. (1994). *Food for Our Grandmothers: Writings by Arab-American and Arab-Canadian Feminists*. Boston, MA: South End Press.

Kaplan, C. (1987). 'Deterritorializations: The Rewriting of Home and Exile in Western Feminist Discourse'. *Cultural Critique*, 6, 187–98.

Karlyn, K. R. (2009). 'Scream, Popular Culture, and Feminism's Third Wave'. In H. Addison, M. K. Goodwin-Kelly, and E. Roth (Eds.), *Motherhood Misconceived: Representing the Maternal in US Films* (pp. 177–95). New York: State University of New York Press.

Keightley, E., and Pickering, M. (2012). *The Mnemonic Imagination – Remembering as Creative Practice*. London: Palgrave Macmillan.

Khalili, L. (2017). 'After Brexit: Reckoning with Britain's Racism and Xenophobia'. *Poem*, 5(2–3), 253–65.

Kitzinger, J. (1995). 'Qualitative Research: Introducing Focus Groups'. *BMJ*, 311(7000), 299–302.

Kraidy, M. M. (2002). 'Hybridity in Cultural Globalization'. *Communication Theory*, 12(3), 316–39.

Kraidy, M. M. (2006). 'Reality Television and Politics in the Arab World: Preliminary Observations'. *Transnational Broadcasting Studies*, 15, Retrieved from http://repository.upenn.edu/asc_papers/303.

Lawler, E. J. (2001). 'An Affect Theory of Social Exchange'. *American Journal of Sociology*, 107(2), 321–52.

Levin, D. M. (Ed.) (1993). *Modernity and the Hegemony of Vision*. Los Angeles and Berkley: University of California Press.

Liebes, T. and Katz, E. (1990). *The Export of Meaning: Cross-Cultural Readings of Dallas*. Oxford: Oxford University Press.

MacFarquar, N. (1999). 'This Pop Diva Wows 'em in Arabic'. *New York Times*. Retrieved on 28 April 2011, from http://www.nytimes.com/1999/05/18/arts/this-pop-diva-wows-em-in-arabic.html?src=pm.

Manier, D. and Hirst, W. (2008). 'A Cognitive Taxonomy of Collective Memories'. In A. Erll and A. Nunning (Eds.), *Cultural Memory Studies: An International and Interdisciplinary Handbook* (pp. 253–62). Berlin: de Gruyter.

Mansour, N. and Sabry, T. (2017). '(Mis)trust, Access and the Poetics of Self-Reflexivity'. In N. Sakr and J. Steemers (Eds.), *Children's TV and Digital Media in Arab World*. London and New York: IB Tauris.

Mansour, N. and Sabry, T. (2019). 'Reading Popular Music in the Arab Region and in the Diaspora'. *Middle East Journal of Culture and Communication*, 12, 3–6.

Massey, D. (1994). *Space, Place and Gender*. Minnesota: University of Minnesota Press.

Massumi, B. (1987). 'Notes on the Translation and Acknowledgments'. In G. Deleuze and F. Guattari (Eds.), *A Thousand Plateaus*. Minneapolis: University of Minnesota Press.

Massumi, B. (1995). 'The Autonomy of Affect'. *Cultural Critique*, 31, 83–109.

Massumi, B. (2010). 'The Future Birth of the Affective Fact: The Political Ontology of Threat'. In M. Gregg and G. Seigworth (Eds.), *The Affect Theory Reader* (pp. 52–70). Durham: Duke University Press.

Matar, D. (2006). 'Diverse Diasporas, One Meta-Narrative: Palestinians in the UK Talking about 11 September 2001'. *Journal of Ethnic and Migration Studies*, 32(6), 1027–40.

Maxwell, J. A. (2005). *Qualitative Research Design: An Interactive Approach* (2nd Ed.). Thousand Oaks, CA: Sage.

Mendelek, M. (2022, January 12). *The Lebanese Trend of Emigration: A New Peak Since 2019?* Lebanese American University: School of Arts and Sciences. Retrieved 16 September 2022, from https://soas.lau.edu.lb/news/2022/01/the-lebanese-trend-of-emigration-a-new-peak-since-2019.php

Mikhail, M. (1979). 'Iltizam: Commitment and Arabic Poetry'. *World Literature Today*, 53(4), 595–600.

Miladi, N. (2006). 'Satellite TV News and the Arab Diaspora in Britain: Comparing Al-Jazeera, the BBC and CNN'. *Journal of Ethnic and Migration Studies*, 32(6), 947–60.

Miller, P. M., Strang, J., and Miller, P. G. (2010). *Addiction Research Methods*. Chichester, West Sussex: Blackwell Publishing.

Morley, D. (2001). 'Belongings: Place, Space and Identity in a Mediated World'. *European Journal of Cultural Studies*, 4(4), 425–48.

Mosher, D. and Tomkins, S. (1988). 'Scripting the Macho Man: Hypermasculine Socialization and Enculturation'. *The Journal of Sex Research*, 25(1), 60–84.

Naber, N. (2005). 'Muslim First, Arab Second: A Strategic Politics of Race and Gender'. *The Muslim World*, 95, 479–95.

Nasr, G. (2018). *Fairouz and the Rahbanis: Nation, Nostalgia and Lebanese Cosmopolitan Modern*. Doctoral Dissertation, Indiana University.

Norman, K. P. (2021). 'Introduction: Taking Stock of Middle East Migration since the Arab Uprisings'. *Digest of Middle East Studies*, 30, 248–50.

Peirce, C. S. (1931–58). *Collected Writings of Charles Sanders Peirce* (8 Vols.), Eds. Charles Hartshorne, Paul Weiss, and Arthur W Burks. Cambridge, MA: Harvard University Press.

Pickering, M. (2001). *Stereotyping: The Politics of Representation*. Basingstoke: Palgrave Macmillan.

Pont, G. and Lacroix, G. (Producers), Mitterrand, F. (Director). (1998). *Fairouz*. [Documentary]. Paris: Arte Television.

Probyn, E. (2010. 'Writing Shame'. In M. Gregg and G. Seigworth (Eds.), *The Affect Theory Reader* (pp. 71–90). Durham: Duke University Press.

Racy, A. J. (1986). 'Words and Music in Beirut'. *Ethnomusicology*, 30(3), 413–27.

Racy, A. J. (1996). 'Heroes, Lovers, and Poet-Singers: The Bedouin Ethos in the Music of the Arab Near-East'. *The Journal of American Folklore*, 109(434), 404–24.

Racy, A. J. (2003). *Making Music in the Arab World: The Culture and Artistry of Tarab*. Cambridge: Cambridge University Press.

Radway, J. (1984). *Reading the Romance*. Chapel Hill and London: University of North Carolina Press.

Robins, K. and Aksoy, A. (2006). 'Thinking Experiences: Transnational Media and Migrants' Minds'. In J. Curran and D. Morley (Eds.), *Media & Cultural Theory* (pp. 86–100). Oxon: Routledge.

Ruddick, S. (2010). 'The Politics of Affect: Spinoza in the Work of Negri and Deleuze'. *Theory, Culture and Society*, 27(4), 21–45.

Russell, S. S. and Teitelbaum, M. S. (1995). *International Migration and International Trade*. World Bank Discussion Papers. Washington D.C.: The World Bank.

Sabry, T. (2012). 'Arab Cultural Studies: Between "Reterritorialisation" and "Deterritorialisation"'. In T. Sabry (Ed.), *Arab Cultural Studies: Mapping the Field* (pp. 1–31). London and New York: IB Tauris.

Sabry, T. and Ftouni, L. (2017). 'Arab Subcultures and the Paradox of Cultural Translation'. In T. Sabry and L. Ftouni (Eds.), *Arab Subcultures: Theory and Practice* (pp. 1–15). London: IB Tauris.

Sabry, T. and Mansour, N. (2019). *Children and Screen Media in Changing Arab Contexts: An Ethnographic Perspective*. London: Palgrave.

Said, E. (1991). *Musical Elaborations*. London: Vintage.

Sakr, N. and Steemers, J. H. (Eds.) (2017). *Children's TV and Digital Media in the Arab World: Childhood, Screen Culture and Education*. London and New York: IB Tauris.

Salaam, K. (1982). 'The Sensitive Luther Vandross'. *The New Black*. Retrieved from http://www.thenewblackmagazine.com/view.aspx?index=592.

Sayad, A. (2004). *The Suffering of the Immigrant*, trans. D. Macey. Cambridge: Polity Press. (Original work published 1999).

Schaefer, J. (2015). 'Middle Eastern Music and Popular Culture'. In S. Altorki (Ed.), *A Companion to the Anthropology of the Middle East* (pp. 495–508). West Sussex: John Wiley & Sons Inc.

Schade-Poulsen, M. (1999). *Men and Popular Music in Algeria: The Social Significance of Raï* (Vol. 20). Austin, TX: University of Texas Press.

Scherer, K. and Ekman, P. (2009). *Approaches to Emotion*. New York: Psychology Press.

Shouse, E. (2005). 'Feeling, Emotion and Affect'. *Media and Culture Journal*, 8(6). Retrieved from http://journal.media-culture.org.au/0512/03-shouse.php.

Silva, N. (2004). *The Gendered Nation: Contemporary Writings from South Asia*. New Delhi: Sage Publications India.

Slobin, M. (1994). 'Music in Diaspora: The View from Euro-America'. *Diaspora: A Journal of Transnational Studies*, 3(3), 243–51.

Small, C. (1998). *Musicking: The Meanings of Performance and Listening*. Middletown, CT: Wesleyan University Press.

Smith, S. J. (1994). 'Soundscape'. *Area*, 26(3), 232–40.

Soja, E. (1989). *Postmodern Geographies: The Reassertion of Space in Critical Social Theory*. London: Verso.

Spivak, G. C. (1999). *A Critique of Postcolonial Reason: Toward a History of the Vanishing Present*. Cambridge, MA: Harvard University Press.

Stewart, K. (2010). 'Afterword: Worldling Refrains'. In G. Seigworth and M. Gregg (Eds.), *The Affect Theory Reader* (pp. 339–53). Durham: Duke University Press.

Stoetzler, M. and Yuval-Davis, N. (2002). 'Standpoint Theory, Situated Knowledge and the Situated Imagination'. *Feminist Theory*, 3, 315–33.

Stokes, M. (Ed.). (1994). *Ethnicity, Identity and Music: The Musical Construction of Place*. Oxford/Providence: BERG.

Stoll, D. (1963). *Music Festivals of the World: A Guide to Leading Festivals of Music, Opera and Ballet*. Oxford: Pergamon Press.

Stone, C. (2008). *Popular Culture and Nationalism in Lebanon: The Fairouz and Rahbani Nation*. New York: Routledge.

Street, J. (2012). *Music and Politics*. Cambridge: Polity Press.

Tabar, P. (2010). 'Lebanon: A Country of Emigration and Immigration'. *Institute for Migration Studies*, 7, 6–26.

Tacchi, J. (2003). 'Nostalgia and Radio Sound'. In M. Bull and L. Back (Eds.), *The Auditory Culture Reader* (pp. 281–302). Oxford, England and Rhode Island: Berg Publishers.

Taylor, C. (1989). *Sources of the Self: The Making of Modern Identity*. Cambridge: Cambridge University Press.

Thiollet, H. (2011). 'Migration as Diplomacy: Labor Migrants, Refugees, and Arab Regional Politics in the Oil-Rich Countries'. *International Labor and Working-Class History*, 79(1), 103–21.

Tomkins, S. (1978). 'Script Theory: Differential Magnification of Affects'. *Nebraska Symposium on Motivation*, 26, 201–36.

Tomkins, S. (2009). 'Affect Theory'. In K. Scherer and P. Ekman (Eds.), *Approaches to Emotion* (pp. 163–94). New York and London: Psychology Press.

Tomkins, S. (1995). *Exploring Affect: The Selected Writings of Silvan S. Tomkins*, ed. Demos, E. Cambridge: Cambridge University Press.

Traboulsi, F. (2006). *Fairouz wa-Al-Rahabina: Masrah Al-Gharib wa-al-Kanz wa-Al-A'juba*. Beirut: Riad El-Rayyes Books.

Trad, M. and Khalifa, R. (2001). *Fairouz: Hayatuha wa-Aghaniha*. Tripoli, Lebanon: al-Mu'assasa al-haditha li-al-kuttab.

Tsagarousianou, R. (2004). 'Rethinking the Concept of Diaspora: Mobility, Connectivity and Communication in a Globalised World'. *Westminster Papers in Communication and Culture*, 1(1), 52–65.

Tsagarousianou, R. (2016). 'European Muslim Diasporic Geographies: Media Use and the Production of Translocality'. *Middle East Journal of Culture and Communication*, 9(1), 62–86.

Verschaffel, B. (2012). 'The Meanings of Domesticity'. In C. Briganti and K. Mezei (Eds.), *The Domestic Space Reader* (pp. 153–7). Toronto: University of Toronto Press.

Vertovec, S. (2009). *Transnationalism*. London: Routledge.

Virdee, S. and McGeever, B. (2017). 'Racism, Crisis, Brexit'. *Ethnic and Racial Studies*, 41(10), 1802–19.

Williams, R. (1977). *Marxism and Literature*. Oxford and New York: Oxford University Press.

Williams, R. (1983). *Keywords*. New York: Oxford University Press.

World Population Review. (2022). Qatar Population 2022. 5 February. Retrieved from: https://worldpopulationreview.com/countries/qatar-population.

Yazida, H. (2010). 'Conceptualizing Hybridity: Deconstructing Boundaries through the Hybrid'. *Formations*, 1(1), 31–8.

GLOSSARY OF TERMS

3almani   Secular
3aysheen   Living
Allah   God
Al-gharb   The West
Al-ghurba   Expatriation
Arzeh   Cedar tree, usually associated with the Lebanese flag
Aseel/Asil   Authentic
Awrat   Shameful (religious undertones associated with Islam)
Baladna/Baladi   Our/my country
Baytuna/Bayti   Our/my home
Dayi'tna/Dayi'ti   Our/my village
Gharab   Go West, or to the Occident
Gharaba   To depart, to go away, to leave
Ghareeb   Foreign/strange
Ghurba   Alienation
Ghurbiyé   Foreigners
Haneen   Nostalgia or craving
Haram   Poor soul, but also has religious connotations in Islam to mean taboo
Heiki   Like this
Ightirab   Expatriated
Iltizam   Commitment
Kan   Was
La samah Allah   God forbid
Mawtini   Homeland
Moukawama   Resistance group, in Lebanon usually known as Hezbollah
Mughtaribeen   Emigrants, immigrants
Rakwet Kahwe   Lebanese/Arabic/Turkish coffee brewed and served in a traditional stovetop pot
Shisha/Sheesha   Hookah
Tabbel   Type of drum
Tagharaba   Emigrate or immigrate
Umma   Nation; people
Watanna/Watani   Our/my nation/homeland
Ya3ni   I mean; or kind of

INDEX

www.ingramcontent.com/pod-product-compliance
Lightning Source LLC
Chambersburg PA
CBHW062021270326
41929CB00014B/2275

* 9 7 8 0 7 5 5 6 4 1 8 0 2 *